RELATIONAL TRANSACTIONAL ANALYSIS

RELATIONAL TRANSACTIONAL ANALYSIS
Principles in Practice

Edited by
Heather Fowlie and Charlotte Sills

KARNAC

First published in 2011 by
Karnac Books Ltd
118 Finchley Road
London NW3 5HT

British Library Cataloguing in Publication Data

A C.I.P. for this book is available from the British Library

ISBN-13: 978-1-85575-762-2

Typeset by Vikatan Publishing Solutions (P) Ltd., Chennai, India

Printed in Great Britain

www.karnacbooks.com

For whom the bell tolls

No man is an island,
Entire of itself.
Each is a piece of the continent,
A part of the main.
If a clod be washed away by the sea,
Europe is the less.
As well as if a promontory were.
As well as if a manor of thine own
Or of thine friend's were.
Each man's death diminishes me,
For I am involved in mankind.
Therefore, send not to know
For whom the bell tolls,
It tolls for thee.

John Donne, *Devotions Upon Emergent Occasions,*
Meditation XVII, (1623)

CONTENTS

ACKNOWLEDGEMENTS

We want to appreciate the commitment of all the contributors to this volume, who have worked with us so cooperatively and generously on this project. it has been a huge pleasure to work with you all.

Thanks also for the team at Karnac for being willing and able to turn the project around in rather a short space of time! And a huge thank you to Ged Lennox and Wes Mudge for the cover.

And finally, thank you to our teachers, supervisors, colleagues, clients and supervisees with whom we learn every day.

Heather Fowlie and Charlotte Sills

Cover design by Ged Lennox, gedesign—gedlennox@mac.com

Photographer—Wes Mudge.
(Photograph of the Antelope slot canyon, in Arizona)

ABOUT THE BOOK

The book is divided into three parts. Part I: *Principles of Relational Transactional Analysis* is divided into eight sections, each one containing two chapters, which address one of the principles described above. Part II: *Relational Transactional Analysis in Context* looks at the implication of taking a relational lens to a number of different formats such as in groupwork or brief therapy. There are also chapters on diversity, politics, and on working across languages. Part III is called *The Implications for Professional Practice* and contains chapters on relational ethics, on training, research, and supervision.

ABOUT THE EDITORS AND CONTRIBUTORS

James Agar is a psychotherapist and supervising transactional analyst who works in full time private practice in the South West of England. He likes listening to free jazz and growing older.

James R. Allen, MD is professor of psychiatry and behavioral sciences, Rainbolt Family chair in child psychiatry, and vice–chair, Department of Psychiatry and Behavioral Sciences at the University of Oklahoma Health Sciences Center, Oklahoma City, Oklahoma, USA. He is a teaching and supervising member of the ITAA, a past winner of the Eric Berne Memorial Award, and past president of the ITAA.

Suzanne Boyd is a teaching and supervising transactional analyst. She has a psychotherapy and supervision practice in the South East of England and has long experience of both in a number of settings including the NHS, the education sector, and private practice. She is a visiting trainer at several psychotherapy training institutes.

Sarah Brown has completed four years advanced training in TA psychotherapy and has a private practice in South East London.

Keith Chinnock, BA (Hons), MSc (psychotherapy), UKCP Registered Psychotherapist, provisional teaching and supervising transactional analyst, Dip. in clinical supervision, is a qualified teacher and a member of BACP, EATA, and the ITAA. He runs a private clinical and supervision practice, and is a tutor and supervisor for the Metanoia Institute and CPPD, all in London. He also contributes to CPPD's Integrative Supervision course.

Rachel Cook is a fourth year student at the Metanoia Institute in London and has a private practice in the New Forest, Hampshire, England.

William F. Cornell, MA, teaching and supervising transactional analyst, maintains an independent prvate practice of therapy, consultation, and training in Pittsburgh, USA. He is a co-editor of the *Transactional Analysis Journal* and has published extensively in a broad range of journals and psychotherapy books. He is the author of *Explorations in Transactional Analysis: The Meech Lake Papers*, editor of James McLaughlin's *The Healer's Bent: Solitude and Dialogue in the Clinical Encounter*, and co-editor with Helena Hargaden of *From Transactions to Relations: The Emergence of a Relational Tradition in Transactional Analysis*.

Richard G. Erskine has been the training director at the Institute for Integrative Psychotherapy since 1976. He is a licensed psychologist, licensed psychoanalyst, certified clinical transactional analyst (trainer and supervisor), a certified group psychotherapist, and a UKCP and EAPA certified psychotherapist. He is the author of numerous articles and books and has twice received the Eric Berne Memorial Award. He lives in Vancouver, Canada.

Sue Eusden, BSc, MA, teaching and supervising transactional analyst, is a UKCP registered psychotherapist in private practice in the Cotswolds, England. She also supervises in Edinburgh and teaches at Metanoia, London. Sue is a founding member of the International Relational Transactional Analysis Association and a member of the ITAA and EATA.

Brian Fenton, Psych. BSc (Hons), Post Grad. Dip. in clinical supervision, is a provisional training and supervising transactional analyst and UKCP registered psychotherapist. He has a particular interest in the development of relational transactional analysis. Brian has a private therapy and supervision practice based in Whitstable in Kent.

Heather Fowlie, MA, MSc (psychotherapy), teaching and supervising transactional analyst, Dip. in supervision, is UKCP registered.

She is head of the TA department at the Metanoia Institute in London. She works in private practice in South West London as a full-time psychotherapist, supervisor, and trainer, and is particularly interested in integrating other models of psychotherapy, especially object relations within a relational approach to transactional analysis. She is a founder member of IARTA.

Katarina Gildebrand is a provisional teaching and supervising transactional analyst. She has a background in mental health, and worked in the National Health Service for 10 years before setting up a private clinical and supervision practice. Her particular interests include the integration of findings from neuroscience with the practice of psychotherapy as well as the role of nutrition in mental health.

Dave Gowling, Dip. Soc. Studies, CQSW (London), is a teaching and supervising transactional analyst, UKCP registered. After twelve years in the printing industry Dave retrained in the mid-seventies as a social worker, working in the child care and mental health fields. During this period he trained as a psychotherapist, qualifying in 1987. He now works as a psychotherapist, supervisor, and trainer in London and teaches on the MSc programme at the Metanoia Institute in London.

Helena Hargaden, DPsych., teaching and supervising transactional analyst, MSc, is a UKCP integrative psychotherapist. Helena is director of relational TA studies in Kent. She is co-author with Charlotte Sills of *Transactional Analysis: A Relational Perspective*, and co-editor with William F. Cornell of *From Transactions to Relations*. She is an international trainer and supervisor and has a clinical practice in London and Sussex.

Birgitta Heiller, PhD, MSc, teaching and supervising transactional analyst, is a registered psychotherapist and chartered psychologist, and currently a co-editor of the *Transactional Analysis Journal*. She maintains a private clinical and supervision practice in Guildford, England.

Rob Hill is a qualified TA counsellor and is about to complete his MSc in TA psychotherapy. He has a private practice in Richmond, Surrey, England.

Geoff Hopping is a teaching and supervising transactional analyst and a UKCP registered psychoanalytic psychotherapist. He is currently a consultant psychotherapist in the personality disorder service at

Whitemoor Prison. His special interests are in group psychotherapy, staff training and supervision, with a particular focus on the "shadow" side of human beings. He has spent some 18 years in private practice as a therapist, trainer, and supervisor and is still actively involved in psychotherapy education.

Jill Hunt, MSc (TA psychotherapy), is a teaching and supervising transactional analyst, Dip. in supervision, UKCP and BACP registered. Jill works in private practice in West Sussex, as a psychotherapist, supervisor, and trainer. She has many years' experience as a counsellor, psychotherapist, and supervisor within the voluntary sector, currently maintaining her interest as clinical director of Arun Counselling Service. She is an associate of Cascade Supervision Training and a tutor within the Metanoia TA department.

Gun Isaksson Hurst, MSc, is a provisional teaching and supervising transactional analyst, CDC, UKCP registered. Gun was born in Stockholm and has lived in the UK since the late sixties. She is in private practice in North London and is an experienced lecturer, supervisor, and psychotherapist. She teaches at the Metanoia Institute on the TA MSc programme. She also delivers independent workshops on themes such as working with early developmental trauma, addictions and eating distress, and group work. Gun is particularly interested in relational psychotherapy with its focus on unconscious processes. Her current interest is in her research to do with "The impact of the work on the self of the psychotherapist".

Paul Kellett van Leer, MSc (psych.), MSc (TA psych.), is a provisional teaching and supervising transactional analyst in private practice in London. Paul trained as a transactional analyst at the Oxford Centre for Psychotherapy Training and at Metanoia, where he is a primary tutor and supervisor. He has published a number of papers to date, developing transactional analysis theory and practice in the light of contemporary psychoanalytic philosophy.

Phil Lapworth is an integrative counsellor, psychotherapist, and supervisor in private practice near Bath, England. His recent publications include *Integration in Counselling & Psychotherapy, 2nd Edition* (SAGE, 2010), *An Introduction to Transactional Analysis* (SAGE, 2011), both with Charlotte Sills, *An Introduction to Gestalt* (SAGE, 2012) with Charlotte Sills and Billy Desmond, and a book of fictional short stories, *Tales from the Therapy Room—Shrink-Wrapped* (SAGE, 2011).

Elana Leigh, BSc, MSc, teaching and supervising transactional analyst, has trained and supervised nationally and internationally across a range of cultures for the past 26 years. Her specialty is long-term training where the task is to take trainees through the rigorous journey of becoming an ethical and professional psychotherapist. Having trained as both a transactional analyst and integrative psychotherapist, her passion lies in integration and diversity in both theory and application. Elana is involved both nationally and internationally on bodies which maintain and advance training standards in the field of psychotherapy. She currently works as a therapist, supervisor, and trainer in Sydney, Australia.

Ray Little, certified transactional analyst, UKCP, works as a psychotherapist in Edinburgh. He combines his psychotherapy practice with facilitating supervision and professional development seminars in Edinburgh and London. He is a visiting tutor on several training courses, a founding member of IARTA, and has authored several articles. He has an interest in incorporating psychodynamic concepts into a relational transactional analysis, with a particular emphasis on working with primitive states of mind.

Marit Lyngra, certified transactional analyst, MSc, UKCP reg., is a psychotherapist in private practice in North London. She is originally from Norway, but moved to London in 1995 to complete her studies in music and performance and worked as a musician and teacher before training as a counsellor and psychotherapist. As a bilingual therapist, Marit is particularly interested in how the different languages of the client and therapist can impact the therapeutic process.

Marco Mazzetti, MD, is a psychiatrist, a teaching and supervising transactional analyst (TSTA-P), a member of EATA and the ITAA, and a university lecturer. One of his main professional interests is ethnopsychiatry, cross-cultural psychotherapy, and psycho-traumatology. He is the head of the rehabilitation service for torture victims "Invisible Wounds" in Rome. Marco works in private practice in Milan, Italy.

Karen Minikin, BA (Hons) (counselling), MSc (psychotherapy), is a provisional teaching and supervising transactional analyst. Karen works in East Sussex as a counsellor and psychotherapist, supervisor, and trainer. She also provides management development for organizations. She originally trained and worked as a teacher in secondary education. Her practical and professional interests include understanding and working with cultural identity, trauma, group dynamics, and integrating humanistic and relational psychoanalytical approaches within transactional analysis.

Katherine Murphy, BA, MSc (psychotherapy), teaching and supervising transactional analyst, UKCP reg. integrative psychotherapist, works as a psychotherapist and supervisor in private practice in London. She is actively involved in the education and training of psychotherapists and has contributed to the development of education and training standards within the United Kingdom Council for Psychotherapy (UKCP). She is one of the series editors for the *British Journal for Psychotherapy Integration*. In 2010 she was made an honorary fellow of the UKCP.

Steff Oates is a teaching and supervising transactional analyst, working from a practice in Cheshire and teaching at a variety of institutes in Europe. She has an abiding passion for the appreciation of transactional analysis as a dynamic and robust theory, flexible enough to move with the times and to integrate with other modalities. She is co-founder of the Northern College for Body Psychotherapy based in Cumbria.

Carole Shadbolt, MSc (psych.), is a teaching and supervising transactional analyst. Carole's career has spanned over 30 years of work within psychological services, originally as a welfare assistant, then as a social worker and then as a psychiatric social worker. She has worked as an independent clinician since 1991, and is both a supervisor and trainer. She has published a number of articles, focusing on sexuality, diversity, and cultural aspects. Carole is interested in and committed to developing all forms of contemporary enquiry into TA theory and clinical practice.

Suhith Shivanath, BSc (Hons), MSc, is a provisional teaching and supervising transactional analyst, UKCP and BACP reg., Dip. in supervision. Suhith brings together her life experience of three continents: growing up in Africa, of Indian parents, and living in Britain. Her work experience includes community development, equal opportunities training, and short-term counselling in the NHS. She has a private psychotherapy and supervision practice in North London, and is a member of the TA academic team at Metanoia Institute. She is a contributing author to *Concepts in Transactional Analysis, Ego States* (Worth Publishing, 2003).

Diana Shmukler, PhD, is a clinical psychologist, integrative psycho-therapist, supervisor and teacher, teaching and supervising transactional analyst, and member of UKCP, EAIP and UKAPI. She is former associate professor of applied psychology at the University of the Witwatersrand, South Africa, and visiting professor of psychotherapy at the University of Middlesex and the University of Utrecht in the Netherlands. Her main clinical interests are adult psychotherapy, couples therapy, teaching, and supervising therapy. She has been practising for 30 years and currently lives in London.

Charlotte Sills, MA, MSc, teaching and supervising transactional analyst, is a psychotherapist and supervisor in private practice, a senior tutor at Metanoia Institute, and visiting professor at Middlesex University. She has published widely in the field of counselling and psychotherapy including, with Helena Hargaden, *Transactional Analysis—a Relational Perspective* (Routledge, 2002), and *An Introduction to Transactional Analysis* (SAGE, 2011) with Phil Lapworth.

Judy Sleath recently finished the four year TA MSc programme at Metanoia, and is currently preparing for her certified transactional analyst exams and to set up in private practice in Brussels.

Jo Stuthridge, MSc, is a teaching and supervising transactional analyst and a registered psychotherapist in New Zealand. She maintains a private psychotherapy practice in Dunedin, and is co-director of the Physis Institute, which provides training in transactional analysis. She has a background in counselling for community agencies and involvement in social justice issues. She has published several articles and is currently a co-editor for the *Transactional Analysis Journal.*

Graeme Summers is an executive coach based in the UK. Since 2005, he has worked for London Business School coaching senior managers worldwide from a wide range of organizations. He was formerly a transactional analysis psychotherapist and was director of training for the Counselling and Psychotherapy Training Institute, Edinburgh. He can be reached via email at Graeme.summers@co-creativecoaching.co.uk.

Biljana van Rijn, DPsych., MSc in TA psychotherapy, is a teaching and supervising transactional analyst. Biljana is head of clinical services at Metanoia Institute in London, where she has developed a research clinic. She teaches on the MSc programme in TA psychotherapy there and the doctorate in counselling psychology and integrative psychotherapy, and offers research supervision. Biljana also works a psychotherapist and supervisor in private practice in West Sussex.

Maja Zivkovic is a qualified TA counsellor and is working towards her MSc in TA psychotherapy. She works as a clinical assessor at Ealing Abbey Counselling Service and has a small private practice in Ealing, West London.

INTRODUCTION

Heather Fowlie and Charlotte Sills

The past twenty-five years have seen a significant shift in the technical, philosophical, theoretical, and methodological emphasis of transactional analysis (TA). This shift has mirrored similar movements in the wider worlds of psychotherapy and counselling, as well as psychology, education, organizational theory, spirituality, and philosophy. The "relational turn", as it is often known, seems to have affected every field of human endeavour, as people have come to accept the enormous significance of being in relationship.

In TA, this relational turn has had inevitable implications for practice. It has involved a change of emphasis from a focus on the development of insight as the primary means of psychological change, to an exploration of and engagement with patterns of relating. Thus it places relationship—to self and to others, including the therapist, at the heart of the therapeutic work.

Background to the relational approach

Why has the world seen such a profound emphasis on the importance of relating? Firstly, there have been remarkable and synchronistic developments in the areas of post-modern science, neurobiology, and the study of human development. Research in these three areas has revealed an inter-connectedness between human beings that was hitherto only recognized in some philosophies and spiritual traditions. For more than two centuries, men (and women) committed themselves to positivist, evidence based, logical ways of understanding the world that left no room for mysteries such as intuition, intersubjectivity, and unconscious mutuality. This has gradually given way to a focus on difference, plurality, and textuality. Recent discoveries in affective neuroscience have provided, and are continuing to provide significant evidence (Rizzolatti and Craighero, 2004; Panskepp, 1998; Schore, 2003; etc.), which underscores the centrality of relatedness. Chaos and complexity theory, which recognizes how small gestures can amplify into large-scale pattern shifts, is encouraging us to think of society simply as a collection of interactive processes rather than structures. What is more, though perhaps we guessed it, the loving relationship between mother and infant has been shown to be crucial in developing the brain and the sense of identity (Schore, 2003).

The findings of all these disciplines coincided with a revolution in epistemology offered by the feminist psychologists of the 1980s, such as Jean Baker Miller, Joyce Fletcher and Carol Gilligan, who challenged "the gendered nature of knowledge creation" (King, 2004, p. 16). They pointed out that traditional child developmental theories (for example, Piaget, Erikson and Freud), all of which stressed the importance of ego boundaries, autonomy, and individuation, stemmed from a psychological research base that was the exclusive province of men—carried out by men on male subjects, whose early childhood experiences required them to separate from their mothers in order to grow up. Indeed Carol Gilligan (1993) quotes an eminent research professor who, shockingly, said "Women and blacks should be left out of psychological research samples" (Gilligan, cited in King, 2011). These feminist thinkers offered another understanding of maturity, which involved mutual dependence, cooperation, and relational skills of support and empathy.

Finally, a confluence of ideas in the world of psychology and psychotherapy has given birth to an approach to psychotherapy that has brought the different schools or traditions together in a previously unheard-of integration. Part of this emergence has been the findings of seventy years of psychotherapy outcome research, which has convincingly shown that successful therapy, whatever the theory or model, is greatly determined by certain common elements. These "common factors" are associated with a therapeutic relationship in which clients have the sense of being in a shared venture and in which they feel respected and understood, even when they have revealed parts of themselves of which they are most ashamed (see for example, Wampold, 2001; Cooper, 2010; Norcross, 2010).

The relational movement in psychotherapy is not simply a result of these developments, however, although it has been fundamentally influenced by them. It has also arisen out of and been generated by other trends, most notably a need to understand something that could not be explained or comprehended within existing psychological theories, and to respond to increasingly complex client presentations. Seen through this lens, relational psychotherapy—rather than a formally organized school or system of beliefs—can be better thought of as a framework or way of thinking about the client, the therapist, the relationship, and about how psychotherapy works.

While only named relational in the last twenty years or so, this framework has been evolving for many years in psychoanalytic and humanistic circles alike. It has major roots in object relations theory in the UK (for example, Fairbairn, 1940; Winnicott, 1958; Klein, 1959; Balint, 1968; Bowlby, 1977) and, in the US, with interpersonal psychoanalysis, a movement originating in the work of Sullivan (1953). Building upon, and to some extent away from, Freud's original psychoanalytic theory, the early object relations psychotherapists placed relationship at the very heart of what it is to be human. In a similar departure, the early interpersonal analysts suggested that a person's learned patterns of relating are at the root of his/her psychological problems and believed that paying attention to these patterns, as they emerged in the therapy, was likely to change them. From these psychoanalytic approaches comes a methodology that focuses on non-conscious processes, through the interpretation of dreams, transferences, and also conscious experience, in order to discover underlying unconscious processes and implicit relational patterns.

The second important psychological root of relational psychotherapy is the humanistic (and existential humanistic) psychotherapy movement (see for example, Moreno, 1945; Rogers, 1951; Maslow, 1943; May, 1983), with its aspirational focus on human growth and the meaning and process of living in society. The interest here was on phenomenology, individual truth, and intersubjectivity, and its methodology of authentic relating, empathic attunement, and respect for the intrinsic value of being human quickly became its hallmark. Inspired by the likes of Buber (1958), Perls et al. (see 1951, 1979), Goulding and Goulding (1979), Jacobs (1989), and Hycner and Jacobs (1995), humanistic psychotherapy saw an increasing recognition of the importance of here and now relating and the significance of experience in facilitating change.

Relational psychotherapy became the perfect vehicle for integrating these two major psychological traditions in a new paradigm. It brings the psychoanalytic world's rigorous attention to the non-conscious inner world of implicit knowing and relating, together with the humanistic recognition that human beings exist in relationship and that real connection with another is the source of well-being and growth.

TA fits with ease into this new relational paradigm. First, it is an integrative psychotherapy. Its principal theories are accessible versions of the psychoanalytic concepts of ego psychology and object relations (for an overview, see for example, Sills & Hargaden, 2003, pp. ix–xxiii). At the same time, it sits within a humanistic philosophy, which honours the importance of a respectful, empathic, authentic relationship between equals/adults. It also makes room for the pragmatic action-orientation of the third major force in psychology, behaviourism—later cognitive behaviourism. Secondly, Berne's original theories put relationship at the heart of psychological life. Transactions, scripts, and especially games subtly capture the blend of co-created present and re-enacted past with masterful simplicity. Berne's later writings somewhat confusingly failed to keep that relationality centre stage. He swung, for example, between seeing script as interpersonally (re-)created and seeing it through the pragmatic, medical model lens of an individual's learned patterns. While his colleagues and clients often experienced him as warm and caring (Soloman, 2010), the major thrust of his TA therapy appeared to have turned towards the challenging of script-bound thinking and to increasing self-understanding. Subsequent transactional analysts (for example, Goulding & Goulding, 1979) recognized the importance of here and now affective experience, including the support of a nurturing therapist and (Steiner & Wycoff, 1975) the necessity of contact, but it was to be some twenty years before the multiple levels of the therapeutic relationship itself began to be explored in earnest.

The history of relational TA

Relational Transactional Analysis is an approach to our work as transactional analysts that combines the fundamental TA theories with ideas from the two major psychological traditions, along with other influential theorists and practitioners such as Jung (1971), Stern (1985), and the intersubjectivists (Stolorow, Atwood & Brandschaft, 1987) and, in recent years, relational psychotherapists (for example, Benjamin, 2002; DeYoung, 2003; and Maroda, 2004).

In their book *From Transactions to Relations: The Emergence of a Relational Tradition in Transactional Analysis*, Cornell and Hargaden (2005) collect together sixteen seminal articles, spanning twenty-five years, which chart the history of this integration and shift within transactional analysis psychotherapy. It names as seminal the work of Novellino (1984, 1990), Moiso (1985), Barr (1987), Erskine (1991, 2001), Shmukler (1991), Woods (1996), Summers and Tudor (2000), Allen and Allen (2000), Cornell and Bonds-White (2001), Hargaden and Sills (2001, 2002), Hargaden (2001), Sills (2001), Cornell (2001), Lewis (2002), and Tudor (2003).

The inspiration for this collection was the publication in 2002 of *Transactional Analysis—a Relational Perspective* (Hargaden & Sills, 2002), which was felt by many to be a much-needed articulation of some of the relational challenges faced by TA therapists as well as the beginnings of a way of thinking and developing a relational methodology. This opened the door to a proliferation of articles that expanded and developed relational TA work. For example, in the book of collected articles (Cornell & Hargaden, ibid.) there is a bibliography of about fifty additional articles. They span almost thirty years, with some authors, such as Ken Woods and Petruska Clarkson, contributing significantly in every decade. The vast majority, however, were written within the previous five years, and there have been many more since then, all of which have contributed to the relational theme and the shaping of a relational TA framework.

In 2009, a number of relational TA practitioners and theorists came together to form the International Association of Relational Transactional Analysis (IARTA), which was founded to promote the development and articulation of relational paradigms within transactional analysis. This group alongside other transactional analysts world-wide, has been energized by the perception of an approach and framework in which we can understand and organize the work that we are doing in our consulting rooms. Out of this work emerges some relational principles that provide a common ground for individual styles.

Relational TA—principles

Relational transactional analysts aim to embody TA philosophy, working from a stance that honours the values of human beings (I'm OK, You're OK), with authentic communication and respecting the capacity of their clients to take charge of their own lives. In addition, relational TA is interested in those processes and methodologies that appreciate and are true to certain principles. These principles seek to understand and engage with the language and power of both conscious and nonconscious relating in the present moment. Within this definition, relational TA practitioners can and do come from any and all approaches within TA, but we operate within what Mitchell and Aron (1999, p. xii) refer to as a "subculture", which shares a "particular set of concerns, concepts, approaches and sensibilities" that unify the practitioners, not "by design" but because the "subculture has struck deep common chords among current practitioners and theorists". Whatever our differences, we hold a number of principles to be self-evident. They are principles of praxis. In other words, they involve our way of understanding as well as how we engage, apply, and put that understanding into practice:

The centrality of relationship. Relational transactional analysis places relationship at the very heart of what it is to be human. Being in relationship is a given. Therefore, we emphasize relationship in all its forms: relationship with the self, relationship with the other, and perhaps especially, relationship with the intersubjective or inter-active, in other words, what happens when we meet each other. The lens of relational practice sees a person's learned patterns of relating to be at the root of his/her psychological problems; and proposes that paying attention to these patterns as they emerge between client and practitioner is likely to change them—both within that relationship and outside it.

The importance of engagement. The practitioner is—and needs to be—an active participant in the work, and is not and cannot be a neutral observer on him/herself, the other, or his/her work. This locates relational TA and relational work in Stark's (1999) terms, as a "two-person psychology" in addition to the "one- and one-and-a-half-person" approaches that characterized traditional TA. The client is not there to be "done to", nor is the practitioner a benign provider of what was once missing for the client—except perhaps in this quality of attention and engagement. Both parties are actively involved in the process of finding new and more authentic ways of relating to each other.

The significance of conscious and non-conscious patterns of relating. We believe that we are consciously shaping and being shaped by each other in relationship and that this happens at many levels of consciousness—from the wholly aware to the deeply unconscious. We agree with DeYoung's (2003) view that the "unconscious isn't a place or thing; it is a self-perpetuating patterning or organising of self-in-relationship that remains out of the person's awareness but shapes all of his self-experience" (p. xvii).

The importance of experience. The most profound change happens through here and now experience (as distinct from cognitive understanding) and, most powerfully, through relational experiences that both *embody* and *enact* different meanings from those that relationships once did for the client. We believe that this is a major way in which relational approaches are reparative.

The significance of subjectivity—and of self-subjectivity. The practitioner, as well as the client, is called upon to get to know, to extend or expand, and to challenge and change her/himself in new ways. He uses the push and pull of his/her own subjective experience with the client to inform when and what interventions or way-of-being-with will best enhance the client's knowledge of self, other, and the world.

The importance of uncertainty. In the search for meaning we think that certainty is not always possible nor necessarily desirable. Relational psychotherapy sees the meanings we have, or will arrive at, as being not only shaped and filtered through our social and cultural contexts, but also co-created in the meeting between therapist and client. This shift from an individual perspective to a multiple and social perspective adds richness, complexity, and uncertainty that enhances the endeavour.

The importance of curiosity, criticism, and creativity. We emphasise a freedom to learn and a freedom to practise. In other words, the practitioner and the client need to be free to have their own mind and to creatively and robustly explore and develop their own ways of relating. Alongside this freedom, however, there is an invitation, or maybe even a responsibility to be curious and critically reflective about the work and in particular the relational patterns that get evoked. As Cornell and Bonds-White (2001) put it: "It is the therapist's and client's mutual curiosity and exploration of an individual's experience that is ultimately curative" (p. 150). Holding the possibilities of multiple meanings in mind, the process of inquiry becomes what is important.

The reality of the functioning and changing adults. Relational TA moves away from the "parental paradigm" where the practitioner may be seen as a temporary provider for unmet relational needs and sees the client as an adult who is capable of a reciprocal and mutual (albeit asymmetrical) relationship with the practitioner. We privilege the activity of relating where both parties are willing to acknowledge the truth about themselves and each other.

The shared concepts outlined above form a framework within which relational practitioners can, in their individual ways, explore their practice and engage with their clients and themselves in true relational fashion.

PART I

PRINCIPLES OF RELATIONAL
TRANSACTIONAL ANALYSIS

Principle 1

The centrality of relationship

CHAPTER ONE

The use of self in psychotherapy

Diana Shmukler

*Chapter based on the keynote address at the first IARTA
Conference, December 2010*

*Through the course of preparing and giving this talk, then continuing to think
more about this opportunity to present a personal perspective to a group of
like-minded colleagues, I have had a few more thoughts to add to the chapter.
As I edit my original notes for publication, changing them from thoughts for
a talk to a written piece, I have added these comments in italics to the original
version.*

*The key addition, I think, is the sense I have that a relational perspective is
beyond an integration of humanistic and psychoanalytic thinking. Possibly
this is what Steven Mitchell meant in his now groundbreaking work* Relational Concepts in Psychoanalysis *(1988), as a paradigm shift. I mean an
even broader frame than his, as I and most of the IARTA audience come from a
humanistic tradition. Although many of us have appropriated and accumulated
psychoanalytic ideas to our way of working—indeed our approach may have
psychoanalytic roots—we are, however, psychotherapists. We do not claim to
be psychoanalysts, we have been trained and work in a variety of ways (usually
face-to-face, once a week) which tend to be interactive and dialogic, rather than
relying on interpretation and insight alone as the mechanism of healing.*

What I mean by this as a perspective on therapeutic action is that in the same way as we talk about relational trauma, relational injury, or relational deficit as the source of the psychological problems, so are we also describing a process of therapy that focuses on relational healing. This is the focus of this chapter. It is about not only the validity (according to the research on the efficacy of psychotherapy) but also the necessity of considering the therapeutic relationship, its creation, maintenance, long-term sustainability and internalization as the essence of the work. The work is about making and attending to relational needs in both participants of the therapeutic dyad.

In a sense, this addendum is a plea for a way of working which invites therapists and counsellors to be alive to the need to fully embody themselves, to strive to be themselves, and express themselves, with all the caveats we have around self disclosure—some of which are described below. Thus, we offer our clients and patients a relationship and the experience of being in a relationship with a real, alive person, who has worked on themselves, developed not only the capacity for listening but equally relevantly for self reflection, and self awareness. Someone who is willing to metabolize feelings, process and think about the process, judiciously disclose their own process, and own up to making mistakes, getting things wrong, not knowing and at times not understanding what is happening. Someone who is willing to endure the discomfort and anxiety that intensive intimate one-to-one relationships with other adults generate in the here and now. Someone who both deeply considers themselves and the impact they have on others while at the same time lets themselves go; in other words is able to give up on their own narcissism, known defences and self-protective mechanisms, in the service of risking authenticity and spontaneity.

What follows is the original talk somewhat adjusted to the written rather than the spoken form

I am honoured to be invited to give this address and very pleased to take the opportunity to put some ideas together at this time in my thinking and professional development. I will come to the title: "The Use of the Self in Therapy", *or It's all about you and nothing to do with you at the same time,* in a minute. I want to introduce this talk however with a description of my own background influences and perspectives, which of course have shaped and determined the views that I hold. Inevitably everything that I have to say is framed and in some ways arises from these factors. For years we have used a process called "Who am I?" as a way of introducing people to each other. This is a very powerful way to create a shared context in which to work. At times I have indeed asked clients early on in the work, often in a first session: "Who are you?"

So this first part is about "who I am".

As is well known to many of you, I grew up within the apartheid structures of what is now known as "the Old South Africa", living in a country which meant that all the inhabitants were profoundly influenced by the prevailing political climate of oppression, injustice, and simmering discontent. Yet for a long period while I was growing up, white South Africans appeared to live their lives untouched and in fact sheltered, shielded, and protected from the underbelly of what was going on in terms of the injustice, violence, and racial discrimination, with its impact on the children and adults of races other than white.

As a young woman I was privileged and lucky to get an appointment very early on at the big and important white English language University in Johannesburg. Partly as a result of the brain drain which began as the apartheid policies strengthened and the academic boycotts increased, I became a professor at a young age. Consequently, I belonged to a group of youngsters in charge of things who were able to influence policies, syllabi, and courses at an early stage in our careers. With that came the opportunities to work in a variety of contexts and with a variety of issues, beyond the ordinary middle class preoccupations we may have had and seen in clinical settings.

My earliest intellectual and academic interests were, in fact, typically white and middle class: I pursued a master's and subsequent doctorate degree in the area of creativity, imagination, and play. However, these were superseded by what were to become more significant and political interests. These involved our bids for academic freedom and getting our courses open to all races so that we could train and teach black therapists and professionals, to work across many communities. We were thus thrust into and had to face constant challenges with regard to the relevance of white middle class ideas and theories in broader communities, families, and psychological issues and problems.

Political issues were to take over and dominate our work. In particular, the violence that erupted with the 1976 riots, and then continued to escalate and spread until eventually every-one's life was affected by violence and thus, of course, trauma.

Against this background I want briefly to describe the way in which the psychological field, and in particular ideas about psychotherapy, have changed in the last thirty years or so, leading to the rapid growth and development of contemporary views of psychotherapy.

As a student of psychology in the 60s it seemed as if there were only two options. The first was behaviourism, and our school produced some of the top and best known people in the world, namely Wolpe and Lazarus, followed by a whole cohort of their students who left for the States to head up well known departments of psychology at Princeton, Yale, and to Canada for Vancouver, Toronto etc.

The other frame, much more interesting to us, was the psychoanalytic view, very much at that time traditional Freudian, which was somehow not acceptable because it was not scientific within a post ex facto view of science, and was also problematic in apartheid South Africa where psychoanalysis was somehow linked to the evils of communism. It was seen, ironically, as in the Soviet Union, associated with liberal and hence anti-government ideas.

During the 60s, however, in between these two approaches, arose what became known as the "Third Wave"—that is either humanism or existentialism. Its development allowed a small group of young go-ahead psychotherapists (we were also trained traditionally as clinical psychologists, which meant testing, behavioural techniques, and so on) to seek a training within the humanistic field, which we saw as extremely compatible with the ideas and politically left-wing views held by many at the liberal universities in South Africa. We were attracted particularly to the offshoots of traditional psychoanalysis, specifically Eric Berne's and Fritz Perls's challenges to conventional psychoanalytic treatment.

As many of you remember, an early exposure to TA theory carried its own thrilling and compelling features. Everything seemed possible, people could change, changing was simple if you applied the right technique, be it re-decision therapy, re-Parenting, re-Childing, confronting old script beliefs and so on. Many of these techniques worked well and in response, to provide ourselves with further training, we formed what we called the "TA/Gestalt Society for ongoing training and development in psychotherapy".

The release of affect, the power of catharsis, and the insight that often followed, indicated that unconscious and out of awareness processes were being unlocked, and these experiences were particularly appealing and powerful.

By the time I came to live in England, I felt I was doing reasonably competent work with this approach. I also felt, however, at times and in some clinical situations that I was getting profoundly stuck and there were things that would happen that I could not make sense of.

Self psychology, in which I grew interested around this time, seemed to form some bridge between humanism and psychodynamic thinking and a way of thinking about these stuck places. It was certainly clear to me, and always had been, that unconscious processes were key to transformative and effective therapy going beyond supportive and superficial changes. I think I was looking for some way to include or integrate psychodynamic understanding into a way of working. What remained a puzzle was how to work with the unconscious if one was not traditionally psychoanalytically trained.

My personal growth point at this time had to do with coming to live in London, a rich home of psychoanalytic thinking, ideas, and practitioners. Once I got over the regret of not having come as a young woman to train as an analyst and perhaps a training analyst myself, I could settle down, with my very gifted, generous, and able supervisor, and learn how to extrapolate the richness and brilliance of analytic thinking into broader arenas of work, thus expanding and extending the way and gain access beyond what still feels to me like an elitism in terms of the availability and acceptability for that magical process—a Psychoanalysis.

Some further and highly significant developments in the broad field have largely influenced the thinking, practising, and development of psychotherapy. These developments provide strong theoretical grounds for relationally based work.

The first is what could be called the effect of the "baby watchers" which supports our understanding of how the self is organized and shaped by the past—historical, familial—particularly in relation to others and in relationship. I will come back to this.

The second highly relevant and key development is the research on the brain, the neuroscience and in particular the developing brain, the traumatized brain and the way in which relationships are key to the child's development and capacity for relationship.

In many ways this brain research has, at last, provided the scientific evidence for a relational or relationship-based psychotherapy as a foundation for the correction of the earlier trauma, disruptions, and disorganizations in relationship.

Finally another factor that needs to be mentioned is that all the research into the efficacy of psychotherapy has emphasized and supported the single most outstanding common factor to be the therapeutic relationship.

* * *

So, I have briefly outlined the major influences on my own clinical work and understanding. I believe these same theoretical factors have shaped and changed the field more generally, in the last fifteen to twenty years, laying a solid basis for an integrative way of thinking, as well as an emphasis on a relational perspective.

I want also briefly to expand on some ideas about creative expression—my very early interest, which, as I became clinically equipped, translated into what I call working with the "inner world" in the "outer world", a notion described long ago by Winnicott (1971) as a "transitional space". I see this creative expression as relating to a more general finding and using oneself—expressing aspects of one's inner world in a way that connects to others in a form of creativity in the shared external world. Although these terms seem recognizable and readily understood, I am still not able to clearly describe what the inner world, landscape, internal process, states of mind fully are. It does seem clear to me, however, that this is what the work is about: finding ways and opportunities for this expression by our clients/patients to use in the shared space, the dialogue we co-create together. And, of course, so too do we, the therapists, express our inner beliefs, perceptions, values, and deeply embedded familial and cultural experiences in relationship.

I offer an example from a recent workshop, which involved the symbolic making or constructing aspects of self which then very powerfully led to greater understanding, expanded awareness, and ability to use the self. Simply, we used a technique from play therapy by asking the participants to make fairies from all sorts of bits and pieces. While they were gluing things on, firming things up, finding the right piece of ribbon and so on, it seemed obvious to me that they were concretizing a form of self structure, by the finding and making—both from the real world and their inner worlds. Where this workshop became thrilling and at times, of course, not playful in the fun sense but in fact deeply serious, was when we linked these creations up with their scripts in the form of stories or children's narratives from a selection of children's books.

This is a long introduction to the *Use of Self,* or my statement that *It is All About You and Nothing to Do with You at the Same Time.*

The use of self

It seems to me that from a relational point of view, what we most powerfully offer our patients and clients is a relationship—a relationship with a real person who is present, alive, responding emotionally and intellectually, and putting themselves in the service of the work. I consider the damage that we deal with clinically to be relational damage, trauma, and injury. The people that we work with come to us primarily because they want help to be more effective in their relationships with others and to understand these better. This is not behavioural work, although of course there are important behaviours that can be learnt and that need to change. This is not lying on a couch four or five times a week, ruminating about what is in one's mind—as enriching, stimulating, and enlivening as this may be. Neither is it beating up cushions, shouting at empty chairs, or pretending to be a child again.

As I see it, it is very firmly and clearly working out current and real issues in as straight, effective, honest, and caring a relationship as is possible. As therapists we have the advantage of not living with our clients; our relationship is tightly bounded and securely held in time, space, and professional contracts. (I will say more about the centrality of boundaries in a minute.)

I have come to the position that the more fully we can be ourselves, the more we bring this quality to the relationship. Thus, irrespective of what or who the client thinks we are, when we are sure that we are as fully ourselves as we can consciously be, then we more easily become aware of being turned into something that we are not.

I will explain a little more of what I mean. Of late, I have felt that when I am working most effectively, in whatever capacity, as therapist, supervisor, teacher, consultant, facilitator, that is when I am most fully "who I am" as the grown-up adult. Of course that does not mean that I do not regress—become Parental in a TA or other sense, it means that I bring all of myself as much as possible to the relationship. This best describes what I mean by being fully yourself, that is, the "all about you" part of the equation.

I also feel that the all about you part has something to do with how we inevitably put ourselves into the client's shoes in the required attempt to understand from their perspective. In doing so we are of course vulnerable to imagining what our solution to the dilemmas would be, perhaps missing or not accounting for the client's ability or inability to follow a course of action. I often have biases in couples work and the best I can do is to declare these. For example I have very strong biases about fidelity which I will declare up front, although I—at least consciously—do not judge infidelity but try to understand what it communicates.

The *nothing to do with you* has, of course, to do with the transference that the client forms. This begins externally with what it means to them that you are the race, gender, age you are as well as the class, accent, and the many other aspects about you that you manifest consciously and unconsciously in terms of what these represent to the client. Then there is the internal aspect. Whoever you may be in your own mind, of course you will be used by the client to represent what they need, expect, or want from you. Where this is an unconscious process it becomes more tricky to identify and understand. You may find yourself thinking, feeling, and more disconcertingly acting in a way that is unusual/surprising or unlikely for you and at times seemingly untherapeutic. This idea that we respond to the unconscious pull leads us directly to the notion of "the use of the object". I do, however, at this junction need to make a comment about self disclosure, generally and also specifically.

Self disclosure is a central issue for the relational psychotherapist. The question of what to consciously and verbally self disclose is addressed in numerous ways in recent literature. My view is that the most significant and useful things to self disclose, judiciously, are your own thought processes: thinking, associations, and feelings that are occurring as you sit with the client and as you listen to their material. Not only is this a powerful way of relating in terms of you and I, but it is a form of intimacy and an experience that most of our clients did not have and probably do not have, where the other shares what is in their mind. This is part of an intimate way of relating. It gives feedback about the effect/impact the other has on you and also provides valuable information about how another—you—operates. It often normalizes the client's experience, especially their anxieties, as well as defusing paranoid fantasies. However, the caveat to this principle, which I feel is most significant, is that there are times and ways of consciously disclosing your process that can be more or less helpful.

In thinking about being yourself and also striving to be as authentic, spontaneous, and real there are of course risks. We can make mistakes. Hopefully these are those therapeutic errors like expressing something "unthought" (Bollas, 1987) but perhaps known, picking up a disowned thought from the other, or getting it wrong simply in the sense that it is about our process. However, if we accept the idea of a two person psychology—right brain to right brain communication and transmission, we must assume that whatever we are thinking when we are working with someone has something to do with them as well as with our own self.

In this connection we are directly led to Winnicott's (1971) late contribution known as *The Use of the Object*. This notion of the relevance of the therapist's response is one of the most clinically important notions to understand. Often however, supervisees confess reluctantly to their negative reactions and feelings, somewhat embarrassed or ashamed of finding themselves not liking, being disinterested, or impatient with a client. They are surprised at my pleasure and welcoming of their responses. These difficult countertransference reactions are the clue to the patient's/client's beginning to want to use you in the transferential relationship to represent past figures, by unconsciously creating a relationship in which you carry these difficult emotional qualities. It is a communication about the past which is usually not in a narrative form, but unconsciously expressed in the attempt to have it both recognized and understood by another, with a different relational and emotional outcome.

It is only or often through the mistakes that we may make, and the enactments that occur, that we can capture and make conscious something about the unconscious process between us. It is in this regard that boundaries are so critical because usually an enactment occurs around some boundary to the work. Conscientiously holding boundaries enables us to catch and, if we can, turn these into productive and powerful opportunities.

Some examples come to mind. I made a recent mistake when as a trainer I found myself, or heard myself, saying something before I had thought about or processed it in any way. The group had already been challenging the boundaries, coming in late after I had specifically spoken about the time boundary and how I was going to hold it tightly. Some fifteen minutes after the lunch break from which they returned, again late, one of the trainees asked if he could go to the toilet.

Already somewhat irritated with them, I heard myself say: "No. Sit down!" I hardly believed it myself. I immediately saw how furious he was; he remained simmering throughout the afternoon, although he complied with my command. I was somewhat exercised by the incident that evening, but decided to wait and see what would happen the following day. Next morning, asking to see me before we began, he thanked me for allowing him to become so angry, without defence, retaliation, or collapse. He had realized that his parents had never allowed him to express his anger. They had always either attacked him or become extremely defensive, leaving him feeling in the wrong and guilty.

Another example also comes from a supervisee, a highly experienced psychodynamically- informed practitioner, who pays careful attention to all forms of boundaries. She arrived recently, upset by what had occurred to her the day before. She had a full clinical day and got a message from a client who was somewhat irregular in her attendance to say she wasn't feeling well and would not be able to keep her appointment later that day. Soon afterwards another of her long-term patients sent a text asking if there were any possibility of coming somewhat earlier for her appointment. In view of the cancellation, without too much thought, she offered her the earlier session. Around the middle of the day the first client contacted her again; she was feeling much better and wondered if it would be alright for her to come for her session. My supervisee had to say that it would no longer be possible and felt guilty about replacing her session so quickly. Now, the really significant point of the story is that the person whose session had been replaced by what can so easily be seen as a slip by her therapist was working on having been replaced in her job by a bullying and frightening boss.

Perhaps the biggest challenge in the effective *"Use of Self"* is how to recognize in the first place, understand, work with, and read your countertransference responses. Because there is a significant unconscious component, it is impossible at times without the help of a supervisor or colleague to recognize your own process. The most important aspect of countertransference is to understand that these responses are unconscious and it is only when we act something out or find ourselves caught in an enactment, often around boundaries one way or another, that we can become aware of our own process and think about what we are contributing.

I will draw this to a conclusion by mentioning Bion's (1990, p. 5) oft quoted phrase about therapy having two frightened people in the room, it being the therapist's task to manage the anxiety of both, i.e. their own and the patient's.

So in finishing I repeat something of what I began with. The task in many ways is to keep working at and developing your understanding of yourself in the role of therapist. What are your own beliefs, defences, and vulnerabilities—known and unknown, and how do you experience and express these to others? Clinically I see this translating into a need for a continuous self reflective process, linked to self awareness of yourself.

Ongoing professional and personal development is not only a continuing professional development (CPD) requirement, but is deeply intertwined and relevant to our capacity as therapists, and the recharging and refuelling necessary for the serious and strenuous nature of the enterprise. Although supervision, training groups, workshops—in other words learning settings, are not meant to be and are not personal therapy, they can be extremely therapeutic.

It is possible that our own ongoing growth and development is a significant element in the motivation for the enterprise. I remain grateful and privileged for finding a profession and work that not only constantly challenges me but also provides me with a forum for creative and enlivened expression.

CHAPTER TWO

A response to Diana Shmukler's keynote speech—the use of self in psychotherapy

Heather Fowlie, Suhith Shivanath, Brian Fenton and Ray Little

Heather Fowlie

I wanted to start with a funny twist on the title of Diana's keynote speech and the title of this conference—"The Use of Self". As the snow began to fall and fall and wasn't stopping, the organizers started to worry about what we would do if the workshop presenters couldn't get here. As today drew closer, we began to panic and hurriedly pulled out bits of old workshops that we had done and bit of old speeches, believing by yesterday that we really would need to step into the breach at the eleventh hour. In the midst of this, one of the IARTA founders wrote on an email, "This wasn't quite the use of self that we were expecting" [laughter].

I thought I would divide what I wanted to say about the use of self into three parts: What are we trying do? How do we use ourselves? And why do we need to use our selves in relational therapy?

In terms of the "What am I trying to do?" I thought about Winnicott (1958), partly prompted by Diana's speech. He suggests that therapy is about two people playing and that the therapist's role when a person can't play is to help them to learn how to. Interestingly, one of the lovely quotes that I like about relational therapy comes from a woman called

Benjamin (2002), who defines relational therapy as "questions that come to the fore as a result of the adoption of a two-person approach". As part of this, she has a diagram, which looks like two overlapping circles. She talks about the overlapping bit in the middle, as the bit that, as relational therapists, we become interested in. In other words, we focus on what is happening for each of us and between us as we meet. What I did not know and found out when I was doing some preparation for this panel discussion was that this is Winnicott's diagram (1952), which he used to illustrate the notion of the therapeutic encounter.

When thinking about "How do I use myself?", I began to think about the times when I am most aware of using myself and noted that this is when I am usually finding it most difficult to do so, or at least do so in a way that is effective. In other words, when I'm not really pulled much, and I am experiencing myself in an Integrated Adult place, using myself feels quite easy. When, however, I experience unintegrated and unprocessed parts of myself and these parts intrude into the work, it is then that I am more profoundly called upon to extend myself in order to use myself. This reminds me of a quote of yours, Diana, that I used on the last page of my CTA case study:

> Engaged in this work we are continually thrown on our own resources. As we use ourselves, we discover our weaknesses and strengths and are forced to grow and develop aspects of our personalities. I think this is the reason that so many of us are continually fascinated and engaged by what we do. If we can keep burn-out at bay, we are privileged to pursue a profession that keeps us at the growing edge of our own need to keep growing (Shmukler, 1991, p. 134).

Continuing on with the theme of How?, I was speaking to a well-known TA practitioner the other day about whether he would write a chapter for this relational TA book, and—half tongue in cheek—he said: "I have read the relational principles [referring to the principles on which this book is based] and I have to confess that I sometimes give clients home work and sometimes I give them things to take home, I sometimes even put people on cushions—am I relational enough?" This got me thinking about who makes the decisions about what is relational.

In a similar vein, a supervisee who works with profoundly damaged people had been to a conference about trauma, and one of the speakers was talking about how she would often use rose oil with clients who were traumatized if they were experiencing flashbacks. The speaker explained that smell gets right through to a person in a way that talking sometimes can't. The supervisee wanted to know if this was okay, in other words, relational, to do this. Whilst I think it is important for all of us to think about when and why we might move to use techniques and objects in this way, I thought her question arose more out of some kind of notion about there being a relational TA police who decide how we use ourselves.

One of the concepts I really like, again it's Winnicott, is his idea that first of all the client sees the therapist as an "objective other". In other words, the client comes to therapy looking for both the "feared and the longed for relationship" (Fowlie, 2005, p. 195). The feared relationship being that you are going to be just like the person that hurt me, and the longed for, that you are going to come and fill this gap in me. And of course if we do either, we remain the objective object. What we have to be, in Winnicott's words, is a "transitional object". If we can hold that space, which makes us disappointing to the client, as we are neither the longed for nor the feared object, then we hold the possibility of becoming a "subjective object". A subject rather than an object. Playing then becomes possible.

I just want to finish with one last story, which should illustrate part of the "Why" we use ourselves. It is a story that Stephen Mitchell (1997/2005) tells—who is often credited with being the originator of relational work. Stravinsky had written a wonderful piece of music, which was impossible to play. Mitchell linked this to Freud who had said that psychotherapy was an impossible profession. A famous violinist was trying over and over again to play this piece of music and eventually he threw his violin down in fury and said, "This piece of music is impossible to play!"; and Stravinsky said, "Of course it is, of course, that is not important, what I wanted was to hear someone willing to try and play it."

And in a way that sums up for me what we are trying to do, we are trying to create a relationship, and maybe within that, the interventions that we make, what we do, is less important than the fact that we are willing to try and create a place where we can play.

Brian Fenton (reads from paper)

Diana's title directs us to a central theme for relational psychotherapy—how to "use our self" in the therapeutic encounter—and the complexity of this experience for the practitioner.

While clients need our minds in different ways (for example, alongside or opposite), these ways can be generalized into two main positions, namely one and two person modes (see Gill, 1994b; Stark 1998).

Roughly speaking, one person psychology derives from philosophical positions where the organizing of our developing self is weighted towards innate and unfolding capacities supported from the outside (Freud, 1940; Kelly, 1955; Piaget, 1960; Rogers, 1959). From this position the therapist has a supportive role in the development of the client's mindset. A two person approach is where two subjectivities more directly shape each other's psyche and the relationship between them is the primary mechanism for development and self organization. Development within this mode, is viewed as more interpersonal and intersubjective, (Bowlby, 1958; Stern, 1985; Vygotsky, 1978; Winnicott, 1985). Note this is a bidirectional process and both parties are potentially changed by the other.

Both these experiences (one and two person) occur simultaneously (Silverton, 1995) and both positions have developmental power. Each perspective can include dynamic unconscious processes and levels of relatedness, and each holds interest to relational psychotherapy. How and where we direct attention at any given time marks the differences between them.

In managing this situation I view dialectical processing as important. For me the relational perspective has emerged in response to our dialectical nature of being self and being self-other. Thus, when we adopt two person models, care needs to be taken to synthesize these with one person models. Dialectical processing itself seems to hold an innate developmental energy that works towards organizing self and other, and in some sense coping with the contradictions of existence. Emergent meaning from synthesizing relational experiences is the foundation of what could be termed relationally constructed Adult. Although initiated interpersonally (i.e. good breast/bad breast), the primary organization of emergent meanings remains a dialectical situation between one person (see Klein, 1959) and two person (see Fairbairn, 1990).

The dual nature of development is demonstrated from the beginning in nonverbal interaction. A touch says for example both that "I am not you and you are not me" (I am thus separate), and simultaneously, there can be a communication within the touch such as "I love you", which is situated initially between the infant and carer, and later internalized within the infant contributing to both the building blocks of interaction itself (see Trevarthen, 1992) and to the formation of what we might term sense of self and other. This one transaction demonstrates interrelated forms of one and two person developmental processing where the infant is finding their self boundary in relationship, and also simultaneously, self is developed and added to through relationship. Relational psychotherapy has to consider then a duality (and multiplicity) of identity formation.

Returning to Diana's title we can see this theme emerge in the consulting room in how we might work with projective processes.

Initially Freud (1940) worked projective process to support the client tell self from other. This derives from a one person attitude where we find self from pushing against the other.

This method is an attempt by the therapist to support the client to go further into their own world and in a loose sense has nothing to do with us. The asymmetrical attitude of the neutral therapist invites reflection on self/other differentiation as well as developmental processes such as idealizing and self object relating.

When we consider that the ability to tell self from other is at the heart of empathy, reflective function (Diamond & Marrone, 2003) and mentalization (see Fonagy & Target, 1998), this capacity becomes particularly crucial to the developing therapist (and is one function of a training analysis).

Diana's emphasis on self reflection and self development implies that knowing self enhances knowing other (from us). In addition, knowing ourselves intimately informs our imaginative leaps in attempting to understand our client's experiences. Further, the effort to understand seems to me to heighten bidirectional effect, bringing transformation to the therapist. In thinking like this we turn our attention to two person psychologies.

In adopting a two person approach, whereby Freud's classical position concerning projection is extended to include that to form our identity, we not only need to be able to tell self from other, we also need to gather and develop self directly through other. Here projection is viewed as a bidirectional co-constructed process (part me/part you—see Hargaden & Fenton, 2005), and as well as being potentially unhelpful, is also potentially developmental (see transformational transference, Hargaden & Sills, 2002). From this perspective, the attitude towards the emerging data (i.e. collaborative reflection on countertransference) invites a different use of the therapist's and client's minds.

In considering two person perspectives, I extend the understanding of phenomenological experience to include notions of being taken beyond ourselves, and into self/other phenomenological experience (see "we-ness", Summers & Tudor, 2000), where self can initially be found in the other. I extend also the notion of self actualization to include notions of self/other actualization. From here the development of the other requires our subjectivity and in a sense is everything to do with us and our capacity to hold in mind, and meet, what is occurring.

In my opinion the relational therapist would do well to include both forms of relating, one person doing to, from a good enough neutrality, and two person from a doing with attitude. As therapists we have the ongoing dilemma of knowing when to use our self to hold and work with projection to allow the client the space to find their own edges, and when and how to share our minds from a more two person approach.

Suhith Shivanath

When I was asked to be part of this panel, and I began to prepare for now, for this moment, I went through all kinds of thoughts and feelings, which highlighted my own internal relatedness with myself. Did I have a right to be here? Did I have anything pertinent to say? Do I have anything profound enough to say? I felt a sense of relief, however, and excitement when I saw Diana's title—"It's all about me, and it's nothing to do with me", since this acknowledges us as subjective beings and that we come to each encounter with clients, with supervisors, with colleagues from within the influences that have shaped us. We have been shaped from birth, and this forms how we perceive ourselves, others, and the world. It influences what we say and how we interact.

As I was preparing for this panel discussion, I came across a quote by Bollas who said that "in order to find the patient we must look for him [and I have added her], in ourselves" (1987, p. 202). As an Asian therapist, I work predominantly across cultures and in some respects it is not always easy to find the client within myself. I spend a lot of my time sitting on the outside, where I am curious and wanting to learn about the individual and their social context. In order to do this, some of my inquiries revolve around getting them to explain the more obvious parts of themselves (as well as the less obvious of course). Conversely, when I work with Asian clients, I have a whole different experience within me: I find myself much more stretched not to make assumptions;

so there is a knowingness of the culture that I think I have which I need to hold back on and question. This is a case in which my subjective self could get in the way and become less helpful, although, of course, I am also potentially more able to empathize with their experiences.

I also think about power a lot. I am mindful of how much power as therapists we hold. Given this, a question arises for me about the need for us to be aware of how much of what we do and say can be re-enactments of social power dynamics. For example, values imbibed through our upbringing within the class system may unconsciously inform how we respond to a client, particularly if their way of being is different from our own and/or how we expect them to be. Relational psychotherapy involves an acknowledgement that we are not, and neither is it possible for us to be, neutral or objective; in fact, our subjectivity is vitally important when working relationally. Our reliance on our subjectivity suggests that we have an added responsibility in this respect, to make ourselves aware of any biases in our thoughts and responses that we have and that may interfere with our ability to be of use to our clients.

So tipping Bollas's quote on its head, maybe the question could be, how do I not find the client in me, and how do I work with that? This reminds me of the importance of having colleagues and supervisors who bring different perspectives to the work. If a client went to see all six of us [pointing to each of the panel members], she or he would probably find different aspects of themselves in each of us. For this reason, I think it is a pity that we do not do groups as much as we used to do.

We are working on the edge of some ideological place all the time. For example, in my work with an Asian male client, I need to account for the fact that decisions that are made in the family are made for the family as a whole, and not for the individual. Do I encourage his individual right to autonomy which may subvert the family system? What then are the consequences for him and his family? How do I want to participate in this? I hold all of these things in my mind. I think that these questions are ethical considerations, and opening up our subjectivities enables us to examine our motives and our responses in open, challenging, and interesting ways.

Ray Little (reads from paper)

As a profession, we are unusual in that we use our psychological and emotional self, that is, our mind, as the tool of our trade. This can exert a lot of pressure on us as therapists, both consciously and unconsciously. Often we are involved in a talionic process in which we are stirred by the client. In addition to more cognitive associations, more primitive emotions such as rage, envy, hate, and eroticism may be stirred. These emotions may be difficult for the therapist to tolerate. We may, for example, be called upon to tolerate the feeling of murderous rage, without acting-out, so that we can understand the feeling, and then find some way of incorporating it back into the therapeutic dyad.

As a result of this pressure, it behoves us as therapists to not only take care of ourselves, but also to know ourselves psychologically and to have the kind of therapy that will enable us, as Shmukler (2003, and in this volume) states, to know what we might project into the therapeutic relationship.

The therapist's stance

The degree to which a therapist may experience pressure will, to some extent, depend on their orientation to psychotherapy. One aspect is to do with the particular stance the therapist takes in relation to the client. From my perspective, there are two broad positions that the therapist can adopt (Little, 2005).

The first stance is to be alongside the client, facing the client's problems together, locating the problems the client is presenting either outside the therapeutic relationship, or intrapsychically. That is working *with* the transference.

The second position is to stand opposite the client and allow the client's problems to be concentrated in the therapeutic relationship, addressing the client's difficulties live, in the here and now. This is working *within* the transference-countertransference matrix. Working in this way involves a greater direct use of the self.

The transference-countertransference matrix is here defined as the client's and therapist's mutual responses to each other and consists of conscious and unconscious processes, both cognitive and affective (Maroda, 2004, p. 66). Winnicott (1965) describes transference and countertransference as containing both a subjective and an objective element:

• We each bring our own history to the relationship, our expectations and experiences—this would be the subjective element.

- We also each respond to the personality and behaviour of the other (in ways that might be recognizable to most people)—this would be the objective element.

From this perspective, everything the client communicates to us is both intrapsychic and interpersonal (Maroda, 2004). Looked at in this light, the transference-countertransference relationship is not only about the reactivation of previous relational experiences, it is also about how the client and therapist are reacting to each other in the here and now. Therefore, we are working with the past in the present.

The term countertransference is taken to mean the totality of the therapist's responses to the client (Clarkin, Yeomans & Kernberg, 2006). Broadly speaking, there are two types of countertransference (Little, 2008, adapted from Racker, 1972):

- *Countertransference Associations,* which consists of ideas, thoughts, fantasies, and associations, which are less emotionally intense, and may occur both during the therapy and at other times, e.g., dreams.
- *Countertransference Positions,* which consists of emotions, stances, and positions, which are of greater intensity and often entail projective and introjective identifications.

The stance of the therapist entails bringing the self to the therapeutic dyad and being stirred and impacted by the client. Stark (1999) believes that the relational therapist can only be available to the client if the therapist remains centred in their own experience (p. 117). Thus, the therapist becomes an "observing participant" (Hirsch, 1987, p. 209), who uses their self, as Stark suggests, "to participate with the patient in an intersubjective relationship that involves mutuality and reciprocity" (p. 23).

The therapeutic stance involves finding a balance between being available to engage with the client and being able to preserve an observing perspective: having "one foot in and one foot out", as a colleague describes the process (Eusden, 2009, personal communication). With one foot in, engaging with the client and through the client's use of projective identification, the therapist will come to understand the client's experience. However, countertransference reactions can originate from either the therapist's or the client's internal world. Therefore, the therapist must be willing to examine their own responses (Clarkin et al., 2006).

The technical question will be to do with the utilization and integration of the therapist's countertransference response to the client into their therapeutic approach. It is the therapist's responsibility to consider and understand his or her responses. First of all we need to allow ourselves to be stirred and impacted by clients. The more we can allow it, the less likely we will be to repress the feelings and/or project them into the client. Second, we need to know our own primitive processes (Little, 2005), thus avoiding acting out the feelings, and instead thinking them out, initially to ourselves. The relational therapist, as Stark states, needs to recognize and acknowledge, at least to themselves and possibly to the client (1999, p. 118), their countertransference stirrings and develop the capacity to use their involvement and experience in a way that is useful to the client.

Principle 2

The importance of engagement

CHAPTER THREE

Therapeutic involvement

Richard G. Erskine

Therapeutic involvement is an integral part of all effective psychotherapy. This chapter illustrates the concept of therapeutic involvement in working within a therapeutic relationship—within the transference—and with active experiential methods to resolve traumatic experiences, relational disturbances, and life shaping decisions. Involvement is in the psychotherapist being fully present, actively inquiring about the client's phenomenological perspective, and engaging with the client in creating experiences that make unconscious material conscious. In this point of view the psychotherapist's active engagement with the client, while using the various expressive and experiential methods, is the most important factor leading to change both in clients' self perception and in their relationships with others.

The chapter takes the form of an annotated transcript providing an example of both working within the transference/countertransference dyad—focusing on an authentic person-to-person relationship—and also making effective use of expressive, experiential, and intrapsychic methods to change life-shaping decisions. Rather than thinking in terms of a one or two person therapy, I find it more professionally useful to think about therapeutic involvement, that unique experience of client and psychotherapist working in harmony, co-creating a mutual transformative experience.

* * *

Paul is a forty-year-old psychotherapist who has attended a couple of previous training workshops with me. In this particular workshop I have just finished a long theoretical presentation when Paul asked to do some personal therapy. Usually he has a good understanding of himself yet, on this day, he is troubled by unresolved thoughts and feelings. The session begins with Paul and me sitting in chairs facing each other. Paul sits with his legs crossed; his body language is relaxed and comfortable.

Richard: Paul, what are you experiencing?
   Paul: You have just given me a smile. You have touched me and I got emotional.
Richard: What kind of emotion?
   Paul: Sadness. Better said, it is sadness and pain. My intention about working with you is precisely because I noticed that I easily enter into transference with you.
Richard: Please tell me your story about transference.
   Paul: I notice that in some moments I have difficulty in relating with you in a natural way. But that it is not your fault. I am conscious enough to realize that I am having fantasies. I notice that I have a big mistrust of you and that I want to withdraw. Then I say to myself, "Look for the contact."
Richard: In these fantasies what are the ways in which I might I hurt you … so the drawing back is absolutely necessary?
   Paul: Let me tell you my internal movie. The first day you made a comment to me about what I had said following Martin's therapy demonstration. I understood that what you wanted me to do was to reflect on why I had said it. But the following day I felt out of my centre. I felt that I was in trouble with you.
Richard: So I must have shamed you.

This is the fifth transaction that I have made. It contains several elements of an involved therapeutic relationship: acknowledgement, vicarious empathy, responsibility for the therapist's errors, and my introducing the concept of shame that could possibly enhance Paul's understanding of his experience. It sets a stage for how the work may proceed; we could build on any and perhaps all of these elements. And it may be too soon; most likely Paul has much more to say before we focus on a particular element or two.

This transaction follows four transactions that are examples of phenomenological inquiry. They are not all questions but each phenomenological inquiry invites an internal search—a discovery and expression of what is internal—a revealing of one's subjective experience. Together these four inquiries form a unit of involvement that supports Paul in further describing his internal process.

> Paul: [Pauses for several seconds.] The fantasy I got was what I call a dark fantasy. I imagine that you think or ... even that you comment to other people that what I do is not right. You say, "Paul does not behave well."
>
> Richard: You mean that at dinner time or on a walk in the evening that I am gossiping about you?
>
> Paul: Not gossiping, but maybe having a commentary with somebody.
>
> Richard: What's the difference? In either case I would be belittling you. In either case, I would be making a humiliating comment.
>
> Paul: Or at least a disapproving comment.
>
> Richard: It seems that what makes your fantasy painful is that I would be doing it behind your back and not to your face.

In the three previous transactions I am clarifying and identifying the significance of Paul's distress. This transaction and the one to follow are examples of two types of empathy: vicarious and emotional. First I am making use of vicarious introspection—using my own experience to cognitively identify and explore Paul's possible subjective experience of belittlement or humiliation. This is coupled with the next transaction, a second aspect of empathy—an expression of my affect: "That would hurt." At this moment we are engaged in a shared affective experience: the essence of emotional empathy. The core of therapeutic involvement is in the capacity of the psychotherapist to express empathy accurately within a tone or facial expression that provides the reciprocal to the client's affect; in this situation affective attunement is in the compassionate tone that responds to Paul's sadness.

Paul: Correct.

Richard: [Said compassionately] That would hurt!

Paul: Of course. If there is something between you and me, and
            you would come and tell me, that would give me a lot of
            security and trust.

Richard: So as a result of the fantasy that you are telling me about …
            you pull away … and you are not centred within yourself.
            [Richard pauses for a few seconds.]
            Paul, those are all the symptoms of shame.

Paul: [Pauses for several seconds, looking sad, and looks to the
            ground and shrugs his shoulders.]

Richard: Can you tell me about those feelings of sadness?

Paul: [Pauses for 10 seconds.] I feel it inside of me as an old com-
            panion. I don't really know where it originated from, but it is
            familiar to me.

I have re-introduced the concept of "shame". Paul has not mentioned
it, but his sadness, long pauses, and lack of eye contact all hint that he
may be experiencing shame. Often, all the person may know is that he
or she is sad, nervous, feels small, or cannot make contact. The origins
of shame may not be immediately available as explicit memory—only
as procedural memory—until there is safety in relationship. It is often
necessary that the psychotherapist introduce a concept such as shame,
envy, revenge, or betrayal so that the client can begin to think about his
or her relational experiences.

Richard: Well then, let's stay between you and me. Here you had trust
            in me and in your internal movie; I betray you by talking
            about you behind your back.

Rather than take Paul to some unknown historical story, I keep the
focus on the two of us in the present moment. I am building on the trust
in our relationship that Paul previously experienced by suggesting to
him that he maintain the sad feelings that have arisen as a result of my
behaviour and that we talk about those feelings and his self-regulating
reactions, as if transference did not exist.

    If there have been misattunements or therapeutic errors, or even
humiliating comments that I have made, they are more likely to be evident, and resolved, if the therapeutic work is in the present, between

us, rather than searching for an origin of Paul's feelings. We can always do the historical work later if it proves necessary. Keeping the dialogue about our current relationship seems most important at this point in the therapy. It is "between us" that Paul can form a new relational pattern; perhaps I too will learn and grow from this encounter.

Paul: That is it. When I lose contact with you and I enter into old stories, I lose my trust in you. [Paul starts to cry.]

Richard: Those tears are important.
[Paul nods while he cries.] Just close your eyes and go where that cry takes you. [Paul closes his eyes … a few seconds pass.] It looks like you are stopping your body from weeping, as though your body knows a sense of betrayal … having trusted someone and they don't live up to your trust.

Paul: [Takes some deep breaths and pauses for thirty seconds with his eyes closed. He opens his eyes and smiles at Richard.] These words touch me. Your words describe that I trust somebody that betrays my trust. I'm sad and I feel like I am shaking inside. [Paul wipes the tears from his face … and after a pause is no longer crying.]

In this last set of transactions I validated Paul's feelings and experiences while also bringing his attention to the connection between his crying, shaking body, and the betrayal of trust from a significant other. His shaking body is telling a significant story that he is not yet putting into language. He has been able to tell a bit about his emotional experience by using the metaphor of an internal movie—a movie in which he is humiliated.

Is his yet untold story solely about how my behaviour has impacted him? Or is it about other significant relationships? Or both? It may be time to explore beyond our relationship (he did mention that this feeling is familiar) and then perhaps return to articulating the quality of connection we have with each other: both his former trust and now his big mistrust of me.

An effective, relationally focused integrative psychotherapy continually weaves the client's and psychotherapist's experiences of their relationship in the present moment with an exploration of the emotional and self-stabilizing results of past relationships in the client's life. It is this dual focus that provides a double opportunity to resolve the troubling effects of relational disruptions with introjected others while also establishing new patterns of relationship with the psychotherapist. I then take the risk of expressing my intuition about why he may be crying. I phrase it as a tentative question rather than as an interpretation.

Richard: Paul, what was your relationship with your previous mentor? You mentioned at lunch that you no longer see him.

Paul: I always kept a secure distance from him. I did not feel sufficiently protected and taken care of to open up for a closer relationship.

Richard: Did you want a closer relationship with him before you kept him distant … or even while you kept him distant?

Paul: It is like a double movement. A wish to be nearer … while a part of me says "Stay away!"

Richard: Have you done that double movement with me these past two days … after I made that comment? Had your mentor also done something that kept you away, or did you sense something would go wrong and never got close?

Here I open two possible avenues of discovery. If he talks about our relationship it will provide the opportunity to explore new possibilities between us. If he chooses to talk about his mentor, we can work on resolving that relational conflict first and then I will also use it as a metaphor about our relationship, eventually bringing our therapeutic dialogue back to what is both present and missing in the contact between us.

Paul: Both are there. I think my observations were correct. But, also, when I can relate with somebody in a relaxed and a natural manner, that is one thing …. But when I notice that I feel uncomfortable and I don't know how to be …. That happened to me on the second day with you. That used to happen often with [he speaks the name of his former trainer and supervisor].

Richard: Then I will assume that I hurt you the other day by either the content or the style in which I spoke to you … or at least in the context of doing it in front of your colleagues here. That was a break in our relationship!

At this point I am bringing the focus back to my failure—to the error I made that ruptured Paul's trust. I have some reparation to do before we turn our attention to his disappointments in other significant relationships or to explore his sense of shame. If I take responsibility for how I have failed or betrayed him and make the necessary corrections, then it may not be necessary to explore his loss of trust with his previous mentor or any other significant person. The healing of his shame or sense of betrayal may occur in how I repair our relationship.

> Paul: I think for me it was your tone of voice.
> Richard: Can you share with me the tone of voice that you heard? I don't remember it.
> Paul: For me it was strict.
> Richard: So it is the tone that is shaming ... the strictness of it? [Paul pauses and nods.] Does the tone say, "You did it wrong"? [Richard says, shaking his finger at Paul to emphasize the tone with a body gesture.]

My gesture is used to validate Paul's experience of the tone—a shaming gesture that describes the strict tone that Paul heard. At this point acknowledging and validating Paul's experience are the most important transactions—transactions that signal my involvement. Any explanation or description of what I felt or meant would be non-therapeutic and may create an even greater rupture in his sense of trust. It is therapeutically necessary that I de-centre from my own experience and stay with Paul's. How Paul makes meaning of our transactions is most important in understanding how he organizes his experience and in eventually co-creating a new set of relational anticipations. My immediate therapeutic priority is in re-establishing a trusting relationship.

> Paul: Yes, that gesture shows how I received it. I felt that at that moment you did not approve my words that I addressed to Martin. It is like you said, "You did wrong by saying that at that moment".
> Richard: It is true that I did not approve of it. That is true. [Small pause.] What do you think?

Being straightforward and honest about my behaviour is important in our relationship. I could imply that the disapproval Paul is experiencing is the result of his misunderstanding and/or transference, but the effect would be a loss of my authenticity and genuine involvement. Truth telling is essential if we are to have a healing relationship. In the next several transactions my honesty and authenticity, as well as making Paul's point of view central, are significant in establishing Paul's security-in-relationship.

Paul: [Pause for five seconds.] You linked this comment of mine with other comments, saying to me that after other pieces of work I also make diagnostic comments of this type.

Richard: That's true. I did say something to that effect. I had seen a pattern in two other workshops.

Paul: For me, this comment was not correct.

Richard: Do you think I made a mistake … and that I was not correct?

Paul: I think you are not precise.

Richard: Tell me about that. You know, I could be wrong.

Paul: [Pauses and starts to talk, but hesitates and stops.]

Richard: You just interrupted yourself there. What did you interrupt inside?

Paul: [Pauses for a couple of seconds, looks to the ground and sighs.] A commentary about what I did in other workshops leaves me defenceless, because we can either reflect on what is happening at this moment … such as my comment on the work that Martin did…this for me is here and now. But when you connect it with other stories and you say, "It is like this", I get lost.

Richard: That makes sense. So, in the future, if I think you are misunderstanding someone, you want me to keep it only in the now. And you need me not to bring in other events … only the current event.

Paul: Yes, that is it. In the present I can find myself and understand myself. And I can understand what you are saying.

Richard: I can do that for you!

Graciousness is an important aspect of involvement. "I can do that for you!" is one of the most wonderful interpersonal transactions, provided there are no strings attached—no "You owe me". A freely given "I can do that for you!" is a form of unconditional positive regard for the other, an intimate connection. It is beyond apology; it is a commitment to future action and therefore reparative.

> Paul: [Paul nods his head.] While we are talking I noticed that my body is tense … and for the last five minutes I have noticed that it has tensed a bit more.
>
> Richard: Well, let's go back to your movie. Run it ahead at fast speed and see what the terrible ending could be from this conversation.
>
> Paul: This conversation or of my movie?
>
> Richard: It could be mixed, so you choose.
>
> Paul: [Closes his eyes and thinks for thirty seconds.] In the ending of my movie I remain alone. And not only alone regarding you, but alone in a deeper sense of being *really alone*. [Pause.] What moved me, especially yesterday, was the theme of belonging that you were illustrating.
>
> Richard: Earlier this week you seemed very relaxed and free … when you made that comment about Martin. Perhaps it would have been much better for you if I just kept my mouth shut.
>
> Paul: [Sighs.] To exchange and also not to agree with ideas and opinions seems all right to me. I see how you work and I appreciate you a lot. I sometimes see a piece of work that I don't agree with, but that does not change my appreciation for you.
>
> Richard: Oh, I did not know that you disagreed with it. I would like to know about that.
>
> Paul: [Laughs.] Some I have told you.
>
> Richard: Yes, but it's the ones you have not told me that I am curious about now. But you have also said it was my tone, not specifically the content, but the tone.

There are many potentially therapeutic directions to follow in these previous few sentences: what was occurring between us in the past five minutes that increased his body tension, his internal movie, his deep sense of aloneness, the theme of belonging, his different opinions, and my errors. Investigating each of these may well reveal useful therapeutic material; each will take Paul to different awarenesses, memories, and beliefs about self and others. I have only seconds to make a choice.

Therapeutic involvement includes making use of all the personal and professional experience that the psychotherapist has accumulated: from our understanding of theory, from supervision, from working with similar clients, from cinemas and novels, from our own personal therapy, and from our unique sensitivities. We then selectively use these experiences to choose our areas of inquiry. Therapeutic involvement includes a sense of somatic resonance with our clients. As an outcome of my somatic resonance with Paul I steered the therapy to what I suspected was the source of Paul's body tension—that tension which may have been building up in the past several minutes. I thought it was important to bring Paul's attention back to the tone of my voice and how he sensed my strict tone. But I was not certain. I wondered if his body tension was a reaction to my tone, or something that has happened between us that we were not yet talking about, or if he was having a bodily reaction to some emotional memory?

Paul: Yes, and the tone was badly done. That is how I received it. [Paul shakes his finger at Richard.]

Richard: Please do that gesture again. [Richard shakes his finger at Paul in imitation of a gesture that Paul has just made ... a gesture that Richard made earlier to emphasize the strict tone that Paul heard.] You did this [shaking his finger].

Paul: [Shakes his head.] No, I was not conscious that I did that.

Richard: So the tone is badly done. Can you translate those words into German and say it? "Badly done"... or something similar? [Paul no longer lives in Germany, but the language of his first twenty-five years was German.]

Paul: *Das hast du falsch gemacht.* (You did it wrong.) [Shaking his finger at Richard.]

Richard: Now do that again with your hand.

Paul: *Das hast du falsch gemacht.* [Shakes his finger, then fist at Richard.]

Richard: Now close your eyes and do it.

I have directed Paul to speak in his original language. At this moment I am relying on my previous experiences in doing psychotherapy with bilingual people. I am also assuming that his body tension is because of what he is not saying. Having him express himself in German may facilitate self-expression and new awarenesses. Closing his eyes may also be effective because it may take him out of the present context and activate memories that have not been conscious until now.

In the last four transactions I am using the method of therapeutic direction. In these transactions the therapeutic work is not directly in the transactions between us but, rather, it is in the client's discovery of his internal processes, a learning about his unconscious or intrapsychic processes. Therapeutic direction should only be used within the context of a securely established relationship—the relational dynamics bracket any intrapsychic work. In the next several transactions, the therapeutic direction is based on the psychotherapist's full involvement with the client.

Paul: [Closes his eyes.] *Das hast du falsch gemacht.* (You did it wrong.)
Richard: Now with the right tone and louder.
Paul: *Das hast du falsch gemacht.*
Richard: Keep going.
Paul: *Das hast du falsch gemacht!*
Richard: Now, keep going and finish the sentence.
Paul: *Das hast du falsch gemacht!!*
Richard: Keep going … keep talking.
Paul: *Das macht man nicht so. Das hast du falsch gemacht!* (One does not do it like this. You did it wrong!) [Takes a heavy sigh and looks like he is close to crying.]
Richard: You know that tone.

This transaction and my next are examples of validating what has been significant in Paul's life. My validating comment opens the possibility for Paul to express emotions that have remained unexpressed. Prior to these last few transactions I was not sure if he was expressing how he experienced my behaviour, the meaning in my tone of voice, or whether he was quoting someone else. From the intensity of his emotional reaction I assumed that he was speaking from an archaic experience, hence my comment, "You know that tone".

Paul: [Nods his head then bows his head and cries for over a minute.]
Richard: You know that tone very well [said very gently].

Paul: [Long pause. He sighs and nods his head.] That is true. [He wipes the tears from his face with a tissue and blows his nose.] It takes me back directly to the two years I lived alone with my father after my parents' separation and my mother moved back to England, when I was fourteen to sixteen. I realize now that there was nobody else. I think that before then, when we lived together, his tone did not hurt me because there were five people. After their separation I was there with him alone.

Richard: [Touches Paul's hand.] Show me again. [After a pause Richard shakes his finger at Paul.]
    "Badly done, badly done."

At this point there are two primary nonverbal transactions that I am doing. I tenderly touch Paul's hand to make physical contact and provide a sense of security between us before he goes on with his story. He may need our physical contact as a safe reference point as he uncovers old memories. Secondarily, I repeat the gesture of a pointing finger while simultaneously repeating the words, "Badly done". My finger pointing and critical words constitute an enactment that may stimulate his memories. An important aspect of a relationally focused integrative psychotherapy is in the psychotherapist's willingness to be actively involved by engaging the client in re-experiencing difficult or even traumatic events. Through a combination of a well established secure relationship and the judicious use of experiential methods, the psychotherapist creates a "safe emergency" in which the client can recover previously unconscious memories, feelings, and life-script forming conclusions and decisions.

Paul: I have one memory that stands out. For me it is so incoherent that I always kept it apart. For me it is not understandable and it only happened once.

Richard: What is that?

Paul: That my father at a certain moment told me: "I would like you to be dead."

Richard: What a betrayal. It may have lasted only a moment, but the memories lasted for years and years and years.

Paul: Yes. It disturbed me completely. I could not understand, but I never forgot.

Richard: Say it again so it makes an impact on me.

Paul: *Ich wünschte, du wärest tot.* (I wish you were dead.)

Richard: Now do it in his tone.

Paul: [In a strict voice.] *Ich wünschte, du wärest tot!*

Richard: And with the same gesture.

Paul: No, I don't remember his gesture.

Richard: But you know the tone and you know the message.

Paul: He said it with total disapproval.

Richard: Not only disapproval of your behaviour.

Paul: [Points to himself with his finger to his chest.] But of myself ... that is what I felt with him. [He places his hand on the side of his face, put his head down and cries.] I feel tremendous loneliness.

Richard: "Tremendous loneliness".

Here I am using the technique of therapeutic highlighting, repeating the client's words, therefore acknowledging and validating what the client has just said as a way to underscore the significance of his words and affect. The previous enactment has stimulated Paul's memory of his father's words, "I wish you were dead!" Now Paul is aware of the context of his "tremendous loneliness" and his anticipation of disapproval.

Paul: I remember this year as the most difficult year in my life; a dark year.

Richard: Did he destroy something that day?

Paul: Not only that day but with everything that happened.
    He never said these words again, but his message was that I was not valuable.

Richard: And I did a mini-version of the same thing when you heard my tone. The tone in my voice implied that you were of no value.

I am again bringing the focus back to the relationship between Paul and me. I am taking responsibility for the fact that for Paul my tone implied that he was "not valuable". It would be easy to keep the focus only on his father's behaviour but if this is going to be a healing relationship, my taking responsibility and making the necessary corrections will be extremely important. The work will now weave back and forth between a focus on us—our present relationship, as Paul experiences it—and a focus on his relationship with his father.

Paul: This was the trigger. Do you remember the first work we did together?

Richard: At this moment, no, but if you keep going I will. You have to press the right buttons on my computer.

Paul: Four or five years ago in London.

Richard: I remember meeting you there, but at the moment I don't remember, so keep going.

Paul: I worked there for the first time with respect to my father and I couldn't talk to him in an empty chair.

Richard: Yes. I remember that you could only talk to me about him.

Paul: Because my experience of that period of my life was that he was this big [Paul opens his arms outward and wide] and I without power.

Richard: Now I remember that session we had. So, is it accurate to assume that when you got the verbal message from your father—at age sixteen—that you were of "no value"… that it had been happening all along, but much more subtly?

Rather than make a pronouncement or an interpretation about the psychological dynamics between Paul and his father, I ask Paul a question that solicits his understanding. This is based on an important principle of a relationally orientated psychotherapy: the absence of certainty on the part of the psychotherapist. Involvement then includes a continual phenomenological inquiry about the client's experience, holding his or her self-expressions and opinions in high esteem. Both client and therapist learn and grow from this shared experience.

Paul: In some manner, yes. When my parents separated and my two sisters went to England with my mother, I chose to be with my father … to not leave him alone … the family broke and that was horrible for him. Two years later, when I was fifteen, his mother died and that for him was like the last blow. I think he was not there for me.

Richard: So it was the last blow to you also. [Paul nods his head intensely and says yes.] A real knockout?

Paul: Enough that I left.
Richard: So yesterday ... were you leaving me?

Here I again bring Paul's attention to our relationship. I inquire about how he may be using his self-stabilizing strategies with me that he learned to use when his father was "not there". It is in our current therapeutic relationship that he can relax his old self-stabilizing patterns that interfere with both full internal and interpersonal contact.

Paul: The day before yesterday. Yesterday I re-encountered myself and therefore I felt more comfortable with you.
Richard: Why didn't you stay distant? Why give me a second chance?
Paul: I feel a need to be near to you.
Richard: So what happens if I continue to make other mistakes like this one? Let's look at the future film. Let's say I make these mistakes again.

Now I am shifting the focus of our therapeutic work to the future. What have we each learned from this session? How will we be different with each other? I have already committed myself to speaking only about a current event and not bringing external events into any discussion.

The therapy that follows has a distinctive cognitive and behavioural focus—thinking together about how to do "it" differently in the future. This is still an integral part of a relational psychotherapy. If done with respect, it constitutes a shared experience: inquiring about how Paul envisions being different and me sharing my perspective of how he can change his reactions.

Paul: I think that with two or three occasions we will repeat ourselves and then I would withdraw in a definite manner.
Richard: So to withdraw is a self-stabilizing solution for you?
Paul: That is one solution, to protect myself.
Richard: Oh ... you call that protection?
Paul: [Laughs.] Yes. Not because you are so dangerous, but because when I connect with this disapproval and loneliness it leaves me knocked out.
Richard: Yes, and then you probably stabilize yourself by withdrawing. [Pause.]
          Can I argue with you?

Paul: OK.

Richard: The real protection … the most effective protection … is to do what you did here today.

Paul: [Nods his head.] Yes. I woke up this morning and I felt that I had to work for two reasons. Because our relationship matters to me.

Richard: And for that I am very happy. I did not know that you were distancing; I could not tell. And the second reason?

Paul: Because I want to heal this wound.

This is a mini-contract from Paul that allows me to take the next therapeutic direction—a direction that takes Paul back to his original relationship difficulties with his father. To facilitate this experiential work, I encouraged Paul to express his hurt and angry feelings directly to his father, which he did with a lot of emotion. I then made use of therapeutic direction to facilitate Paul's awareness of his original script decision.

Space prevents a detailed inclusion of this latter half of the psychotherapy. The expressive methods I employed will be familiar to TA practitioners versed in re-decision therapy. Many of these experiential methods are illustrated in Integrative Psychotherapy in Action (Erskine & Moursund, 2010).

With Paul, the experientially expressive methods included facilitating the full access to and expression of his retroflected pain and anger at his father through a bodily-active method using voice and action (hitting a pillow with his fist and speaking out about his pain and anger for the very first time). Then a "two-handed" discussion—a vehicle for the expression of intrapsychic dialogue—enabled him to realize both sides of the impasse facing him: his need to be close and his self-stabilizing urge to withdraw for safety. This two-handed experiential discussion identified and clarified for Paul the relational pattern that was being enacted in the present with me and significant others since he was an adolescent.

The safety-in-relationship which I established with Paul, along with the physically expressive and emotionally evocative methods, Paul's experimentation in new behaviour, and a new awareness of the implications of his life-shaping script decision, all jelled together to result in Paul making a life-changing re-decision.

The focus of the psychotherapy moved between our relationship, the past relationship between Paul and his father, and back to our current relationship.

As I emphasized earlier, the healing of our client's relational disruptions occurs in two dimensions: by working within a contactful therapeutic relationship and intrapsychically by the client expressing his or her feelings and needs to an introjected significant other. When we focus the psychotherapy both on the current client/therapist relationship and make judicious use of expressive methods, we strengthen the possibility that our clients can find both security-in-relationship and the courage to reorganize self-stabilizing behaviours and change script decisions.

* * *

In this psychotherapy I have focused on both the centrality of the therapeutic relationship and the use of experiential and expressive methods. Without a quality relationship the experiential methods would simply be doing something to the client. Within a caring therapeutic relationship the expressive and experiential methods are used in a co-creative process with and for the client. When the psychotherapist is fully contactful and completely involved in the relationship with the client, the client can then risk experimenting with active methods that create a therapeutically useful re-enactment of old relational failures and traumas.

This chapter is a condensed version of a longer paper entitled "Integrating Experiential Methods in a Relational Psychotherapy", Vancouver: Institute for Integrative Psychotherapy, 2011, pp. 56, www. IntegrativePsychotherapy.com

CHAPTER FOUR

Countertransference self-disclosure

Ray Little

Introduction

The particular relational principles and concepts that influence my approach include aspects of the psychodynamic and humanistic traditions. I consider that many of the problems that clients present have their roots in earlier relationships, particularly with their primary caretakers. A variation of these difficulties is then perpetuated in their current relationships. Therefore, I believe a relationship has the potential for transforming their difficulties, creating a narrative with different meanings.

Furthermore, I see the mind as made up of relational schemas (Little, 2011) and that human development occurs within a "relational matrix" (Burke & Tansy, 1991, p. 370). My clinical focus is to attend to these schemas within the transference-countertransference relationship. The client and therapist begin to create a unique coupling that involves an engagement between two subjectivities. This engagement offers the opportunity for the client to meet the new object, work through the old object relationship, and reclaim the self.

I will here focus on the countertransference element of the transference-countertransference matrix and the application of the

47

therapist's use of countertransference self-disclosure from a relational perspective.

The debate about self-disclosure has evolved because of clinical and ethical concerns as well as deep-rooted and contrasting philosophical differences about what helps clients. Those from a psychodynamic background might be more familiar with anonymity and the theoretical discouragement of certain aspects of self-disclosure, considering this to be an intrusion into the client's internal world, whereas for those from a humanistic tradition, self-disclosure may be part of the therapeutic frame and they may be more at ease with it. Perhaps the theoretical task is to find a balance between these two positions.

In line with contemporary understanding the term countertransference is taken to mean the totality of the therapist's responses to the client (Clarkin, Yeomans & Kernberg, 2006), and is determined by:

1. The client's transference to the therapist of ego state relational units (Little, 2006), which may generate a reaction.
2. The reality of the client's life and the therapist's reactions; for example, a bereaved client may provoke sadness.
3. The therapist's own transference dispositions, as determined by his or her ego state relational units.
4. The reality of the therapist's life that may influence how the therapist behaves with the client, e.g. suffering a cold and not wanting to see anybody.

Engagement in relationship

Stark (1999) translates Mitchell's (1988) delineation of his three psychotherapy models in the following way. The "drive conflict model" she describes as the *enhancement of knowledge*, in which the therapist responds interpretively, "the developmental-arrest" model as the *provision of experience*, in which the therapist responds empathically, and "the relational-conflict model" as the *engagement in relationship*, in which the therapist responds authentically. She suggests that the therapist is continuously shifting between these three modes of action.

In a relational-conflict model, and thus a relational transactional analysis model (see Hargaden, 2010, for an exposition of the commonalities between these two), what occurs in the therapeutic dyad will take account of the total experience of both the therapist and client.

This stance entails a further relational principle, which is the engagement in relationship.

Engagement in relationship, as outlined in the introduction, concerns helping the client to understand their impact on the therapist and also the therapist's impact on the client. Engagement also entails the therapist being centred within his or her own experience. The therapist makes use of his or her countertransference, seen as an important source of information about both the therapist and client. The transference-countertransference matrix is seen as co-created within the therapeutic dyad and represents a unique coupling. A further ingredient is the need to be able to shift between being the old object of earlier relationship and the new object; between the repeated and needed relationship, to understand the nature of the present engagement. As Stark describes, the therapist will be "drawn into participating with the patient in her enactments and yet ... preserve a perspective that enables her to have some understanding of what has been mutually enacted in the relationship" (p. 118). Self-disclosure of the therapist's countertransference in the process of engagement is a significant therapeutic option.

Self-disclosure

It seems that, for some therapists, self-disclosure has become equated with the relational approach. "There is a common misperception that to work relationally means to self-disclose relentlessly" (Wachtel, 2008, p. 245). Wachtel reminds us that in a relational orientation self-disclosure is permitted, not required.

As therapists, we cannot avoid revealing ourselves. The way we talk, our gender, our dress, the furnishings of our consulting rooms are all aspects of ourselves that we reveal. Further, the therapist's interpretations are disclosures, since they demonstrate the existence of a different and separate mind. When the therapist sits opposite the client, in contrast to using the couch, disclosure of the therapist's subjectivity is inevitable. The client will interpret the therapist's behaviour and responses to their expressions and behaviour; as does the therapist. This process will be both conscious and unconscious.

Further to the inevitable disclosures, we need to consider the therapist's deliberate self-disclosure. My goal in exploring countertransference self-disclosure is to invite us to consider what we might be disclosing, when and when not to disclose, and if we do, how we do and the motivation for it.

Self-disclosure of the countertransference

According to Maroda (2004), focusing on and incorporating the revelation and analysis of the countertransference into psychotherapy technique increases the opportunity that dynamic conflict will be resolved within the therapeutic dyad and enhances the here and now relationship.

Aron (1996) poses the question, "When is it useful for an analyst deliberately to self-disclose?" (p. 223), and provides various questions to consider. In summary, he invites us to think for which clients it might be useful, at what point, and under what conditions. He further invites the therapist to reflect on the ethics involved.

Therapeutic frame and method

The process and degree of countertransference self-disclosure that a therapist will allow him or herself, will be influenced by their therapeutic frame, and how boundaries are understood, as well as by the therapeutic method, in particular how the purpose of therapy is conceived and accomplished. Maintaining our therapeutic frame enables us to detect any erosion resulting from unconscious processes.

Gorkin (1987) offers the following arguments in favour of self-disclosure:

- Self-disclosures may confirm the patient's sense of reality.
- They may help to establish the therapist's honesty and genuineness.
- They show that the therapist is not so different from the patient, that the therapist too is human.
- Self-disclosures clarify the nature of the patient's impact on the therapist.
- Self-disclosures may help to break through treatment impasses and deeply entrenched resistance.

On the other hand self-disclosures by the therapist should take account of the client's process, their developmental level of functioning, the current state of the therapeutic relationship, and the nature of the transference-countertransference matrix. In my view an aim of relational therapy is to deepen the transference-countertransference relationship. Self-disclosure may not be judicious if it forecloses on deepening that relationship, or is used defensively.

A technical choice point

There may be a tension between self-disclosing, on the one hand, and staying with, and working with the client's projections on the other. If I self-disclose I may disrupt the projections that the client needs me to understand, but self-disclosing may also facilitate a different process. This represents a technical choice point.

Clinical example I: Non-Disclosure. The countertransference response I had to a stoic man who was talking about his musical interests, was the urgent desire to tell him I played guitar, as I knew he did. This was interesting because, at that point, his stoicism made it difficult for me to warm to him. Reflecting on this led me to understand that he wanted to connect with me. At that point, I could have self-disclosed and told him of my interest in guitars. This may have enabled him to identify with me. Instead, I chose to talk of what I understood of his needs at that point, and how he probably wanted to connect with me. I offered him my interpretation of my countertransference response. This man used projective identification extensively to rid himself of his needs and maintain his self-reliance. I had received his projection and converted it into an aspect of myself that identified with him. In so doing I understood the communicative elements. The aspect of my countertransference process that was particularly mine was the interest in guitars. What he projected was his need to connect. At an unconscious level, I had combined the two. His use of projective identification worked because an aspect of me identified with his projection: it is an interpersonal process.

Clinical example II: Countertransference Disclosure. In the case of a client who lacked awareness of her impact on others, my self-disclosure gave her an opportunity to receive feedback in the present moment. At the end, of a stormy session during which the client attacked me in a sadistic and persecutory manner, she asked me gleefully if I was angry with her. It was as if she would feel triumphant in having provoked me. I felt a pull to comply and say I was angry. However, I said, "No I don't feel angry. I feel frightened and bullied." I felt we had a strong enough attachment to tolerate the disclosure. She was shocked by the feelings I disclosed. The client's expectation of being faced with an angry person was familiar. The fear that I felt was the client's disavowed feeling, which she had learnt to repress when faced with her bullying parent.

In the first example, in not disclosing my countertransference, and instead examining my experience of introjective identification, I could then understand what the client was unconsciously struggling with and attempting to communicate through projective identification. In the second example, in my disclosing, the client had the experience of knowing how she was impacting on me, and from that she could then perhaps begin to know her own response of fear to her internal sadistic bully with which I was identifying.

Gabbard and Wilkinson (1994) suggest that one of the purposes of self-disclosure is to inform the client of the "interpersonal and intra-psychic use that the patient is making of the therapist" (p. 143). They further suggest that this form of self-disclosure can be defined as "clinical honesty" (p. 143). This is echoed by Maroda (2010), who describes addressing the need for "affective communication and personal feedback" (p. 159) as one of the tasks in treating borderline personalities. Gabbard and Wilkinson highlight that, in working with borderline clients in particular, self-disclosure of the countertransference will have an influence on several areas of the therapeutic work, including transference exploration, patient revelations, and neutrality.

Technical neutrality

Greenberg (1986) highlights the nature and importance of neutrality within a relational-conflict model. Within this, an important area for consideration is whether the therapist's disclosure promotes or detracts from the therapist's ability to maintain technical neutrality (Little, 2011). It is an attitude of mind, not a set of behaviours, entailing a non-judgemental stance which attempts to find a balance between engagement and observation as well as balancing an attitude and stance between being perceived as both the new object and the old object (Greenberg, 1986). The client will invite the therapist to repeat old experiences but will also long to be exposed to new experiences. At times, the therapist will seem more like someone from the past and at times someone new. Technical neutrality involves acceptance of all parts of the client; not being invested in any one aspect over another.

Old Object

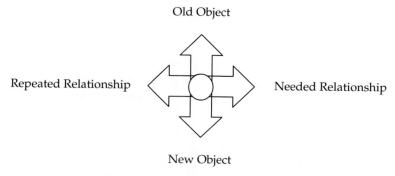

Repeated Relationship   Needed Relationship

New Object

Figure 1. The position of technical neutrality.

This enables the client to work through the old object relationship, find the new object, and reclaim the self. Neutrality is measured by the client's experience of the therapist as both the old and new object (Figure 1).

Technical neutrality is an aspect of the "therapeutically required relationship" (Little, 2011) and represents that which it is appropriate for the therapist to provide, as opposed to that which was needed from the primary carers but was missing, insufficient, or part of a traumatic experience. This will need to be understood and grieved. One way of understanding the working through of these processes would be to consider this a mourning process.

Self-disclosure may impede or enhance neutrality and the working through process. For therapy to get underway the therapist will need to be seen as a good enough new object who offers containment, and for therapy to come to an end the therapist will probably need to be seen as the old object (Greenberg, 1986). The therapist might not interpret the existence of the bad/old object in the early phase of therapy so as to enable the client to settle in. A good enough relationship needs to be built before the client can bring any disavowed feelings directly into the therapy.

Counter-therapeutic self-disclosure

The space between the therapist and client is a dynamic and changing expanse of conscious, non-conscious, and unconscious processes (Summers, 2011, this volume), verbal and nonverbal communication.

Self-disclosure may open up or close down this space and may be in the service of the "therapeutically required relationship" (Little, 2011), or a defensive manoeuvre by the therapist.

Newly practising therapists from a humanistic tradition may have a tendency to self-disclose in order to anchor the therapy in the working alliance (Greenson, 1967). They may be uncomfortable with the client's transference perception of them and try to impose what they see as reality, thereby discouraging the development of the transference-countertransference relationship. Alternatively, therapists may self-disclose to gain approval from the client (Myers & Hayes, 2006, quoted in Maroda, 2010, p. 109), as with the therapist who demonstrates to the abused client that they do care for them, unlike their abusive parent. This projects the sadistic persecutory object outside the consultancy room, so that the client can continue to be seen as a victim and the therapist as the idealized perfect other.

There are benefits and costs to the therapeutic relationship as a result of the therapist's self-disclosure which need to be assessed individually. Self-disclosure by the therapist needs to be a choice, and we need to be "attentive to the consequences" (Wachtel, 2008, p. 247).

Therapist self-disclosure may be experienced as intrusive or abusive, and too much for the client to tolerate. At times, we may feel under pressure from the client, or from our theories, to disclose. If we feel obliged, we are probably caught up in something that needs understanding. If we feel under pressure from our theories, then they are an object that may be tyrannizing us in that moment. We need to think carefully and choose whether to disclose.

If the countertransference contains split off, expelled elements of the client's psyche, it may be more therapeutic to contain these elements until they are understood. Carpy (1989) suggests that if the therapist is able to tolerate the projected feelings that are the basis of the countertransference, this "by itself can help the patient, and produce psychic change" (p. 289). By tolerate, he means "the ability to allow oneself to experience the patient's projections in their full force, and yet be able to avoid acting them out in a gross way" (p. 289).

Clinical example III. I will now describe an invitation to self-disclose that the therapist believed could lead to a reinforcement rather than an experience that has the potential for growth. A depressed young man had spoken of something he was wrestling with at work. The therapist commented that he seemed caught between a rock and a hard place, and seemed unable to make a choice between two options. She noticed that she did not feel involved as he spoke, as if he was holding her at arm's length. Towards the end of the session, the client asked if she was angry with him because he could not make up his mind. The idea that the therapist might be angry with him left him anxious and he sought reassurance before leaving the session.

The therapist did not feel angry with him, but she was aware that if she answered the question with a "Yes" or "No" that would keep them in his script (Berne, 1972). The therapist thought that his fear of her anger needed to be addressed. A "Yes" would only have confirmed the client's beliefs. A "No" may have given him temporary reassurance ("She's not angry this time"), but left the fear intact. In this example, the therapist is actively engaged in the relationship and is able to hold in mind the meanings implied in the request for disclosure and the impact of this request.

If a client perceives the therapist to feel a particular way, and the therapist does not feel that way, the therapist should consider what in his or her behaviour served to trigger the client's perception. The client is probably interpreting some aspect of the therapist's behaviour.

Self-disclosure in the context of separateness

With some clients, the clinical task is to support their individuation and separation (Mahler, Pine & Bergman, 1975). Self-disclosure can serve as well as hinder this developmental goal. Many clients struggle with being separate in relationship and some will try to merge with the therapist to avoid separateness. A request from a client to the therapist to disclose their feelings, thoughts, or fantasies may be an attempt to merge and close the gap: an attempt by the client to enter the therapist's mind. It is important to explore carefully a request for the therapist to disclose their feelings and thoughts. Similarly the therapist's self-disclosure may also be a strategy to close the gap to avoid something potentially uncomfortable.

Clinical example IV. A client, who was depressed and distressed, asked me if I thought he was borderline. This was an idea he had picked up from his partner. He asked in an anxious manner, and I felt obliged to answer. A thought I had in the moment was: he wants to know what is in my mind in order to close the gap between us. I responded by saying "You want a diagnosis rather than have an experience with me." Then

I went on to say, "If I said yes, how might you feel? And if I said no, how would you feel?" He was silent for a few moments, during which time he became tearful, and said, "I want to know who I am." This represented his core issue.

Conclusion

In conclusion, I believe we cannot avoid disclosing, or revealing ourselves. However, it is often a choice to decide in what way and when to disclose our countertransference. We need to bear in mind certain questions when considering disclosure:

1. Would self-disclosure represent a repeated traumatic relationship for the client?
2. Would it enhance or interfere with the "therapeutically required relationship"?
3. Is disclosure a defence, avoiding something?
4. Is there something behind the request or my impulse to disclose?

If the therapist considers that self-disclosure is a feature of their therapeutic approach, then whatever style they adopt, or whether they disclose with a particular client, needs to be a considered choice. I agree with Aron (1996) that whether or not we disclose, our position needs to be open to reflection and comment by both client and therapist, a position aligned to the relational principle of engagement.

Principle 3

The significance of conscious
and nonconscious patterns of relating

CHAPTER FIVE

Dynamic ego states—the significance of nonconscious and unconscious patterns, as well as conscious patterns

Graeme Summers

Introduction

In this chapter I will explore the significance of levels of consciousness with particular reference to ego state theory (Berne, 1961). In doing so I will also describe a dynamic ego state model developed specifically to account for nonconscious as well as unconscious, preconscious, and conscious patterns of experience.

Dynamic ego states

Inspired by the work of Daniel Stern (2004) and the Boston Change Process Study Group (BCPSG) (2010), the Dynamic Ego State Model is my attempt to account for some recent developments in developmental psychology, neuroscience, and positive psychology within a TA theoretical frame (Figure 2).

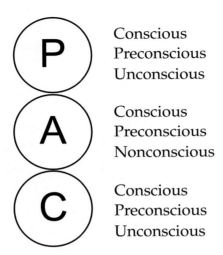

Conscious
Preconscious
Unconscious

Conscious
Preconscious
Nonconscious

Conscious
Preconscious
Unconscious

Figure 2. Dynamic ego states (Summers, 2008).
Note: In the colour version of this model the Adult circle is displayed in green (which denotes health) and the Parent and Child circles are displayed in red (which denotes defensive fixation).

The Dynamic Ego State Model builds upon the foundations of co-creative TA (Summers & Tudor, 2000) to propose that:

- Ego states are "patterns" of experience. They are relational possibilities and probabilities.
- Adult ego states represent our flexible, creative, and resourceful self or sense of self.
- Parent and Child ego states represent our rigid or compulsive psychological defensive patterns most often used in times of stress.
- Personal development is a process of expanding Adult relational capacity and reducing Parent and Child probabilities.

I have chosen the term "dynamic" for two reasons. Firstly, it echoes Freud's (1913) use of this adjective to describe the unconscious when referring to active repression from conscious awareness and so accurately reflects its usage in relation to Child and Parent ego states within this model. Secondly, it helps the consideration of personality in terms of ongoing vitality (both within and between people) rather than reified personality structure and therefore reflects the phenomenological, field theoretical, and social constructivist basis of co-creative TA.

I do not use the term to denote affinity with Blackstone's idea of the "Dynamic Child" (1993) especially since my conceptualization of the Child ego state is radically different from her formulation.

Unconscious/nonconscious distinction

I was introduced to the distinction between nonconcious and unconscious through Daniel Stern's (2004) writing which helped both clarify and develop my thinking in relation to co-creative TA. I resonated with his suggestion that we consider aspects of implicit relationship that are *not conscious but also not defensive or pathological* as nonconscious while reserving the term unconscious for that which is dynamically and defensively repressed. This useful distinction helps account for nonverbal health, healing, and creativity which may or may not become verbalized by therapist or client. Stern's proposition is that interpersonal experiences may be transformative (in therapy or otherwise) without ever being named or made explicit.

Applying this to co-creative TA, I think of Parent and Child ego states as largely implicit unconscious processes in which the deepest unresolved transferential dramas unfold within the therapeutic dyad. Through unconscious co-transferential enactments the therapist becomes part of the problem with the client in order to become part of the solution. The heart of the transformational process, however, takes place within implicit nonconscious inter-relations through the co-creative (but not necessarily conscious, verbal, or explicit) Adult-Adult "moments of meeting" (Stern, 2004, p. 165) and new ways of being with another that develop in parallel with co-transferential replays.

I draw on Little's (2006) use of "structuring" and "non-structuring" internalizations to distinguish between Child-Parent and Adult ego states respectively. In this formulation Child-Parent relational units that develop defensively in response to (inevitable) unbearable or unmanageable experience are differentiated from good-enough self-other interactions that are generalized and represented internally. I build upon this conceptual frame to locate the Child-Parent ego states and Adult ego states, each underpinned by RIGs ("Representations of Interactions that have been Generalized" (Stern, 1985 p. 97)), within implicit memory in the unconscious and nonconscious respectively. Using this theoretical base I consider "working in the relationship" to mean that therapist and client work together at the intimate edge of bearable/unbearable experiences. Therapeutic work involves co-creating viable experiential alternatives to co-transferential defensive transactions to enable the client to be more fully present in relationship with himself/herself and with the therapist. These therapeutic experiences may or may not become explicit: "It is more likely that the majority of all we know about how to be with others resides in implicit knowing and will remain there" (Stern, 2004, p. 115).

I remember a moment in my own therapy when I talked about a painful experience in a somewhat stereotypical northern English, working class male, matter-of-fact way. In response, my therapist visibly softened, showing subtle signs of sadness in her face which, in turn, helped me soften. Although this interaction was not explicitly discussed, in hindsight I believe it helped me feel recognized at an emotional level, and yet the absence of explicitly discussing the experience simultaneously acknowledged my allegiance to my culture of origin. Such refined choices of interaction, assuming they are even available to consciousness, concur with Stern's caution that "an attempt to make this moment of meeting explicit, especially immediately after it occurred, could undo some of its effect" (2004, p. 191).

In *Change Process in Psychotherapy* (2010), BCPSG write: "The task of therapy is to change implicit relational knowing" (p. 193). They see the development of the implicit relationship between therapist and client as the medium to "make more of the patient's world relationable" (p. 194) and to "create new relational possibilities" (p. 194).

As I have already noted this does not necessarily imply that previously repressed unconscious experiences were once conscious or that they become conscious in the therapeutic journey. I consider that repression has different meanings depending on whether we use Freud's (1913) or Fairbairn's (1952) conceptualization of the ego. Indeed, within a Freudian frame repression means repression from consciousness; however, within a Fairbairnian frame we can also understand repression as meaning repression from relationship. This latter conceptual frame helps distinguish between levels of unconsciously repressed experience that may be consciously recoverable and those that may be relationally recoverable through change in implicit relational knowing but still unavailable to explicit consciousness.

The additional significance of acknowledging a nonconscious implicit realm of experience and relating is that it supports the conceptualization of the expanded/expanding Adult ego state and further differentiates from restricted notions that Adult ego state is merely to do with consciousness.

Tudor (2003) creatively builds upon the one ego state model of health pioneered by Erskine (1988) and adapted within co-creative TA. I agree with much of his chapter on the "Integrating Adult", especially his articulation of the implication (within this model) that we are "conceived Adult". He states that his reference to conception more accurately refers to the notion that the foetus "… adapting to its reality in utero may be thought of as having a neopsyche or Adult ego state" (p. 204), and admits that "this may be the point at which the Parent, Adult, Child metaphor breaks down and we need to present new metaphors by means of new nomenclature". (p. 207).

I do, however, think he creates some confusion when he subsequently describes integration as "the capacity to reflect upon and make sense of our worlds" (p. 216).

He further states, "It is this capacity to reflect on ourselves and others, to spit out those experiences or introjections that are no longer relevant, and to assimilate the past in service of the present, that defines the 'Integrating Adult'" (p. 218), and "In my view an essential quality of the 'Integrating Adult' is, precisely, a critical consciousness which is alert and does not accept what is assumed given or received" (p. 219).

All of this makes sense in relation to reasonably well-functioning, chronological adults but seems a tall order for a foetus! In the main, Tudor's descriptions of "integrating" lean heavily towards explicit consciousness and necessitate a level of developmental achievement way beyond that of a foetus or neonate.

This contrasts with the co-creative TA assertion that Stern's (1985) description of four senses of self "supports the possibility of working at nonverbal levels of self development within an Adult frame of reference" (Summers & Tudor, 2000, p. 31).

So while Tudor usefully builds on the co-creative ego state model, especially in terms of discussing the importance of Adult reflective and critical consciousness (in later human development), I think the nonverbal and implicit aspects of the original co-creative TA formulation of ego states need to be re-asserted.

My interpretation of integrating incorporates much less developmentally sophisticated processes. I think in terms of biological notions of organism-environment co-regulation which is more of a Gestalt formulation: "We cannot do anything to take into our bodies those necessary things we require, whether it is affection, knowledge, or air without interacting with the environment" (Wallen, 1970, p. 10). From this perspective, I think the foetus example holds true and that human co-regulation then takes on more sophisticated forms from birth onwards.

On further reflection, however, I am less inclined to use the prefix integrated or integrating in relation to Adult. I think it is important to account for experiences, relational or otherwise, that we hold as somewhat unintegrated fragments but are not defensively organized. In the ongoing process of lifelong learning we hold many fragments of experience (ideas, feelings, images) at different levels (conscious/ pre-conscious/nonconscious) that we may or not be able to integrate, but we are nonetheless able to tolerate the fragmentation, not-knowing, and uncertainty. In contrast, I think that certainty is often an expression of a Parent ego state used to defend against the experience of the unknown.

In everyday learning we often need to dis-integrate our familiar ways of meaning-making to create an "open space". Such familiar ways may be habitual preferences of thought, feeling, or behaviour that we need to deconstruct in order to learn something new. Incorporating the concept of nonconscious processes within the Adult, I therefore propose that dynamic Adult ego states can be considered to have integrating, dis-integrating, and non-integrating capacities that play a pivotal role in healing, learning, and living, in and out of awareness.

Conscious/pre-conscious distinction

The conscious/pre-conscious distinction, like the dynamic unconscious, also dates back to Freuds's dynamic model of the psyche. In *The Interpretation of Dreams* (1913) Freud saw the pre-conscious as a screen lying between the unconscious and conscious systems. He proposed that the unconscious can only reach consciousness via the pre-conscious system and is therefore the main domain of psychotherapeutic work. The preconscious is often used to refer to experiences, thoughts, or memories that, while not in present consciousness, are readily accessible through an introspective search and then available for conscious attention.

Tudor suggests that "the neopsyche is the seat of consciousness" (2003, p. 218). Whilst I think this is true in terms of deeper reflective consciousness, I also think that a person can be conscious in a more limited way when using Parent or Child ego states. For example, I may well be conscious that I am being critically condemning of another person. However, I may not be conscious of the way in which I am unthinkingly copying the attitudes of an authority figure or that I am adopting this attitude as a psychological defence. I could also scan my pre-conscious experiences whilst using a Parent or Child ego state to gather evidence in support of my defensive position.

I recall an executive coaching client whose direct reports were telling him (via a 360° feedback process) that "he wasn't there much and when he was there he was critical". This feedback was not surprising to him—he was already conscious that he related in this way. What he realized through our coaching work was that he was re-enacting a relational pattern he had experienced many times with his own father. Not only was this a useful cognitive insight, it was also painful for him to remember this aspect of his childhood and to recognize that his archaic experience of his father was now strongly echoed by the people who presently work for him.

As illustrated in the above example, the conscious/pre-conscious distinction is particularly relevant to the TA concept of contamination (Berne, 1961). Contamination occurs when an individual mistakes their Parent or Child for Adult. Decontamination involves the process by which Parent and Child patterns of experience become consciously differentiated from Adult and therefore available for reflective consideration. At this point, Eusden (2011, and in this volume) suggests a person can develop the capacity to have "one foot in and one foot out" and to "mind the gap" between deeply felt co-existing psychological realities.

Eusden and Summers (2008) proposed the notion of "Vital Rhythms". Here we related Panksepp's (1998) classification of emotional systems to ego states and hypothesized that each system can be regulated within Adult or within the archaic Child-Parent relational units, the former being more functional. Glynn Hudson-Allez (2008) also refers to Panksepp as she links the capacity to use secure attachment (which I consider an Adult capacity) to the effective co-regulation of panic states. As the client's unconscious/pre-conscious archaic strategies for managing emotions become apparent within the unfolding co-transference, opportunities emerge to co-regulate these affect states within the developing Adult-Adult attachment of the therapeutic relationship.

Note that one of the strengths of Berne's (1961) PAC model is accessibility. I have witnessed many people make important insights about their own patterns as they use this deceptively simple model to recognize how problematic patterns in the present have meaningful roots in earlier experiences. Such insights can provide the basis for immediate changes and/or serve as a prompt to further personal development. Equally, the move from pre-conscious to conscious awareness may be the consequence of deeper emotional work:

"It is noteworthy that in the field of psychotherapy, the focus of therapeutic action has begun to shift from models favoring cognition to models that emphasize the primacy of interpersonal factors and bodily-rooted affect. These models suggest that insight is the result not the agent of change. This gives a new meaning to Berne's recommendation first to change then to analyze" Allen (2010, p. 44). In this case, cognitive insight, and the conscious Adult re-working of personal narratives can serve to reinforce personal transformation that has already been made at deeper experiential levels.

The conscious/pre-conscious distinction within Adult has particular significance in relation to the recent explosive emergence of positive psychology (Seligman, 2003). Here we move our focus away from problematic experiences (that may require healing or transformation in order to unlock creative potential) towards patterns which are already functional and creative. Within the terms of this chapter, the emphasis here is on bringing pre-conscious competence into awareness.

Fredrickson (2009) found that when people experience positive affect (e.g., joy, interest, happiness, anticipation), their peripheral vision expands. She linked this, and other empirical findings to the "broaden and build" strategy which suggests that positive emotions encourage exploratory thought and behaviours that in turn build new skills and resources. The notion of building is a pro-active, skill-based process that is prompted by and reinforcing of positive affect. Fredrickson also reports that positive affect is generally experienced with significantly less intensity than negative affect (e.g., anger and fear). Whilst I do not necessarily regard anger and fear as negative, this does remind us, as practitioners and clients, to also attend to the flow of possibly less intense yet positively experienced emotions that can support personal development.

Numerous strengths inventories have been developed in recent years with the intention of helping people discover and clarify what is right with them rather than what is wrong with them. Again, the intention here is to invite pre-conscious health into consciousness.

Within my coaching practice, solutions focused inquiry (Jackson & McKergow, 2007) often proves useful. A female senior manager wanted to raise the profile of herself and her department. She identified that she needed to make more connections with key people operating at the executive level above her but felt repulsed at the idea of politically motivated "schmoozing". I asked about the good relationships she already had with some of her seniors and how they had come about. She realized that they had all developed through collaborative cross-functional projects, where together they had made genuine contributions to the work of the organization. Following on from this insight she was able to develop a viable strategy for profile raising that felt congruent with her values and natural ways of being.

Positive psychology has many overlaps with TA (see for example Napper, 2009), both in the affirmation of human well-being and encouragement to act and not just think or feel. From a psycho-educational perspective there is congruence here with Susannah Temple's (1999, 2004) work on functional fluency, a term she uses to describe "the behavioural manifestations of the integrating Adult ego state" (1999, p. 164). Temple has devised research based classifications for identifying a range of social behaviours. This approach offers a methodology for expanding Adult flexibility at a conscious behavioural level.

Conclusion

There are many ways in which people heal, learn, and develop within which "The explicit and implicit intermingle at many points" (Stern, 2004, p. 187). As I consider this in relation to ego states my main proposition is that while Parent and Child ego states are relational possibilities experienced, expressed, and maintained largely through unconscious implicit interactions, it is nonconscious implicit processes that form the ongoing experiential basis for Adult ego states. My secondary proposition is that pre-conscious searching for meaningful connections can be made with respect to our healthy functioning as well as our troubles.

Damasio (2010) states: "Mind is a most natural result of evolution, and it is mostly nonconscious, internal, and unrevealed. It comes to be known through the narrow window of consciousness … which is an internal and imperfectly constructed informer rather than an external, reliable observer" (2010, p. 117).

With this thought in mind I conclude, as ever, with great respect for the unknown that lies within and between us despite our earnest attempts to understand and make use of the aspects of our experience that we are able to perceive.

CHAPTER SIX

Aspects of selfhood

Paul Kellett van Leer

There are more things in Heaven and Earth ... than are dreamt of in your philosophy.

—Shakespeare, *Hamlet*, act I, scene 5, lines 165–166

The unconscious ranks amongst a few rare concepts in the history of Western civilization that have transformed our understanding of ourselves and the worlds we inhabit. Freud's radical account—developed as a consequence of his scientific project for a metapsychology of human nature (1895)—swept away the modernist myth that we are the rational authors of our deeds and thoughts, the masters of our feelings and desires, and helped usher in the dawn of postmodernism. Henceforth, the unconscious would be the centre of gravity for a vast panorama of human creativity.

Berne took a reactionary position regarding the unconscious, developing a model of selfhood that he believed a fantasized eight-year-old version of his patients could comprehend (1972). Ultimately, he refused to accept the limit imposed by the notion of the unconscious on his project for an autonomous Jeder who is the author of his own show (ibid.) and erased the word unconscious in the hope of disavowing this limit. While certain schools within TA have continued in this vein, others have since developed TA so as to begin to account for unconscious dynamics. Transactional psychoanalysis, forged through the work of Moiso and Novellino, for example, reviewed Berne's original writing and drew out implicit references to unconscious processes, and this project has been furthered by the relational turn within TA (see Cornell & Hargaden, 2005, amongst others). These approaches, however, remain true to Berne's original philosophy and architecture so that, consequently, there are more things in the concept of selfhood than are currently dreamt of in our TA philosophy.

In this chapter, I outline a summary developmental narrative that offers a rationale for a structural model of selfhood comprising conscious and unconscious structures, as well as nonconscious aspects including the pre-conscious and sub-conscious enclave (see Figure 3).

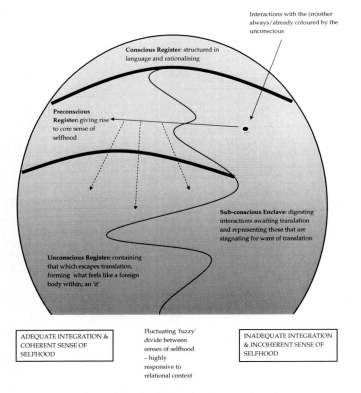

Figure 3. A Structural Model of Selfhood (after Laplanche, 2007: 40 & 41).

This account is based on that described by Laplanche (2007), in turn developed from Freud's "apparatus of the soul" (1923). I relate certain foundational TA concepts to this model and outline some consequences for transactional analytic practice.

The development of selfhood

Elsewhere, I have summarized an account of the infant's initial symbiotic state, involving his or her internal alienation and the subsequent restructuring of selfhood through the acquisition of language (Kellett, 2006, 2007a). This account portrays an internal world of the infant without words, without culturally-based stories, and without an unconscious. From this position, interactions with the (m)other—an adult subject to language, stories, and an unconscious—appear *enigmatic* to the infant; shot through with unconscious dynamics that cipher all interaction, pointing to an incomprehensible "something" beyond the infant's translation. Furthermore, the nature of this unconscious something is beyond even the (m)other's conscious grasp, leaving the infant alone in his or her survival-level need to make meaning: an existentially impossible task (Laplanche, 2007).

Consequently, those aspects of interaction with the (m)other that remain incomprehensible cannot be represented, threatening the coherence of the infant's developing sense of selfhood. This incomprehensible, un-representable remainder is subsequently "walled off" (Hargaden & Sills, 2002) and experienced as a foreign "it" that coalesces to form the foundations of the infant's unconscious, restructured upon the acquisition of language and consequently infused with disavowed desires that fall foul of the injunctions of the social matrix in which the child is inscribed (Kellett, 2007a).

The conscious

The conscious aspect of selfhood involves making meaning, resulting in the dialectic functions of rational reflection and rationalized defence. These functions are performed within linguistic structures, and thus subject to the *a priori* rules of a language that itself pre-exists the individual. These words, for example, are inscribed within a language game that circumscribes what and how I can write (Wittgenstein, 1953). The number of words is limited in line with a variety of considerations concerning issues of authority, power, and legitimation (Lyotard, 1979). The words chosen must be ordered in such a way as to obey appropriate rules of grammar, and I am not free to choose any words to frame my meaning, nor any meaning for the words I choose. While there are a number of ways in which we might denote the transactional analytic dyad, for example, "therapist" and "client" are currently accorded a dogmatic status within psychotherapeutic literature, and so—though these words produce problematic associations with consumerist values (Kellett van Leer, 2009)—I must use them here in deference to this status. Using other words, while we have the impression that it is "I" who speaks, it is rather "I" that am spoken.

With the exception of unconscious discursive formations, all speaking in analysis is a function of the conscious aspect of selfhood, so that all *rationalized* speaking potentially functions as a defence. Consequently, speaking in analysis requires a counter-cultural mode of engagement, just as engaging with the unconscious demands a counter-cultural mode of listening, as we shall see. Take, for example, "Do you know what I mean?"—and derivatives, such as "You know?"— commonly voiced by the client, though occasionally by the anxious therapist in need of reassurance. While I have previously outlined various analytic responses to this utterance (Kellett van Leer, 2009), suffice it to say here that the therapist needs to meet all such utterances with a benign curiosity, acknowledging that *neither client nor therapist can assume they understand the utterances of the other*, and inviting both to wonder who or what is being spoken and, indeed, who or what is speaking.

Thus, the therapist needs to fashion a speaking that evokes multiple meanings, inviting reflection rather than a quest for certainty. In this regard, meaning remains fluid; a constellation of symbolic possibilities that the analytic engagement keeps in play, rather than collapsing to a single truth. Such speaking takes time to develop, and this is true for each moment of each therapist-client relationship (Ogden, 2009). In this sense, Berne's (1961) dictum that the client must possess a robust-enough Adult to fruitfully engage with analysis highlights the demand upon the client to tolerate an unfamiliarity modelled by the therapist, and a capacity to develop a benign curiosity in and about themselves. As for the therapist, he or she must find a way to bracket the client's demand for the therapist to take the position of a more familiar other, something we will return to in our consideration of the sub-conscious enclave.

The pre-conscious

The pre-conscious comprises the distillations of interactions that have been integrated within a coherent-enough sense of selfhood, manifest as an enduring sense of identity, or personal narrative, which gives rise to the sense of a core "me" that transcends temporally situated relational contexts. In this way, the pre-conscious finds parallels with the Bernian notion of personality (Berne, 1961); the integrating functions of the Adult, fixated aspects of archaic ego state relational units (though functionally these extend into the sub-conscious enclave) and the fuzzy boundaries (Kellett, 2007a) of contamination (Berne, 1961) or "felt meaning" (Hargaden & Sills, p. 34).

The function of the pre-conscious also echoes aspects of life script (Berne, 1961): the recruited, culturally-embedded, dramaturgical tale that promises to decode the cipher of what was intolerably incomprehensible for the infant (Laplanche, 2007), thereby offering a distracting comfort even in adulthood. Thus, upon conscious reflection—frequently evoked by confrontation (Berne, 1966)—the felt sense of an enduring core self may shift, representing a decontamination (Berne, 1961). Since this aspect of selfhood receives the attention of most traditional TA techniques, let us move on to those that have been relatively neglected.

The subconscious enclave

The sub-conscious enclave functions as a working register, a mode of being in which the incomprehensible elements of interactions with others are *actively* engaged with in an attempt to assimilate these within a coherent-enough sense of selfhood. These include first attempts at translating recent interactions, repeated attempts at translating old incomprehensible interactions, and the demand—often surprising to the client—to (re-)translate repressed aspects of selfhood that return as a result of movements in the unconscious. As such, the sub-conscious enclave represents at best a transitory domain of interactions-in-translation or, at worst, a fragmenting chaos that threatens to overwhelm a coherent sense of selfhood.

A common class of incomprehensible interactions involve script messages such as drivers (Kahler, 1974) and injunctions (Goulding & Goulding, 1976). The infant finds integration of such imperatives all but impossible, and so must either accept or refuse; forcing him or her into a compliant or rebellious adapted Child state respectively (Berne, 1961). This position leads to a repetitive going-over—akin to Berne's (1964) broken record—a nightmare of re-living in an increasingly despairing attempt to resolve and thus escape the dire consequence of submission to such impossible imperatives.

This repetition manifests, partly, in some of the more common projective transference dynamics (Moiso, 1985). By means of transference, the client *recruits* the therapist (Kellett, 2007b) to perform a role specified by the client's script, a role that is conceivable within the therapist's script. Transference thus represents a manoeuvre—outside awareness and patterned by the client's favourite games (Berne, 1964)—to recruit the therapist as a familiar, lacking other, and/or an idealized, gratifying other. The therapist's response to such invitations is crucial, since refusal to engage (invariably a defensive response on the part of the therapist) or entanglement in the game (often the result of the therapist's nonconscious attempt to coerce the analysis in order to work through his or her own transferential issues) returns the client to the lonely despair of the repetition of the impossible.

Rather, the therapist must maintain a semblance of performing their assigned role with the aim of eventually voicing an effective interpretation (Berne, 1966), one that contains the client's despair and offers a creative space for reflection and working through. Such a profoundly delicate project is the subject of current debate. Little (2005) for example, has outlined a distinction between working in and with transference, offering one way in which to think about the vicissitudes of technique in this regard. Suffice it to say here that interpretation—ideally made by the client, though initially more usually the therapist—performs *the crucial and decisive action of detoxifying impossible relational introjects* (Berne, 1966). In the meantime, the client must experience the therapist as elusive, allowing for the transference to (in)form, rather than fix the analytic process.

The unconscious

The unconscious is structured *like* a language (Lacan, 1973 [1998], p. 48) one that the client and therapist must attune to and decode (Berne, 1961). For the client, this requires a willingness to voice whatever comes to mind, with as little censorship as possible. For the therapist, this attunement requires an orientation to listening characterized by a free-floating attention that allows the therapist to alight, often surprisingly, on certain utterances, words, turns of phrase, inflections, movements, expressions, and all manner of quirks. Thus, both client and therapist have the opportunity to follow the associations that arise in connection with what comes into focus, gently unfolding the structure of the client's unconscious.

It is important to remember that, in this regard, the client's unconscious is *unique and beyond the direct reach* of either client or therapist and, as such, not subject to co-creation. As Hanly (2007, p. 60) has said, "Co-creation occurs, but it is limited to *manifest* associations, resistances, and transferences. The underlying unconscious psychic reality [of the client] *is not vulnerable to co-creation*" (italics added). To this end, the therapist-client relationship must "turn on, tune in and drop out" (Leary, 1970): turn on to the truth of the client's unconscious, tune in to its language, and drop out of the distractions of conscious defence.

The language of the unconscious

The structure, or grammatical laws, of the unconscious is commonly manifest in slips comprising *missing* words, *substituted* words, and *fused* words. Missing words are those that are (a)voided, representing repressed symbolic connections. The client's speaking will coalesce, in time, around *repeatedly* missing words—incomplete sentences, or absent words marked by "you know", for example. The therapist's enquiry at such key moments is likely to be discounted (Schiff et al., 1975), redefined as a grammatical correction by the client, thus defending against a return of the repressed. In this case the therapist can always offer his or her own hunches as to the missing word. Whether the therapist gets it right is beside the point, since the attempt models the therapist's freely directed curiosity, inviting the client to do similarly.

Substituted words reveal associative links in the unconscious structure that lead to the revelation of uncomfortable truths encoded within. For example, a client spoke of the "*virtuous* circle" he felt trapped in with his father. When I repeated "virtuous" the client referred to what he had *intended* to say ("vicious"). My ambivalent "Hmm" was enough on this occasion to overcome this initial defence and invite his reflection on the potential significance of the word "virtuous". Consequently, the client began to weep, signalling a movement in the unconscious and corresponding yielding in the conscious defence. He then admitted that, were he to be himself—to follow his own desire—he believed that his father would feel betrayed, hurt, and disappointed—implying something the client's sense of selfhood could not tolerate.

Fusion involves words that are scrambled or mixed together in various ways, such as "crive", uttered by the same client, compounding the words "crave", "strive", and "cry", words that found a complex resonance upon later exploration.

Dreams and enactments

The manifest content of dreams represents a cipher for the uncomfortable truths of the unconscious. The non-rational settings, actions, substitutions, and combinations of a dream's content require the dreamer's similarly non-rationalized associations to symbolize these truths. A client, for example, had a dream involving a spot-lit orchid. When I asked her about this flower, no associations came to her mind. I then asked her what the word for "orchid" was in her mother tongue—the client is not a native English speaker—and she immediately associated it *phonetically* with a word corresponding to "testicles" in English. It is also crucial to remember that the manifest content of dreams signify more than one true meaning; indeed, seemingly contradictory meanings can each represent important truths for the client.

Enactments (Mitchell, 1988) are, in part, a product of projective identification, occurring at the edge of the analytic boundary and impacting the therapist in ways that fundamentally differ from the transferential invitations outlined above. Novellino (2003) argues that such unconscious communication represents an Adult function and is not connected with reinforcing the script. While the unconscious is not a function of the Adult according to the model proposed here, Novellino's description of unconscious communication complements the idea that, while other domains of transference represent dynamics of the sub-conscious enclave, projective identification is an emergent function of the unconscious, offering the possibility of transformation, as Hargaden and Sills have suggested. This perhaps overly-neat distinction nonetheless offers a way to tease out differing flavours within the nonconscious domain, as the following brief vignette illustrates.

> I had worked with a client once-weekly at 08.00 for almost three years when I set my alarm incorrectly and slept soundly through his session. The following week, he asked why I had not "let him in".

I apologized for my mistake, explaining what had happened and inviting him to talk about the impact this experience had on him. He said, "Everyone finds me exhausting." The following week the client had a dream that included a scene recounted as: "Someone is laying out tubes, like those of a dying machine—I mean drying machine [laugh] you know—anyway, from the car into the house … a complex web … sellotaped to the pipe at the back of the car … not very clever …

My initial rationalization and apology—eliciting a compliant understanding from the client—represents a defence grounded in the rationalizing conscious aspect of selfhood. In the pre-conscious, our senses of selfhood similarly interlock; the client's imago of himself as too demanding and mine of myself as an inadequate (trainee) transactional analyst. Regarding the sub-conscious, both dream and enactment reference the client's toxic experiences of his depressed and intermittently suicidal mother—a dreaded relationship in which the exhausted other appears dead—a (m)other who is not available to "let me in". For my part, the insidiously poisonous shadow of the perfect (qualified) therapist feeds a script-based shame and game-based instinct to apologize and accept the position of the failed other. In these differing ways, we both had the opportunity to consolidate our script beliefs and collect familiar payoffs (Berne, 1964).

Finally, regarding the unconscious, the client later associated the dying/drying machine with a memory of his parents arguing about divorce while his mother was attending to the laundry. This led to an acknowledgement of the role of his mother's depression in his father's decision to leave the family, allowing the client to recognize his not very clever defensive strategy of being angry with his father as the *cause* of mother's depression. This strategy had, in the past, allowed the client to avoid feeling rageful towards his mother—feelings that threatened his fragile sense of selfhood—resulting in a complex web of fantasies about, and avoidance of feelings; a situation he found utterly exhausting.

Concluding remarks

As relational transactional analysis finds words for a more comprehensive narrative of selfhood, it faces the task of forging a model that accounts for unconscious, as well as conscious and nonconscious domains. This chapter outlines a structural model of four aspects of selfhood developed by Laplanche, rooted in a developmental account and describing several fundamental emergent functions. I have also outlined several consequences of this model for the analytic engagement, with the hope that transactional analysts may find these reflections evocative, just as we aim to evoke reflection in our clients.

Principle 4

The importance of experience

CHAPTER SEVEN

The importance of experience

Dave Gowling and Jamie Agar

Writing this chapter together comes out of our participation in a long-standing peer supervision group. Over the years, we have used the group to better understand, accept, and even anticipate how profound change can occur for the client when the psychotherapist is willing to be dazed and confused by unexpected and intense turns in the dance of the clinical relationship. We believe that client and therapist are both changed by this experience and thus new meaning can be made between the two parties, which is reparative for the client.

What we intend to show in the weaving of theoretical concepts and clinical vignettes is the deeply moving experience of mutual transformation which can occur in a two-person psychotherapy (Stark, 1999). In keeping with the relational principle on which this chapter is based (the importance of experience, as outlined in the introduction), we describe our relational understanding of the terms *experience, enactment, and embodiment*.

Experience

Psychotherapy can be understood as a kind of participative experience or "experiment in intimacy" (Gilbert, 1992, personal communication) that the therapist offers the client within a contractual framework. This is an invitation for direct, personal participation in the clinical relationship that the therapist intends will create a lasting impression and promote beneficial structural changes in the client.

We like to think about provision of this lasting impression in terms of how Stark (1999) outlines differing modes of therapeutic action. She describes the therapist offering and moving between one-, one-and-a-half-, and two-person ways of relating, according to the contract or therapist's and client's shared understanding of the client's change process.

Briefly, traditional psychoanalytic techniques and classical TA interventions such as Berne's therapeutic operations (1966) could be seen as being based upon a one-person psychotherapy. Here, the therapist is the observer of the client's process, and as such is an authoritative expert, healer, and container of knowledge. The client learns from the therapist's observations and is the recipient of this knowledge. A TA example of a one-and-a-half-person psychotherapy might involve cathexis reparenting methods (Schiff et al., 1975). Although the psychotherapist is more involved in these ways of working, she is still doing something for or to the client. Stark cites the work of Buber (1923/1996) in describing both the one and-one-and-a-half approaches as having an "I—It" quality, where the therapist thinks about the client rather than relates directly with her.

What Stark emphasizes in her two-person approach is the primacy of the relationship itself. She is in essence asking how we bring the past fully into the present moment, anticipating the emergence of the familiar old and disturbing dynamics, in the hope of creating an alternative experiential outcome. It is here where both therapist and client exist in an intersubjective matrix, each mutually influencing the other; two subjectivities meeting. She calls this the "I—Thou" relationship (Buber, 1923/1996).

We think it is important to reiterate that Stark does not privilege one approach above the other and that the therapist will move between one-, one-and-a-half-, and two-person modes according to the work at any given time.

Each person's interest in and ability to focus their relational attention depends upon their unique personal and professional identity. My ways of relating are not yours and there is no particular formula for being with others and no given relational truth. We can only bring our attention to any given relationship from the person that we are and not from the person that perhaps we want to be, or more importantly, think we should be.

Relational principles highlight two crucial elements in the realm of clinical experience: enactment and embodiment.

Enactment

An enactment may be understood as a two-person "transference drama" (Berne, 1961/1975, p. 117). As Stark (1999, p. 133) says, rather than think of the client as acting out her pathology, we might consider that she is trying to communicate something about her internal experience that is both intentional and cannot as yet be verbalized. Indeed, both client and therapist bring their real needs to the relationship and these real needs exist for both beneath their racket (English, 1971) needs and social needs.

What does the client bring to induce the therapist's unconscious process?

> Robert was seeking therapy to decide whether to stay with or leave his long-term male partner of twenty years whom he had recently married in a civil partnership. He was qualified as a community mental health nurse and was taking prescribed medication for bipolar disorder. Nine months prior to contacting me he had made a serious suicide attempt and was unexpectedly found by his partner, James.
>
> During his initial consultation Robert told me that he had previously received help from a mindfulness-based psychologist whom he referred to rather cursorily as a "charlatan". This got my immediate attention and stayed with me: who was being called a charlatan and why?
>
> I was suddenly reminded that when I have a break from work I sometimes wonder about and even doubt the significance of what I actually do for a living, sitting in a room and making conversations with clients and supervisees. So I knew that I could also think of myself as a kind of charlatan and was, in fact, doing so in the moments following his comment. I was bothered by Robert's remark; even a bit scared. I found myself remembering lyrics from a song by the Doors (1968), "No one here gets out alive".

Robert didn't elaborate, and when I asked him about his relationship with his previous therapist several sessions later he didn't answer my question and was quick to reassure me that I had come highly recommended and that he had great faith in me. I acknowledged his polite reply, but I wasn't reassured. I noticed my discomfort and continued to watch for what was being avoided by both of us.

In supervision with colleagues, I discussed Robert's tragic script (Steiner, 1974) and 3rd degree game (Berne, 1964) and considered the implications for our emerging relationship. What future was there for our civil partnership? I felt my anxiety rising as my supervisor playfully sang the opening lyrics to a famous Irving Berlin song (1936), "There may be trouble ahead ..."

What sense do we make of this?

Limbic resonance and regulation join human brains together in a continuous exchange of influential signals. This takes us into the realm of Stern's (2004) "implicit relational knowing". "Mirror neurons provide possible neurobiological mechanisms for understanding the following phenomena: reading other people's state of mind; especially intentions; resonating with another's emotion; expressing what someone else is experiencing, and capturing an observed action so that one can imitate it" (p. 78). Characteristics of mirror neurons include resonance, empathy, sympathy, intersubjectivity, and contagion.

So every brain becomes a part of local networks, which link individual mirror neuron systems. Each system resonates with concordant and complementary memories, emotional states, and relationship patterns of other systems. Each of us can signal and even lure others into our emotionally-laden virtual worlds that were shaped by an original protocol (Berne, 1961). Those with whom we are in an ongoing relationship, such as client and therapist, can be particularly vulnerable to the other's influence.

Therefore, in relationship, one brain/mind/body influences another, one heart changes another; we are constantly involved in a limbic revision (the dance).

Is it this unique mammalian ability to read the other's mind that allows us to sink into the depths of our co-created unconscious? To be disturbed and to hold empathy and understanding, while in the mutual contagion to manage our feelings of being possessed by self- and other-induced demons? We can sensitively enter into what sits beyond the immediate presentation, as long as we are able to take the risk. In embracing our disturbance, we open ourselves to a rich vein of emotional knowledge, about ourselves, our client, and our relationship.

> Of course in my own mind, I could hypothesize what Robert was trying to tell me about the two of us. We could talk explicitly about his troubles such as his fear of becoming depressed again. He even acknowledged that his fear of the condition could serve to trigger another major depression, but he didn't believe that this knowledge would stop him from hypo-activating, becoming that familiar depressed self he had described sitting in his living room on the day he'd almost killed himself. I felt Robert's rage and despair, but mostly his defiance.
>
> He had kept the chair where he had sat when he'd overdosed earlier in the year. No, he hadn't got rid of it. He had kept it and had it re-upholstered, he said, looking directly at me. He knew about CBT and rated himself a "six out of ten at the moment", but he knew he'd be getting depressed again, a "one or lower". He said that's why he was seeking therapy—he hoped that I could take it.
>
> I met his intense gaze, and it felt personal. A challenge to me to do something. Or nothing.
>
> I had accepted his invitation and here we were, poised face-to-face on the dance floor with a warning of "trouble ahead". In that moment, it was as if I'd lost my mind to what I was seeing in Robert's eyes—his familiar state of torment, self-loathing, and suicidal ideation.

Enactments may seem mindless and even terrifying to the therapist and yet become "a powerful therapeutic tool that conveys important information to both patient and therapist about the patient's internal state" (Stark, 1999, p. 133) as well as that of the therapist. Whatever may be ahead might emerge at, for instance, the moment of "the Switch" in the game (Berne, 1972).

In a two-person exchange, re-enactments of past relational experiences, whilst obviously unconscious, are viewed both as inevitable and as offering powerful opportunities for relational repair. It is often at the moment of the Switch in a game that these opportunities become most profound. If the therapist can keep finding her mind under the pressure of whatever is emotionally provoking them, the opportunity for the mutually influencing unconscious to emerge and the development of an intersubjective narrative becomes possible.

The primitive, defiant Child in Robert might maintain his script-bound identity [A_1] by keeping hold of that chair, while another part [A_{1+}] sought rescue and redemption, and projected [P_{1+}] this onto me through idealization.

Thus, when the primitive P_1 is projected onto the other, it provides release from the internal tension. As another client once said, "I bring you all the shit". This can be the point of escalation into apparently destructive rackets and games; and yet we project in order to do one of two things: to rid ourselves of our badness (P_{1-}), or to protect that which we feel is good in us, but under threat (P_{1+}).

As Schore (2003) says, our job as therapists is to allow (do we have a choice?) the patient to experience "dysregulating affects" (p. 92) in tolerable doses and within a safe enough environment, so that over-whelmingly traumatic feelings can be regulated and integrated into the client's emotional life.

Transformational transference: facing the music

We think that the above example illustrates the heart of projective iden-tification. The client splits off from their C_2 experiencing (Hargaden & Sills, 2002, p. 26) and attempts to project it into the therapist. This has worked if the therapist begins to feel something which has an "other-than-self", a felt sense where she is compelled to think, feel, or behave in certain ways, which may be "rigid" and/or "chaotic" (Siegel, 2010). Of course, this can feel extremely risky.

In the grip of this experience, we catch ourselves in an enactment; we make a mistake, and we are involved in creating or potentially creating a rupture in the alliance. In this moment, the therapist becomes vulnerable and defensive. Shock at being attacked or dismissed can lead to anger with self, self-doubt, and humiliation or even a teetering on the edge of a defensively driven hostile attack on the client. We may begin to view the client through a very different lens, one that sees her as awkward, resistant, hostile, and essentially unavailable to be involved in the relationship.

> An instance of this occurred, when in what seemed like an awful and unguarded moment I called a client "an awkward sod". This "slipped out" under what felt like extreme provocation as yet

again, in session, my effectiveness was questioned, criticized, and dismissed. I was angry, and so was she. The session finished with two very disgruntled people in the room. I attempted to stay as aware and as mindful as I could of my own internal process, but without much success.

In the following week I ranged between uncertainty, fierce self-criticism, hostile rejection, and blame; I certainly convinced myself that my client would not return (even though we had worked together for nearly two years).

At the next session I settled nervously into my chair and braced myself for her familiar hostile attack. Instead, she said that last session had been "marvellous", and that she had never had an experience before of someone confronting her in that way and staying engaged. She had always been able to escalate to the point where the other would give in to her. She felt contained, but most importantly she said, "I've never felt held like this before."

In moments like this, we hold to a framework where we stay open to the disturbing experience. We are not seeking to offer an unobtainable, re-parented relationship, but a reworking of the inevitable ruptures to any relationship. As an object, we will inevitably and necessarily disappoint the other. It is our mistakes, lack of foresight, and defensive manoeuvres which create the opportunity for re-enactment and healing.

Embodiment: the dance

The enactment re-creates and, in the enactment, the client can take many different meanings from the immediacy of the therapeutic error. The creation of this new narrative *embodies* a new experience.

The Oxford English Dictionary (2010) defines the word "embody" in the following way: "an expression of or to give a tangible or visible form to an idea, quality or feeling". The Boston Change Process Study Group (2010) eloquently describes the brain/body/mind's "intention unfolding process" (pp. 167–168) which occurs when one person is making words with another. They maintain that language is inherently rooted in brain/body/mind action and quote the philosopher Husserl who states that, "Movement is the mother of all cognition" (pp. 167–168). Just as Winnicott (1952) stated that "There is no such thing as a baby" (p. 99), we might also say that there is no such thing as a body (without a mind).

> A client at the end of her second marriage who was dealing with an acrimonious separation, divorce, and single parenthood, returned to therapy after the Christmas break and told me she had been ill with vomiting and diarrhoea in the week leading up to Christmas Day because she "didn't have the stomach for it".

In the split seconds before finding her words, this client looked inside for intuited and imagined bodily movements, which would resonate with her mind's intention. What followed was her explicit use of language and gestures to convey to me an approximation of what she had mentally intended.

Early life embodiment occurs through eye-to-eye and skin-to-skin contact. The right limbic brain and its emotional attractors become encoded through early transactional moments of meeting with primary caregivers. These form neural pathways, which shape the baby's sensory, memory, and attachment patterns. The infant forms particular emotionally encoded preverbal views of her relational world. In the consulting room, this manifests in many different ways.

> Midway through a session with Jane, a client I have worked with for several years, I offered what I thought was an empathic response. She looked at me, said, "This is absolutely no use," stood up and stormed out.
>
> I felt lost, humiliated, and furious, and after a few days I was surprised when my client rang to confirm her next week's appointment.
>
> As we explored what had happened between us, Jane said that, in that moment, she had expected me to be critical and realized that I was, in fact, being compassionate. On reflection, I realized that I could have been drawn into a stern and Parental response, something which was not unusual between us.
>
> Movingly Jane then said, "I have just realized that if you are for me, I believe you are against me."
>
> She went on to say that every expectation of intimacy and closeness embodies a sense of her self, dropping away from herself, becoming an empty shell, devoid of feeling, but terrified of human

contact. She went on to understand that she has to turn me into a cruel and unkind man. Only then could she have some sense of relationship, some sense that she existed, through her hatred towards me.

Jane now has a "strange feeling" in her body that I may be okay, and she approaches sessions with her familiar fear, but also with some tingling excitement. I feel moved. This represents the integration of transition and embodiment: a feeling of a sense of change; a loosening of affect and the melting of body armour. Jane says that now she feels able to talk with some courage, and my sense of this is that we are both more heartfelt towards each other.

I can think of this technically as the multiple layering of decontamination upon decontamination, and deconfusion upon deconfusion. Although, in our narrative we are often telling the same story that we have told many times before, we experience, not redecision, but subtle, often indescribable senses that we are different.

Jane says, "I hope this lasts, but it is lovely to feel different."

Conclusion

The past emerges into the present when we bring an unconscious re-enactment into the here and now to become a rich and disturbing enactment. Therapist and client remain full of uncertainties, doubts, and a sense of swimming in a murky sea, but with some growing awareness of the profound implications of what is taking place between them.

As a dear colleague Sue Eusden (2010, personal communication and in this volume) remarked, "What we hope as therapists is that through supervision and personal therapy we are able to keep at least one leg, one foot or maybe even one toe in conscious Adult awareness."

When we "face the music and dance" in a negative projective transference, this is often all we can hope for. Ensuring our emotional, physical, and mental health is most probably our deepest commitment to the client's transformation.

CHAPTER EIGHT

Person to person: a meditation on a two-person practice

Katherine Murphy

> *A person makes his appearance by entering into relation with other persons.*
>
> —Buber (1987, p. 85)

> *... so ancient is the desire of one another, which is implanted in us, reuniting our original nature, making one of two, and healing the state of man.*
>
> —Plato (1920, p. 318)

Background thoughts

One of the editors asks me if I wanted to contribute to this book on relational TA and, if so, what I might like to write about. I hesitate; I am just back from a month's break but not yet arrived. I don't feel conversant in TA conceptual language any more and have not been so involved in the TA world. Equally the principles speak to me and I see them as common across many forms of practice irrespective of theoretical orientation.

How would it be if I write about the "person to person", I offer. You mean adult to adult?, she questions. I pause for thought. No, I am thinking about something different from that: more than that though not exclusive of that way of inter-relating. I am more thinking about an inter-human (Buber, 1987) stance that is at the heart of the interpersonal encounter and is, in my view, central to healing or changing through meeting. Something to do with therapeutic ways of *being with* and *being together* which are different from particular structures of experience, and more than ways we can treat the other as an object to be known and used.

Later in the day, I am at yoga class of over eighty people, each of us working separately yet together, both one and the whole. We are invited to set our intention for our practice, becoming as present and engaged as we can in body and mind, body with mind, breathing naturally and fully. As I struggle to centre into this place in my self, an unbidden thought floats through my mind. Working person to person is a kind of setting of intention by the psychotherapist: a commitment to and a willingness for a way of relating as a way of working. The therapist acknowledges both that human beings are inextricably interconnected and intertwined with each other, that we are in continual states of mutual and reciprocal influencing, co-creating experiences, and we are also inescapably different, separate, and in some ways unknowable to each other. With this in heart/mind the therapist commits to a form of practice that is an interactive therapeutic dance. It involves an exploration by both partners of what is experienced subjectively individually, as well as how a situation is experienced together. The therapist sets their intention to be available for various kinds of meeting including a full-bodied turning-towards-the-other while the patient/ client, too, moves into a full-bodied turning-towards-the-therapist/ other such that:

> "Both patient and therapist transcend socially proscribed roles, and in moments of encounter that take them both by surprise they may truly meet—and such meeting confirms their very being" (Hycner & Jacobs, 1995, p. 205).

I take down from my shelf Rogers's *On Becoming a Person*, Yalom's *Loves Executioner*, Hycner and Jacobs's *The Healing Relationship in Gestalt Psychotherapy*, Stern's *The Present Moment*, the Boston Change Process Study Group's (BCPSG) *Change in Psychotherapy*, Maroda's *Psychodynamic Techniques*, and Benjamin's article on *Intersubjectivity* as starting points for my own reflections on the person to person as an orientation to two-person psychotherapy (Boston Change Process Study Group, 2010). While looking for something else I find a paraphrase of something Paolo Friere (2000) wrote in relation to education that captures my sense of this. For a moment I riff on education and psychotherapy as forms of freedom to learn.

Friere talks of the teacher-of-the-students and the students-of-the teacher being in a dialogue and that through this process they become teacher-student with student-teachers. The teacher is both teaching and being taught and the students are teaching while being taught: both jointly responsible for a process in which all grow.

In similar vein the BCPSG talks of how "... the complex process of fitting together requires an active negotiation between the two partners, such that analyst and patient are working together back and forth in finding direction and fit. This is a hit-or-miss endeavour" (2010, p. 204).

As I read through the various books scattered around me I am reminded of the observation that if you ask psychotherapists from a variety of orientations to describe what they do and to bring their work alive in ordinary prose their descriptions sound surprisingly similar (Rozenzweig, 1936; Norcross & Goldfried, 1992). When you ask them to speak conceptually they not only sound different but can become argumentative in their differences. To my eyes and as I experience them, descriptions of work, unadorned with theoretical commentary, often have the feel of two people being together, working together, actively negotiating their separateness in their togetherness, equal participants jointly responsible for a process, in service of the patient's therapeutic needs, surprised by moments of meeting. In these moments I see the person to person.

So, setting my intention, I go to meet Rachael, a client of long-standing. We are now in the closing stage of this work.

Rachael: Knowing me Knowing you (ABBA, 1976: "Arrival")

Driving to my practice several miles away from my home I listen to a weekly radio programme where eminent people from all walks of life choose eight discs of music they would take with them on a desert island. They discuss their choices with the host/interviewer of the programme. The novelist Howard Jacobson is reflecting on his life through the music he has chosen. Perhaps because I am about to see Rachael, she comes into my mind. She would enjoy his choice of classical music. Over the years she has brought some of these pieces into our work as a way of telling me something that she had not yet found words for. Music was a shared pleasure between her and her husband who died prematurely several years ago. It is the anniversary of his death on the date of our next week's appointment. I have been deeply touched with what she has wanted to share and give expression to in this way, and it has also been my pleasure to be hear pieces of music I did not know. In the course of the interview Jacobson describes his need for a loving other and a sense of not feeling he exists unless he can see a look of love, for him, in the eyes of another. Another fleeting resonance with Rachael. I remember how irritating I found her in the early days and months of her psychotherapy. I re-experienced my recoil from what I saw as her large hangdog eyes dripping with unexpressed yearnings, her passivity, the palpable hunger for someone to respond to her and enjoy her, her impulse to initiate flaccid, the desperate waiting. No amount of under-standing of her early world inured me from the strength of my initial unforgiving responses and the pull to withhold. However, I understood these feelings from transference countertransference perspectives, with their child developmental underpinnings, and also knew that the fact that I had them meant they had echoes not only to her early years but also to something that was mine. I did not enjoy her bringing my under-belly to light. Yet disgust has dissolved into delight and withholding softened into immediacy and I open the door to Rachael this morning with both memories and affection.

Rachael settles herself as she usually does; shoes off and feet folded under her on the chair. She likes it that in spite of her aging she can still do that. She glances at me with a rueful shrug, sighs and shifts around in her posture. She sighs again and looks at me. I am taken by the striking earrings she is wearing and how surprisingly stylish she is. She begins to tell me about the radio programme I had been listening to and how much it had stirred her. She hesitates and then asks, falter-ingly, if I heard it too. She is still not sure if she is allowed to ask me frank questions even though we have navigated this many times and she knows I will be respectful of her curiosity and truthful in my reply. "I heard snippets," I respond. I pause, looking at her, "And some of his music reminded me of you." There are moments of quiet. Her eyes fill with tears. She talks softly of the sound of his voice, a sound she had not heard for years yet so familiar. It was the sound of her father and his family, and her early childhood. The sound of many people now dead and a time passed. She sits quietly. I feel full of feelings: poignant sadness and bittersweet sensations. Time passing—life and death; flourishing and decline. We are both busy with this. Her fight with her own aging and in the presence of a psychotherapist a generation younger than her; my ancient parents, ten years older than her, on the cusp of their deaths; the shape of my aging to come. And the evocativeness of sound. How I know my own version of this. After thirty-something years in London I can still hear a New Zealand accent in a crowd and feel both a warmth of recognition and a nostalgia for something now gone. More quiet. She moves on; there is something both slow and graceful about how she is and perhaps how we seem to be.

She refers to Jacobson's feeling of not existing unless another looked at him with love. A piece that had reminded me of her. With tears in her voice, she says, "I don't think I am quite like that, or not any more, but I desperately miss the little remarks that Steven [her husband] would make about how I looked or something I had done. His confirmations, even when he was horribly sick and dying. I need some confirmation .... It helps fix me." I am taking in what she is saying. I have never heard her speak like this, neither in content nor in tone. I think about the times I have been an explicitly confirming voice for her. I do not feel as though I have been a replacement for Steven but the thought flickers in my mind. I wonder about the "fixing". Rachael is a gifted amateur photographer and I guess she is using fix in the way photographers do, but I check somewhat tentatively. "The fixing ... I think you mean as in fixing a print when you develop it ..." She smiles, "Yes, you fix something that is already there, that is emerging ..." She pauses, looking at me. I experience her gaze as clear. There is no hang-dog in this look. I do not want to withdraw. I look at her. We both breathe deeply. I wait. "That is what happens here," she says. She sobs quietly. I feel tears in my eyes. "That is what can happen here," I say, "and there is something about the way that Steven was with you, day to day in your marriage that has gone, none of us do that particular fixing." Another long pause. Rachael continues, "I don't think that gap will ever close ... and I no longer need it to ... there are other fixings and they are not the same."

I know I have not been a substitute for Steven and that we have developed our form of fixing. I comment on her beautiful earrings. She chuckles. We chuckle. She leaves for this week. I am glad I am not seeing anyone for an hour. I sit for a long time savouring the past hour, the last years, of the painstaking meeting and the stumbling towards getting to know her, knowing me, knowing her. And sometimes we have been surprised by true moments of meeting.

Rachael has read this piece and we have discussed it together. She has given her permission for me to present it in this current form.

Principle 5

The significance of subjectivity and self subjectivity

CHAPTER NINE

Subjectivity and intersubjectivity

Suhith Shivanath

Introduction

In this chapter, I will explore the issue of power within the therapeutic relationship. I am focusing particularly on the socially constructed power relationships (gender, race, class, being able-bodied, sexuality, etc.), and how these sometimes become vehicles for the expression of known and unknown material between clients and therapists. In order to illustrate this complex link between culture and unconscious communication I will write about a dynamic that emerged between my white English client and myself, an Indian therapist who is an immigrant to Britain. I will use the concept of modern oppression put forward by Batts (1998), together with projective identification (Hinshelwood, 1994) and Hargaden and Sills's (2002) work on primitive processes and culture, which they locate in the Child ego state (Berne, 1961).

Projective identification

Hinshelwood (1994), in reviewing different meanings of projective identification, states that Klein (1946) believed that it served the purpose of evacuating the bad parts of the self together with bad objects. She suggested that, for the recipient, the nonverbal unconscious communication has the feel of a primitive attack, a sense of being pushed away, which elicits a response to reject or retaliate. On the other hand, Hinshelwood suggests that Bion (1959, 1967) believed that projective identification can be a more benign vehicle for communication; that it is an unconscious attempt to gain the empathy of the therapist. Casement (2001) potentially pulls both definitions together under one unifying term which he calls "communication by impact" as an "essential way of communicating what otherwise may remain unspeakable" (p. 73) and perhaps inaccessible.

In working with these primitive processes, an observing ego, or Adult ego state (Berne, 1961) becomes an essential "third" (Mitchell, 2000) that therapists can use to be interested and curious about their own subjectivity. It enables them to be mindful of their moment by moment responses to the client, as well as making themselves available to nonverbal visceral communications. This can be particularly challenging when in the throes of projective identification.

Subjectivity and intersubjectivity are key concepts to working relationally. We give up the idea of an isolated mind because the therapist's responses to the client are material for reflection. Thus both are changed through the impact of their meeting.

Brandchaft (2004) talks of this as being a creative process through the use of language and metaphor in order to discover new meanings, and for understanding how we continually shape and influence one another. In the case example below, I will show how I became decentred from my Adult functioning and how my regaining of this third space became a key factor in the working through of this process. I needed to engage with my own subjectivity and my history in order to make sense of the overt and covert communication from my client. This was part of the bi-directional process where my client's subjective experience needed to impact me at an emotional level in order for me to understand her. I link this to my process in supervision to show how cultural issues were also at play there in the intersubjective field, and how my understanding of the parallel processes became part of my making meaning of my client's communication by impact.

The need to disturb and be disturbed

Liz came to therapy because she was unhappy about the quality of her life, and her relationships with others. She and I gradually chipped away at her need to keep the world out, to compartmentalize, and to stay in control. Over a period of three years, she came to understand her terror of getting close to anyone, including me. She believed that this would somehow lead to her "losing" and everyone else "winning", which would mean her being humiliated and rejected, and having a "total meltdown".

Often, I felt I was on the outside watching and commenting on how she was in session. She sometimes spent entire sessions simply describing her work. My own subjective response was to feel pushed away and not know what use I could be to her. I invited her to wonder about what it meant for her to be with me, but her blocking responses led me to believe that there was not much room for reflection. Despite this, I had a sense of her taking me in visually—she often looked at me intensely.

Over time, she slowly let go of some of her workaholic structure, and put in place some leisure time. As she did so she began to express a wish to "move forward, faster"; she was disgruntled with my not "giving her answers" and "leaving" her to find her own way. She was able to understand cognitively that wanting to be told what to do was akin to wishing for a re-creation of her original experience in her family where she was kept busy fulfilling her parents' wishes.

In retrospect, perhaps I missed the significance of her wish for an active input from me. Perhaps she wanted me to protect her from a growing terror of not knowing what the future held for her, and she wanted me to be a potent, organizing figure like her father had been. She was letting go of her internal omnipotent control, which exposed her infant terror of not being held well enough. I got caught and distracted by the concrete terms in which she put her questions (do you not have a plan for me?) together with the lack of affective cues in her presentation. It is also possible that I missed her because I too had been a "grown up little girl" who sequestered her early needs in the service of maintaining a connection with her mother.

One session she came in a disgruntled mood and told me how she was fed up with London being full of foreigners speaking in languages she didn't understand, standing around in groups, getting a lot of support, and that she felt like a foreigner in her own country which was "not on, and not fair". She spoke animatedly for some minutes—then she suddenly looked at me—saw the impact she had made on me and stopped speaking.

To me this felt as if something destructive and attacking had entered the room. This was not the client I had got to know and like. It reminded me of the distressing times when I first arrived in London. I had experienced a number of instances of overt racism, which deeply shocked me and left me feeling unwelcome. As I experienced her attack, somewhere in the back of my mind I knew that I was supposed to figure something out; but what was her unconscious self asking me to process? What I did know was that I was indeed like "those foreigners"—an immigrant to Britain. I felt confused, furious, and hurt. I was unable to process, and my attempts to get the session back on track felt devoid of any vitality. I had been forced into uncharted territory.

The recovery of my mind

I was in supervision with two senior practitioners who are white and British. I took my thoughts and process to both in order to help me stay grounded. I presented my thinking about projective identification and the primitive cultural parent (Hargaden & Sills, 2002). We explored possible symbolic meanings of Liz's words and how I might process these with her. For example, was she taking me in as a new introject, and I was therefore an invading foreigner to her defensive self? Was she getting in touch with the sequestered part of herself which felt foreign? Was part of her experiencing me as giving her too little? Was this an envious attack? Had "those foreigners" become a symbolic third? Was she letting me feel experientially how oppressed she felt? These possibilities were all helpful, and yet something was missing for me. I still felt stuck and shocked.

I later spoke about Liz's words with my peer supervision group, which consists of practitioners who have personally experienced prejudice and racism. I felt understood by their empathic responses to my hurt and anger. Consequently I felt calmer and this helped me to regain my thinking. The sense of being accepted and empathized with had helped me feel contained, and I began to recover my ability to think, and to shift away from my symbiotic/transferential responses to both my supervisors and to my client.

I realized that my projection on to my supervisors was that they, as non-foreigners, could not and therefore would not, relate to my feelings. It felt as if it was my job to protect them and not embarrass them with my feelings and needs, while at the same time I felt angry that they had not sensed my feelings.

In the transference, I had unconsciously located my supervisors as culturally and professionally more powerful than me, and I responded from my supervisee and minority group status. Here, the child (less powerful) takes care of the caregivers (more powerful)—an enactment of a second order structural symbiosis (Schiff et al., 1975), which is depicted as the P_1 (injunctions) and A_1 (survival decisions/defences) of the child taking care of C_1 (core self) of the mother.

This reflected my defensive structure developed early in my life to survive and manage primitive responses and impulses as a way of holding on to my caregivers.

Batts (2009) offers a useful model for understanding the active relationship, power, and status differential between people and its impact on observable behaviour (see Figure 4). She uses the term "target groups" for people broadly speaking who are oppressed or discounted and "non-target groups" for culturally accepted groups. Importantly, she sees this concept as a dynamic process where in some circumstances we may be part of a target group, and in other circumstances we may be in a non-target category. For example, a gay man in a largely heterosexual group may feel and display behaviours belonging to target categories; at other times in different situations when in a non-target category (for instance as an executive with his employees) he may feel and display behaviours pertinent to non-target categories.

Using this framework to understand the transferential dynamic I set up in supervision, I understood that I avoided contact with my supervisors, because I did not believe that they could understand my experience and feared that they would try and help me identify something that I should have done (dysfunctional rescuing). I therefore tried to get round this by presenting my thinking (system beating, do what they want me to do), and kept my feelings hidden. My supervisors' part in this was that they had moved on to talk about the client's material too quickly for me, and they had not enquired about my feelings (denial of the significance of cultural differences).

Having realized what I had done with my supervisors, I could see how this could have been a parallel process with how Liz was presenting with me. Like Liz, I had presented to my supervisors more cognitively, with subdued affect, from my less powerful category (target)

Non-target	Target
Dominant categories in any culture	Target of oppression
Dysfunctional rescuing	System beating
Blaming the victim	Blaming the system
Avoidance of contact	Antagonistic avoidance of contact
Denial of cultural difference	Denial of cultural heritage
Denial of the political, economic, psychological, historical, etc. Significance of difference	Lack of understanding of the political significance of difference

Figure 4. Modern "isms" and internalized oppression (Batts, 2009, pp. 69–80).

in response to their more powerful position (non-target). With my peer group who had similar life experiences and understanding of being regarded as other, I felt accepted at an emotional level, and thereby gained a reflective space within which I could reconnect with my Adult thinking. I wondered, therefore, whether I needed to accept Liz and her unconscious communication, and give space to our relationship and allow a connection to emerge from within this accepting space.

I was now able to take in and consider at a visceral level Liz's lack of space within her early experiences with her parents, in which she was not able to discover, explore, and allow herself to develop. My hypothesis was that she needed me to understand how terrible and terrified she felt at the prospect of an unpredictable world opening up and I had been party to exposing her to her vulnerable self. Her "protective self" (Fowlie, 2005, p. 198) was probably also letting me know how furious she was with me for this exposure, and used a socially sanctioned weapon against me by aligning me with the foreigners and herself as a more entitled member of the population.

Unpacking the culturally framed encounter

Liz's projective identification process triggered an introjective attack within me. It fuelled a wish to push the bad back into her. It brought together within me experiences of being discriminated against and other times when I had been invited to collude with an antipathy towards new immigrants. Both felt distasteful. This confusion of being one of them as well as one of us symbolized the push and pull aspect of Liz's way of being with me.

As Liz had let me in and her defences began to dissolve, I think that I represented a threat to her survival mechanisms (push me away) as well as a source of hope for something new (pull me in). She "bigged herself up" as a defence against feeling the utter terribleness and grief of her early life. She had been subjugated by her internalized Parent-Child dynamic, and she unconsciously used a socially constructed oppressive structure to let me feel her disempowerment and lack of entitlement at an individual level. I, in turn, felt hurt and angry in relation to her. The hopeful aspect of this exchange is that she trusted me enough to externalize the oppressive structure within her, and the power dynamics were now sitting between us.

I struggled to contain my thoughts and feelings, and of course the question that remains is whether we can ever know how much these responses belonged to me, and how much they belonged to Liz. In some ways, the real importance of this event was the experience in itself. She used her social and cultural power of white English identity to communicate at two levels: she pushed me away as well as letting me know how squashed she had felt in her family. I had enabled this by being the other, as well as by staying "relentlessly empathic" (Stark, 2000, p. 87). She had got close to me, but could not merge with me. I would always be different.

Part of the unconscious invitation to collude with her might have been an attempt to twin or pair up with me, against those foreigners, which meant that my existence as an Indian woman had to be negated. Did this parallel her experience in the family of being negated? Was this an invitation from her Parent ego state (P_2 cultural parent) to form an interpersonal relational unit (Little, 2006), which would enable her Child ego state to continue to be loyal to her introjected father?

I needed to find my way through these possibilities and to recognize that "this is all about me and nothing to do with me" (Shmukler, 2010).

I had to enter the intersubjective field with Liz, and be impacted by her, and to recover my ability to contain and understand what had happened between us. Apart from the holding offered by the ethical frameworks of psychotherapy, I believed that I had enough faith that Liz and I would find a way through to maintaining a connection and make meaning from our encounter. Much of the metabolizing of this experience happened nonverbally, but over time I offered Liz my thinking about her impact on me.

I was impacted by Liz's willingness to engage with me around this piece of writing. Making my thoughts and feelings available to her in this way was new to both of us. Prior to our meeting, I felt concerned that she may feel exposed or used, but hoped that she would feel thought about and held in mind. Our recovery with each other has been part of her current ability to manage uncertainties, and express her feelings in deeply moving ways.

While she had some discomfort with recognizing that I had these thoughts and feelings about what had happened, and with seeing herself written about in this way, mostly she felt touched and privileged. I, in turn, felt moved by the way she held the sheets of chapter almost as a tangible representation of our relationship. She said she appreciated seeing me as human and that she had felt both cared for and not cared for enough. Her statement raises an interesting hypothetical question for me, around working with the tension between filling any developmental deficit versus holding the gap, and containing and surfacing the affect that emerges from the deficit.

Conclusion

Power is a difficult topic in psychotherapy since the aim of our work is to liberate individual psyches from their internal oppressors. Locating the power bestowed on us within the therapist-client, supervisor-supervisee relationship can feel disturbing for both parties. In my work with Liz I learnt experientially the importance of paying close attention to my internal responses, as well as to what I might have missed. When in the throes of projective identification, it can feel almost impossible to think clearly, and the use of other minds (colleagues and supervisors) is an essential component of teasing out self from other.

Most importantly of all though, is the need to include in our reflections our cultural identities and our individual memberships of target and non-target groups, as a way of acknowledging the permissions and prohibitions that are embedded in wider society and become part of our unconscious way of operating. This recognition surfaces the often unspoken relational dynamics between therapist and client which means that we can consider openly those "no go" areas that that have for so long been part of the individualistic bias in psychotherapy.

CHAPTER TEN

Rackets and racket feelings: breaking through the racket system, a case of transformation of experience in short-term therapy

Katarina Gildebrand and Suhith Shivanath

In this chapter, we explore the role of the relational approach used in a time limited setting, and with reference to the racket system (Erskine & Zalcman, 1979), reflecting in particular on the significance of unconscious and nonconscious memory processes. Through the use of a case example, we will discuss the relationship between the client's and the therapist's racket systems (Holtby, 1979), and reflect on the requirements on us as practitioners to help clients interrupt the repeating nature of rackets.

Conscious and unconscious memory systems

The racket system, for the most part, operates out of awareness and is underpinned by memories held in what are known as implicit and explicit memory systems. These two seemingly independent memory systems were discovered by Dr Brenda Milner in the 1960s (Carey, 2008).

Explicit memory *refers* to the conscious, intentional recollection of previous experiences and information, and to memories potentially available for such recollection. It is employed in what we commonly refer to as "remembering" or "recalling a memory". Once an explicit memory has been established, we may inhibit its retrieval by repression as a defence against becoming overwhelmed.

Explicit memory only begins to operate somewhere between the ages of two to three, accounting for the phenomena referred to as infantile amnesia or the inability to recall events from our earliest childhood. In addition, a number of factors may inhibit the laying down of explicit memories including the experience of stress, such as trauma, long-term neglect, or physical illness. If the stress is severe the memories retained will be stored in what is known as implicit memory only and will remain unconscious.

Our earliest learning is limited to implicit memories. This memory system contains "non-symbolic communications and behaviours, including transference manifestations, non-verbal behaviour, the 'unthought known' (Bollas, 1987), and enactments of early experience" (Allen, 2010, p. 25). It operates through different mental processes from explicit memory, informing our experience as it becomes activated through internal or environmental triggers. This memory system has no sense of time; it is experienced as real and in the here and now, and frequently without conscious awareness of influences from the past. It holds the memory of our earliest interactions; our first experiences of human relations that our bodies, but not our minds, can remember. It informs our behaviour and contains our expectations of relationships with others, as manifest in the unconscious enactment of the transference relationship.

The racket system serves to conceptualize and track ways in which we interpret experiences constructed in early infancy and childhood so that life becomes more predictable and therefore more manageable. Our implicit and explicit memories are used and distorted in the service of maintaining our defensive structures. This frequently takes the form of negative internal dialogues and in the extreme, this may result in suicidal ideation. Kalsched (1996, p. 3) suggests that "When other defences fail, archetypal defences will go to any lengths to protect the Self—even to the point of killing the host personality in which this personal spirit is housed". Generated by the belief system, and manifest as part of the rackety display, the internal self attack may be even more vicious than the experience of the original relational failure. This defence mechanism distorts reality and serves as a potent protection from awareness of the unbearable pain of the original abandonment. This rigid framework limits our options and may leave us isolated and sometimes desperate, yet unavailable for intimate contact with others.

Interrupting a system at any given point has the potential to reverberate and have an effect on the whole system. The beauty of tracking a person's individual racket/defence mechanisms is that it focuses on beliefs (thinking), phenomenology (feelings and sensations), and repetitive encounters (behaviour). It offers the practitioner a diagnostic as well as a treatment planning tool, in terms of working out how to help the client to interrupt their self defeating patterns.

One of the facets of working relationally involves the practitioner's willingness to engage with their own defensive structures. The intention is to enable the processing of responses to clients, and avoid any acting out, since it offers an opportunity to be open to connecting with our own (and therefore others') vulnerabilities. Working relationally offers opportunities to bring into consciousness how the two narratives might connect and play out. The therapist's self-awareness and use of supervision becomes key in bringing any stuck points into awareness in order that a co-created closed loop may be interrupted.

In our own experience with clients and in supervising practitioners working within a time limited framework, the most common countertransference process that has a basis in the external reality is one of urgency, or the perceived need to get the client to feel better quickly. Putting ourselves under such pressure may resurrect the therapists' archaic relating patterns. For example we may be influenced by our own core sense of feeling under-resourced, or trying hard to do as much as possible, or hurrying to get the client somewhere. The therapist's analysis of their own vulnerabilities, and of holding their own process in awareness as far as it is in our capacities to do so, is arguably even more important in short-term work since the opportunities for re-enactments may be heightened by a potential sense of urgency by both parties.

Within the public sector, and the likes of the UK's Employment Assistance Programmes (EAP), time limited therapy is mostly the only option open for the majority of clients wishing to receive counselling. The therapist's attuned attention in itself can allow the client to disconnect from their defensive processes as manifest in the racket system. Here the client may reconnect with previously disowned aspects of themselves. These connections and withdrawals include the requirement for the therapist to be able to tolerate their own countertransference responses, including, as suggested above, a sense of urgency and/or a lack of empathic responses with the client, as demonstrated below.

The case example illustrates the interlocking racket systems of the therapist and client, and how this at first felt like a block to effective work, and then informed the therapist about her contact and engagement with the client.

Case example: "the angry man"

John was a very angry man. In his early fifties, he came to see the therapist for six sessions provided by his employer, because he stood to lose his job if he did not "shape up". He was scared and bewildered, fearing that he might end up hurting someone, and indeed lose his job. He described his experience over the last few years as "not being himself".

John had joined the police as a young man. He loved his job, and had been well liked and respected by his colleagues, as well as by many of those he dealt with in his role as a policeman. His particular strength was his ability to gain the trust of young offenders, by showing respect and a belief in their ability to better themselves. Then times changed. With financial cutbacks, John's duties changed drastically. He was moved from one area to another, therefore unable to sustain relationships with the youngsters he had previously worked so successfully with. His numerous attempts to do something about the situation were unsuccessful. He felt unheard by those in positions of authority.

John was born to a mother who was depressed following his birth. She looked after his bodily needs but did not interact much with him, except when he had a tantrum. His early experience of a close relationship, embedded in his implicit memory, was of a distant and passive mother. He learnt that being angry got him his mother's (albeit negative) attention and he learnt to substitute sadness and fear with anger. In addition, John's father was a violent man, and as he grew up, John increasingly took the role of protector of his mother and siblings. Here again he learnt to suppress his fear in order to support his mother. Once this had become a pattern, he was no longer aware of his initial feelings of sadness and fear.

As an adult, each time he had an angry outburst, he attracted negative attention which left him feeling bad and out of control. At the same time he justified his behaviour by telling himself he was right. Each time he lost his temper, he reinforced his defensive beliefs about himself and others.

One day, in response to his increasing feelings of frustration and helplessness, and despite knowing that such behaviour would put him at risk of losing his job, he attacked a colleague, feeling temporarily justified in his actions.

On first meeting with his therapist, John presented as being angry at everything and everyone. The smallest thing could set him off; he avoided going out in case he got into a fight. He reported that he had a pattern of getting angry "inside", and was terrified of losing control again. Having always considered himself to be "a calm and balanced sort of guy" he was greatly unsettled by this development.

To help her formulate an assessment of John's presentation, the therapist used the racket system (see Figure 5 below). The racket system is a useful assessment tool that can help to map out the client's belief system about self, others, and the world, and how this becomes manifest in their observable behaviour, together with their internal experiences and fantasies. In this way, "each part [of the racket system] reinforces the other parts, setting up a dynamic" (Tilney, 1998, p. 100).

His therapist noticed that she did not feel scared of him despite his apparent aggression; perhaps his anger was only skin-deep, protecting a more vulnerable experience of himself, or perhaps she was protecting

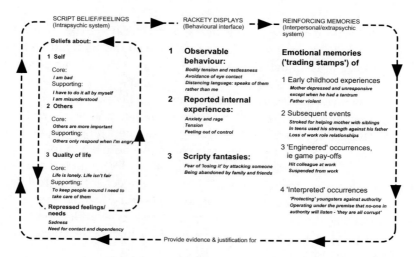

Figure 5. John's racket system. (The Racket System, Lapworth, Sills & Fish (1993) adaptation of Erskine & Zalcman (1979) Racket System reproduced with kind permission.)

herself from the awareness of the impact of her own fear in response to his anger, in an attempt to be the good therapist. She was, however, very aware of an incredible tension in him. She found herself tightening up and holding her breath, resonating with his restless state.

The therapist felt the pressure of the limited time available, and was concerned about not being able to help John; she perceived herself as inadequate whilst at the same time feeling angry with the EAP for only allowing six sessions.

To help her with this, she explored her responses with her supervisor. By encouraging exploration of the countertransference/racket response, the therapist was able to link her lack of connectedness to her own past; she had been born to a mother not able to fully attend to the demands of a new baby. She had developed a capacity to look after her mum by being good and avoiding being "a burden", involving a predisposition to shy away from expressions of deep anxiety as present in John. This helped the therapist to make sense of her own feelings, and to identify with John's internalized unavailable mother, and how he needed to defend against his infant feelings. This created points of interconnection in terms of potential for interlocking racket systems (Holtby, 1979). The therapist realized how she might have become—in the co-transference—his unavailable mother and/or his defended cut-off self.

What had been repressed for the therapist became explicit and in awareness; both client and therapist had concluded that others are more important as an avoidance of dependency. Had the practitioner not become aware of this aspect of her own racket system (i.e., her own implicit memories), she may have acted out from her perceived sense of time urgency and tried to push John towards understanding rather than feeling his feelings. Instead, she held this awareness, allowing herself to experience John with a greater sense of connection; her empathy for her client and his experience had been re-awoken. Through the process of supervision, the practitioner was able to reconnect with her feelings of sadness and compassion in relation to John's story. By having experienced this level of disconnection, the practitioner now understood that her lack of response paralleled John's inability to experience his own suppressed feeling.

In his therapy, John seemed somehow defeated despite his tough exterior. His therapist, now with a greater sense of connectedness, noticed how she felt unaccountably sad in his presence. She wondered whether this was her sadness, or a disowned part of John's experience. She considered sharing her experience of sadness with him, but wondered if that may invite his need to look after her, as he looked after his mother. Instead, she decided to use her sadness to inform her next intervention, saying "I have a sense that you are very sad". By resonating with the therapist's attunement and acceptance, John was able to connect with his real feelings, as he broke down in deep sobs. He began to get in touch with his grief and previously suppressed feelings over his loss of a meaningful role at work. No longer needing to cover his sadness with his racket anger, he went through a difficult time, as feelings of grief and helplessness that he had suppressed for years came flooding out.

This realization enabled John to understand his longer-term therapeutic needs, and the therapist helped him to identify available resources in order that he may continue to be held elsewhere, while he processed the material that had surfaced in their short-term piece of work.

Summary

The use of a relational approach within a time limited framework may present an opportunity for the client to reconnect with their sense of self agency, through the experience of being connected to and being contained by an attentive other. This can have the effect of interrupting the defensive mechanisms, as manifest by the racket system.

For therapist and client, the perceived pressures of fixing the problem within a time limited frame may encourage out of awareness responses which could hinder contact in the here and now. It has the potential for inviting the racket in each party with predictable negative outcome for both. Since these processes are unconscious, as therapists we need to pay close attention to our countertransference, and make use of the minds of others, through supervision, to disentangle the past from the present.

In the case study above, the therapist's use of her own processes in her supervision helped her to break through her own racket system. In subsequent sessions, John and his therapist were able to establish a deeper connection, which helped him to get in touch with and begin to experience feeling contained in his expression of previously suppressed feelings. For him this opened possibilities of experiencing a different reality in contrast to the perceived inevitability of the path he had been on. We agree with Hargaden (2002) who states that "the relational map offers the opportunity to chart the terrain for understanding experiences without trying to control them [...] and understanding of the transferential relationship is central to this model" (p. 62).

Principle 6

The importance of uncertainty

CHAPTER ELEVEN

What do I do now? Grappling with uncertainty in a postmodern world

Jo Stuthridge

I recall vividly the first time I sat in a room alone with a client. I was twenty-five years old. I remember the terrible weight of responsibility and the fear of not knowing what to do. I clutched desperately at theory to ease my anxiety. I reached for maps and models to save myself from drowning in uncertainty. I assumed that the truth about the human mind was out there somewhere, if only I could find the right book or teacher …

Classical transactional analysis training provided me with a raft of ready concepts that explained the client's problem. I was equipped with a prescriptive map and clear directions. I developed some confidence and skill at identifying drivers (Kahler, 1974), injunctions (Goulding & Goulding, 1976), script patterns (Berne, 1972; Steiner, 1974), and games (Berne, 1964). Armed with a water-tight contract, I had a reliable compass and a strong sense of purpose. As a community I think we shared a belief that our theory provided a simple, clear, and accurate reflection of the psyche. We could translate a client's life history into a few concise diagrams. We had tools for making incisive interventions. We could cut through "the jazz" as Berne (1966a) put it, or surface layers, to reveal the hidden truth of things. We knew what we were doing.

These days, working with uncertainty is considered a crucial skill for the relational therapist. This essay will attempt to address questions like: whatever happened to certainty?, why is uncertainty valued?, and how can a transactional analyst apply this principle in a consulting room?

Why is uncertainty so much in vogue today? Therapists from different persuasions sing in praise of "not knowing" and the courage it takes to tolerate doubt. Mitchell (1993, p. 43), in a wry moment, writes that where analysts once thumped their chests with convictions about unbearable truths, "it now sometimes appears that the capacity to contain the dread of not knowing is a measure of analytic virtue; the fewer the convictions the better and braver!". Why the about-turn? Surely our clients pay us to know something. The answers to these questions lie in major shifts in the philosophy of science, which have shaken up the epistemological foundations of psychotherapy.

The problem with certainty

Certainty is no longer considered possible in a postmodern world. Heisenberg's (1958) uncertainty principle taught us that it is not possible to measure position and movement of particles simultaneously. The more we know about one, the less accurately we can measure the other. Relativity theory proposes that reality changes as a function of the observer's participation. Niels Bohr (1963) introduced the notion of complementarity to denote the relation between two conflicting perspectives, which together form a whole. The assumption that nature could be objectively observed was shattered and replaced by notions of uncertainty, subjectivity, and contradiction as elements of science. Thinkers in most fields, including psychotherapists, have been forced to question what it is possible to know.

The observer as participant

In Berne's world of rationalism and objectivism, it was assumed that the therapist could occupy a detached position and know with some certitude how the client's mind was organized. The problem existed independently in the client, quite separate from any influence of the observer. Berne emphasized the importance of careful objective observation, using methods consistent with the science of his time.

Ideas like "Formula G" (Berne, 1972) were direct pleas to scientific rationalism.

A quantum view of the world argues that therapeutic neutrality and objectivity are fallacies. Relational perspectives assume that observer and observed together form a whole. This means the therapist's participation and their unique character will influence the outcome (Wallin, 2007). Instead of locating the problem "out there", a two-person (Stark, 1999) epistemology locates the problem in a process of mutual interaction, specific to the context.

Pluralism versus truth

In a modern world, we assumed that knowledge was absolute, singular, and universal. In a postmodern world, we have to accept that knowledge is pluralistic: there are many ways of understanding. Transactional analysis, like mainstream psychoanalysis, has witnessed a proliferation of models and schools of thought. Previously, therapists believed that theory could provide a single true reflection of the mind's inner workings. Today, therapists must accept that meanings are only ever constructions or interpretations.

Mitchell (1993) notes that the heterogeneity of theory reflects the ambiguity of human experience. Experience always has more than one meaning. Unconscious meanings are even more ambiguous and open to multiple ways of seeing. The therapist can never be aware of all the possible options in any moment, or of the impact of his own unconscious. The central principle of the contemporary philosophy of science is that uncertainty is inescapable.

Living with uncertainty: a constructivist relational solution

When I sit with a client today, I live with a form of uncertainty that is far more frightening than the uncertainty I began with as a young therapist.

If we accept that the therapist's subjectivity will influence the process and that there are always multiple meanings of experience, then uncertainty must be accepted as a constant and uneasy companion. Living with uncertainty raises existential ghosts like meaninglessness, relativism, and transience. Is it even possible to know another person? Are all meanings equal?

Therapists seek the certainty of theory for the same reason we cling to script: to avoid unpredictability in life and other existential dilemmas (Heiller & Sills, 2010). Hoffman (1998) suggests we seek certainty to avoid the responsibility inherent in a therapist's role, because "The responsibility to choose in the context of profound irreducible uncertainty is frightening" (p. 25). Furthermore, according to Hoffman (1998) the therapist must act from moment to moment, whether she chooses to be silent, listen, or speak.

A constructivist relational perspective embraces uncertainty and offers the therapist some liberating possibilities. I use the term "constructivist relational" as an umbrella to cover relational and constructivist approaches both within and beyond transactional analysis. Uncertainty is one of the key threads that unify this diverse group of writers. Donnel Stern (1999) beautifully defines this option as an alternative to the traditional search for objective meaning:

> Psychoanalysis is not a search for hidden truth about the patient and the patient's life. It is instead the emergence, through curiosity and the acceptance of uncertainty, of constructions that may never have been thought before (p. 100).

Vincent Kenny (1997) introduces a constructivist approach to transactional analysis, defined as "the way of understanding" (p. 116). He contrasts this with a classical worldview, defined as "the way of certainty" (ibid., p. 116). Kenny, like Stern, sees uncertainty as pivotal to postmodern psychotherapy.

From a constructivist relational perspective, meaning in therapy is an outcome of a mutually creative co-constructed process. Constructivists argue that to understand, means to construct or create meaning, rather than expose "the truth". Meaning is not waiting to be uncovered like buried treasure in the client's mind (Wachtel, 2008, p. 25) but instead evolves in a dynamic process in the present.

Berne's (1966a) description of the therapist's task epitomizes a distinctly modern view: "After clearing his mind of extraneous matters ... he then tries to penetrate the reality of the situation in which he finds himself" (p. 74). From a postmodern approach, there is no single underlying reality to penetrate. The situation changes when the therapist walks into the room. Rather than "clearing one's mind", the therapist utilizes her subjective experience, including "extraneous matters", to understand the client. Subjectivity is vital to understanding, rather than an unfortunate contaminant. The question is, how can I use my experience to understand what is happening between us?

From a relational perspective, the therapist offers a willingness to engage in a process, rather than certain knowledge. The transactional analyst agrees to an encounter between two subjects or two scripts. In Jessica Benjamin's (1999) words, the therapist offers "a willingness to risk not knowing and failing to understand, an engagement of two subjectivities" (p. 207).

Benjamin (1999) argues that the task is to get beyond a "struggle of your meaning versus my meaning"(p. 208), which she defines as complementarity. Complementarity involves an attempt to force the other to play a role in our script. The achievement of mutuality requires recognition of both subjective viewpoints. In transactional analysis terms, we can conceive this dynamic as a movement from complementary transactions (Child-Parent or Parent-Child) to Adult-Adult relating (Berne, 1961).

For the transactional analyst, embracing uncertainty means wading into the mire of co-created script enactments. The therapist must be prepared to involve herself in an emotional process, sink into the mud and occasionally get stuck. A relational approach assumes that games or enactments offer a vehicle for understanding the client's unconscious communication (Hargaden & Sills, 2002; Zvelc, 2010). A mutual enactment might be defined as an intersection between two scripts. The asymmetrical structure of the therapy relationship ensures that the focus is always on the client's well-being, but the therapist's role can no longer be denied.

With uncertainty as a guiding principle to practice, useful questions to ask oneself are: who are you being for me and who am I being for you?, what are we doing to each other?, and how can we find a different way to relate? Script enactments always carry the potential to either reinforce or transform a script. The outcome largely depends on the therapist's ability to mentalize or move out of the emotional grip of the entanglement. At the point where entrapment in the impasse gives way to recognition of the other as a subject we create an interstice where new meanings can emerge. The self as an agentive subject, or author of one's script, emerges in the cracks between two subjects.

Uncertainty and creativity

Donnel Stern (1999) invites us not just to accept but to welcome uncertainty. An uncertain stance is crucial to access "creative disorder". Stern argues that uncertainty frees the mind from the totalitarian control of defensive thought systems. Following Stern, we might say that certainty is an instrument of script, while uncertainty is the key to collaborative creative therapy.

Stern draws on the experience of artists and creative thinkers to advocate an open, receptive attitude in the therapist. When we stop using theory like a focused beam of light to look for something (like injunctions or drivers), we can construct new meanings from the shadows of "unformulated experience". For example, while writing this chapter I found new thoughts often appeared while doing the dishes rather than focusing on the task at hand.

John Keats's (1817/2002) famous concept of "negative capability" also holds that an attitude of uncertainty is necessary to creativity. "I mean Negative Capability, that is when man is capable of being in uncertainties, Mysteries, doubts without any irritable reaching after fact & reason" (p. 41). Once we stop grasping for certainty, the unknown can excite a creative venture.

Therapy is like any creative process. It involves an oscillation between, on the one hand, uncertainty, flux, and doubt, and on the other hand, a more deliberate attempt to construct meaning. Uncertainty dismantles script convictions and frees us to re-invent ourselves. I believe the trick is neither to abandon theory nor to grasp at it. Instead, we need to play with theory, hold it lightly and be prepared to let go at times.

When the bough breaks

Sarah began her first session by warning me that she had already found a therapist. Although she was happy with this therapist, she requested a one-off session to explore me as a second option. Sarah clearly possessed a brilliant mind and the first therapist had offered a cognitive approach that she felt would suit her well. She laid out her problem clearly. She wanted to understand her own part in a recent relationship crisis and she wanted to know how I might help her. Terrific, I thought, I'm the second option and I'm about to be interrogated. As Sarah quizzed me on my approach to therapy, I began to stumble over my words. I felt somewhat inadequate and intimidated.

Sarah appreciated my explanations of psychodynamic therapy but reiterated that she felt a cognitive approach would work best for her. I said I believed I could help her, but not in the way she wanted. I wondered why she was here. Overall, I felt that what I had to offer was not wanted, and I did not expect to see her back. Towards the end of the session, perhaps in a bid to give her something, I expressed concern for her apparent isolation. Sarah was clearly touched and later told me how the mix of challenge and compassion rapidly undermined her defences. There was an edgy quality to this first encounter.

The following week Sarah phoned and asked for a second appointment. After she explained that she intended to finish with the former therapist, whom she had seen only once, I agreed. From a classical perspective, I could have developed a succinct diagnosis and treatment plan at this point. Her behaviour suggested a be strong driver, countering don't feel and don't be a child injunctions, in the setting of a schizoid personality adaptation (Ware, 1983). Sarah's proposition to see me as a second option could be interpreted as an opening move in a game. Perhaps I would insist on a contract before proceeding any further. Working from this objective stance, the therapist stands on dry and certain ground.

Conversely, working from a relational perspective, the only way to understand Sarah was to immerse myself in what promised to be a fraught emotional experience. Embracing uncertainty is like letting go of a liferaft. It means letting go of complacency and the security of theory. Above all, working at the "intimate edge" (Ehrenberg, 1992) requires a willingness to be vulnerable. The relational therapist resembles the bumbling television detective Columbo more than Sherlock Holmes (Mitchell, 1993).

In the second session, a subtle tension developed between us. I felt caught in a set of complementary transactions. I could either submit to Sarah's agenda, feeling pressured to agree with her compelling and erudite analysis or resist by questioning her logical approach. I alternated between submission and resistance, listening for long periods then interrupting occasionally. Sarah felt pressured by the time-frame and appeared to experience any contribution I made as an unnecessary intrusion.

At one point, I inquired about her emotional experience as a child and her outpouring of words slowed to a trickle. She felt there was little to say. However, the vacuum in the session spoke volumes. I felt moved by her soundless expression of a lonely childhood. The following session Sarah told me she had left feeling dreadful. She felt her answers were inadequate, as if she had nothing to offer. She feared I would not want her as a client. Her experience uncannily mirrored my own feelings in the first session.

By the third session clouds of distrust loomed overhead, threatening our fragile alliance. Looking for a way out, I tried to articulate my experience, speaking from the very margins of understanding, without knowing where it would lead. I told her that I felt pulled by her desire for logical analysis and to be heard without judgement but feared this would lead to further deadening and isolation. Sarah expressed her fear that by insisting on feelings, I might "unravel the threads of her self" or strip away her thin garments of self-esteem. She was terrified of a descent into despair. Hearing her fear forced me to question the certainties that I had been forming in spite of myself. I realized that by pursuing my path of affective engagement I risked doing to Sarah what her mother had done. She might experience me, like her mother, as failing to accept her as she was. Ironically, Sarah described a mother who had treated her like a miniature grown up, ignoring her fears and feelings. This session opened up a more fluid space between us. The dialogue moved beyond complementarity and began to spark at points of mutual recognition. Meanings evolved that neither of us had imagined.

From a relational perspective, Sarah and I appeared to be re-enacting her struggle with her mother. We took turns at playing the domineering mother, leaving the other to feel like an unwanted child. I felt unwanted in the first session and tried to give her something. Sarah felt she had nothing of worth to give in the second session. I shared these thoughts with Sarah and she wove the weft in this story. She knew the deep pain of feeling unwanted by her very young parents and about giving to compensate for her sense of being burdensome. Sarah's parents separated when she was four. She felt like a burden to her single mother and a visitor in the home of her father's new family. I suggested that Sarah had unwittingly repeated her experience of living between her separated parents by placing herself between two therapists, two cities, and two countries (she was an immigrant). She recognized the same feeling of being unwanted by her current partner. She was unconsciously arranging her life to fit the script.

These meanings emerged from our co-created experience in the present. There was a part of me who could play the unwanted child, while the therapist who still clung to her theories made a ready recruit for the part of mother. From an intersubjective position my challenge was to recognize my client's subjective experience without imposing or relinquishing my own. This meant recognizing Sarah's fear of being "crushed" by her emotions, while helping her to trust the process. My early feelings of inadequacy hinted that Sarah's biggest fear might be of overwhelming the other, rather than being overwhelmed. This theme was enacted over a struggle with the fifty minute boundary, which she described as "a constant reminder to me of my general sense that I am simply too much for others to handle". We wondered together if this unwanted baby had been too much for her young parents. My supervisor commented that her need to begin with two therapists reflected a fear of putting all her eggs in one basket, because the original basket could not hold her.

Conclusion

Embracing uncertainty as a transactional analyst involves a willingness to participate in a live script production, rather than viewing the client's script objectively as an intrapsychic relic. Uncertainty does not imply anything goes. Meaning resides neither with the therapist, nor with the client but rather evolves from intricate encounters between two subjects.

If I had assumed the certainty inherent in an objective stance and stuck to a rigid treatment plan, I could have reinforced Sarah's script. The child who feared she was too much for others might have thrashed at the boundaries without finding a voice. The uncertain path led us through Sarah's script in painful nuanced detail. Her deadening monologues, which she later compared to the dead birds her cat brought in (looking for praise), gave way to a more lively relationship.

Clients arrive in therapy stuck in emotional certainties or a script. Through "being in [the] uncertainties, Mysteries and doubt" which reside between self and other, therapy can facilitate movement from the imprisonment of script to a lively encounter with the endless possibilities of intimacy.

I would like to thank Sarah for her consent to use this material and acknowledge her contribution to this client vignette.

CHAPTER TWELVE

The importance of uncertainty

Charlotte Sills

Faust: Wohin der Weg?
(Where leads the path?)
Mephistopheles: Kein Weg! Ins Unbetretene.
(No paths! Into untrodden ways.)

—Goethe, *Faust 1*, p. 364

Uncertainty is an existential given of life (Heidegger, 1927/1962; Heisenberg, 1958). In the previous chapter of this volume, Jo Stuthridge elegantly overviews the arguments that very little is certain in the world. So in this paper, I focus not on the impossibility of certainty but on its undesirability. I explore the necessity in relational psychotherapy of a balance between the certain and the uncertain, in order for transformation to happen. I will then discuss some of the implications for TA theory, a major strength of which is to seem to offer certainty and a particular sort of knowing about human beings and their behaviour. Can we, as transactional analysts, re-vision our concepts so that while they can continue to provide that theoretical support for our work, they can also allow for the unpredictability of relationality, unknowing, and emergence?

If certainty is impossible, why do human beings spend their lives trying to find or create it?

Human beings need stability. Without the certainty of structure and stability in our lives, there could be no order, no society. Chaos would ensue and we would suffer from unmanageable anxiety. In our everyday lives, when we are in situations where there are insufficient boundaries and unpredictable structure, anxiety arises and Adult functioning (Berne, 1961) suffers.

But *why* do we need certainty? Why is there a persistent psychobiological hunger for "Structure" (Berne, 1964)? Is it simply because we need it to manage our lives? The relentless pull to certainty seems to imply more than this. A possible answer occurs to me. It is linked to what we are beginning to understand about early infancy, the growth of the brain, self-regulation, and a secure sense of what one might call "I'm OK. You're OK".

The evidence from research into neurobiology (see for example Schore, 2003) and into human development (Stern, 1985; Trevarthen, 1992) supports the need of the infant for an adequately stable, strong, and reliable carer who will physically and emotionally soothe and nurture him, mirror his experiences, and help him make sense of the world. This soothing containment creates the conditions essential for the development of the brain, the nervous system, and the immune system. It facilitates the regulatory brain functions that allow a person to become autonomous. Berne (1964) described how stimulus hunger (a physical need) is later transmuted into recognition hunger. I suggest that, similarly, the original human need for a containing relationship is represented in the hunger for structure and certainty in the growing individual. This being so, a person's capacity to tolerate uncertainty would relate to the sense of internal "self-containment" that has emerged from their earliest relational experiences.

However, total stability leads to endless repetition and stagnation. There needs to be novelty and difference in order for anything generative to occur—whether this be psychological or biological. Without novelty—or "incident" as Berne called it, nothing new can happen. Creativity exists in the place where there is enough certainty to support stable functioning and enough uncertainty to allow for something new to emerge. Stacey (1993) calls this delicate interface "the area of bounded instability". It is the "edge of knowing and not-knowing" (French

& Simpson, 1999, p. 2). Not-knowing is not the same as ignorance; it is a willingness to explore—to give the human "seeking system" (Panksepp, 1998) free rein, while supported by the stability of what is known.

The importance of uncertainty in therapy

Human beings are meaning-making creatures—from our earliest moments we seek to make sense of our world, to manage it, to make it more predictable. In TA understanding, we write our scripts—the result of the interplay between our hungers (for structure, relationship, and incident) and our early experiences (Berne, 1961). This is our frame of reference (Schiff, 1975). Script becomes pathology when it is not amenable to updating with new information and experience, and when our nonconscious relational patterns impede our healthy relating.

Exploring "what is": A therapist's job is, in large part, to help a client become more aware of how much he lives his life through the filter of his script. He then has the choice either to continue it, or re-decide. As relational therapists we seek to do this by offering an authentic relationship in which the client can get to know himself and the limitations of his script, through, in large part, an exploration of the relational dynamics that get evoked between himself and the therapist.

These relational dynamics, while containing a hope for something different, are also likely to involve a strong pull to reinforce the certainty of our script expectations. We view the world through our own theoretical, social, cultural, familial understandings and prejudices, as well as the embedded norms of our language. In the consulting room, this is experienced perhaps most strongly in the way that both client and therapist organize and shape themselves and each other. Conscious and nonconscious relational dynamics replay as transferences, countertransferences, and co-transferences, as each of us responds to the other, tries to make the world familiar, and to get recognition or strokes (Berne, 1961) predictably. Some of these transferential engagements will make themselves known through bodily sensations or feelings—experienced by the client or evoked in the therapist; some through enactments, associations, or dreams. All this is not immediately accessible to understanding and it requires a willingness to stay with what is, patiently tolerating the unfolding /not yet revealed/unknown until meaning is discovered or co-created.

My client, James, sits in front of me and tells me a long, painful story about his relationship difficulties with his wife. The details are graphic, the dialogue recalled word for word. The wife, who has her own problems, is analysed perceptively by James—as is his own behaviour. An organizational development consultant, he is very familiar with thinking psychologically. He makes meaningful links to his childhood and his script and he sheds an occasional tear. Then he does the same for Jennifer—vulnerable, unemotional, a product of her upbringing with a father "high up in the military". From time to time, James looks at me meaningfully as if to check that I am paying attention.

I listen intently—but I have a vague feeling of unease. I wonder if I have any other role than appreciative listener. We are in the second year of the therapy and for the first year I felt very active. I believed that my presence as an acknowledging, validating other was a vital part of healing the "undeveloped self" (Hargaden & Sills, 2002, p. 25) created by a relationship with an abusive, alcoholic mother. Why am I now not sure? What is the difference between then and now? Gradually I allow my impressions to become conscious. The difference is that there is nothing new happening in the consulting room. Last year, James was voicing the story of his early years for the first time. Now his stories are pre-thought, pre-spoken. There is too much certainty in them.

Opening a space: Therapy at its creative best is an opportunity for both therapist and client *to have a conversation that neither has had before* (R. Wainwright, 2010, personal communication). Engaging in authentic relationship offers the opportunity for the certainty of old patterns to be brought to consciousness and explored. As soon as there are two people genuinely in the conversation, there is the opportunity for a creation of new meanings and new experiences. But the nature of the dynamics requires time and the capacity to sit with not-knowing, and this is unsettling. As Bion (1991, p. 578) says: "Not-knowing leaves the space empty for new insight, as long as we can deal adequately with the way in which our fear of this emptiness drives us to fill it with knowing." Bion (1990) also said, with his usual dry wit: "In every consulting room there ought to be two rather frightened people: the patient and the psycho-analyst. If they are not, one wonders why they are bothering to find out what everyone knows" (p. 5).

I try some interventions to bring some uncertainty into our relational field. "Why are you telling me about Jennifer?" I ask. He looks puzzled. "I'm wondering what this story is telling us about our work," I say pathetically. Rather irritably James explains that he is very worried about his marriage at the moment and wants to talk about it. Later he asks whether he has missed anything in his analysis; is there anything I want to add? I find I have nothing to say. The truth is that I am slightly panicking. There is an empty space where my clinical thinking should be. I feel hypnotized, deprived of my separate mind.

Risking sloppiness. Not only does the therapist have to sit with not knowing, she has to risk inelegance! The sign of a new thought or idea is not a carefully crafted sentence, it is often stumbling and groping. This takes time, attention and experiment. The Boston Change Process Study Group (2008) say that this sort of "unformulated experience" (Stern, 1997) needs to be tentatively reached for; they call this attempt at finding the right words "sloppy work". "It is a process that can rush forward, hesitate, stop, restart gently, and so on" (BCPSG, 2008, pp. 137–138). The therapist who is committed to using her own responses in the service of the work has to be willing to sit with internal sloppiness, a loss of coherence as she struggles to symbolize her experience. She may use supervision to help her bring her mind to bear on it (see Hunt, Chinnock, Shadbolt & Boyd, Leigh in this volume) and sometimes, if for example she believes the client needs to know the impact he has had, she may choose to share her inelegant reaching in a collaborative dialogue.

I think again about James. With his unpredictable and frightening mother, no wonder he has developed a habit of controlling conversations so that nothing unexpected can happen. He engages with me—as with all his relationships—not with his spontaneous responses to here and now, not with his "truth-in-the-moment" (Symington & Symington, 1996, p. 3, cited in French & Simpson, 1999), but with his certainty. I realize that it is my job to encourage/hold the absent polarity of unpredictability but in a way that James can tolerate and risk joining with. As Fletcher (1998) says, a helping relationship has "the capacity to freely and whole-heartedly engage with another's subjectivity … while maintaining and being in touch with one's own—to the extent that one could add to those ideas and create something new".

At the next session, James again starts to describe his life. I suggest that we may have both missed something important to understanding his situation. I ask him to tell me his story again but this time slowly, pausing frequently to sense his body and notice how he is feeling. He and I both start to notice gaps and uncertainties in his story and a more complex, uncertain experience begins to emerge for him. For my part, I rediscover my own mind as I engage with James's felt truth. We begin to create an interchange that is "largely spontaneous and, above all, unpredictable" moment by moment (Novellino, 2010), in which the space is opened to the "safe emergency" (Perls et al., 1951, p. 288).

Implications for transactional analysis

The importance of uncertainty has significant implications for TA theory and method. Our traditional approach—with its clarity of diagnosis, treatment-planning, and clinical certainty, is at one and the same time both its greatest strength and its greatest weakness. It is a wonderful way of describing what is happening and planning a way forward—but it can risk foreclosing on possibilities and jumping to premature conclusions that close down rather than open up the therapeutic space. Relational therapists need to hold their theory lightly, to use it to analyse or "loosen" stuck patterns (from the Greek *analusis*—a loosening of bonds) but without letting it get in the way of being in the moment with our clients.

One of the themes of this book is the revival of the inherent relationality in many of Berne's original concepts (ego states, games, life positions, time structure, and so on). Here, I would like to highlight some of the theories that have the potential for supporting unknowing.

The psychobiological hungers. The primary hungers according to Berne (1964) are for Structure, Incident, and Recognition (or relationship), and they are usually presented as a type of list—even a checklist—that client and therapist can use to identify health and ill-health. I suggest that, instead, we need to look at hungers as an ongoing, dynamic dialectic of existential realities, energies, and needs that balance each other and constantly change according to circumstance.

Our need for structure/stability/safety/a secure base is negotiated with our need for incident/novelty/difference/to explore our world. Cornell speaks of the same theme when he reminds us to "respect the ongoing tensions between novelty and change and the need for famili-arity and chosen adaptations to social and familial structures" (2010, p. 245).

The meeting of these two needs creates the area of bounded insta-bility, which takes place in relationship—a constant context, from the moment of conception to the moment of death. Relationship can provide the stability and safety of structure—the predictability and recognition of rituals and pastimes and the arbitrariness of games and script. It also creates novelty and excitement in the form of authentic meeting: inti-macy. Mutual recognition is the heart of authentic meeting. "By its very nature, the outcomes of mutual interaction are fluid, unknowable—the essence of creativity ... " (Fletcher, 1994, p. 79, cited in King, 2004).

Empathic Transactions. Berne described TA as a "systematic phe-nomenology" (1961, p. 244). In his first therapeutic operations, inter-rogation (less threateningly known as inquiry!) and specification (1966, pp. 33–35), Berne hinted at a method for the sort of collaborative exploration that requires both client and therapist to engage without hurrying to know the outcome. The re-visioning of Berne's therapeu-tic operations by Hargaden and Sills (2002, pp. 119–121), into empathic transactions, has gone far in providing a framework and methodology which accounts for the two-person nature of a relational approach. They acknowledge, for example, that either client or therapist can make an intervention, suggesting that an advantage of the client making their own confrontation or explanation is that "a client who has observed her own patterns and reactions [...] can offer the explanation at a time when they are able to hear it—when it is 'not unthinkable'" (pp. 124–125).

However, there is still a lack of support for uncertainty in the meth-odology. I suggest that the phenomenological method of inquiry (Spinelli, 1989) could effectively address the gap within the empathic transactions.

Phenomenological inquiry is comprised of three elements:

Epoche or bracketing: the therapist brackets his assumptions and pre-dictions, in order to stay with the truth-in-the-moment.

Description: a commitment to discovering "what is", to staying with inquiring into the phenomenology of the client (and indeed the thera-pist) as it occurs in the therapy room, without interpreting, guessing, hurrying to understand.

Horizontalism: which holds that anything and everything may be relevant.

The therapist who commits herself to this inquiry has the courage to wait until pattern or meaning emerges, which is gradually recognized through the use of Berne's/Hargaden and Sills's third and fourth transactions: confrontation and confirmation.

The Contract: This commitment to waiting in the place of bounded instability points to the importance of a clear container in which the creative play of therapy can take place: the contract. Here lies a paradox for the relational therapist. Convincing research into psychotherapy outcomes indicates that a shared agreement about goals and tasks (Berne, 1966)—in other words a contract—is an important part of the working alliance, which is central to effective therapy (see for example Bordin, 1993; Norcross, 2010). On the other hand, by definition, if a goal is capable of being articulated at the start of therapy—or even at the start of a particular session, it must, by definition, be part of the present mind-set. It leaves no room for new ideas, new meanings, and new directions to emerge from a new conversation. As Einstein (1879–1955) warned, we cannot solve our problems with the same thinking we used when we created them. It is important, therefore, that whatever contract is agreed, it leaves room for this possibility of emergence, so that the achievement of well-defined goals can have a place when appropriate, but so also can the uncertainty of exploring and allowing multiple ways of relating and multiple truths.

The contracting matrix (Sills, 2006, 2010; Chinnock, this volume) offers a framework for the relational therapist to make such flexible, dynamic contracts. The vertical axis of the matrix is from Hard to Soft contract—from observable and definable to subjective and phenomenological. The horizontal is from Known to Unknown—in other words, at one extreme, client and therapist are clear about what the goal is to be and can articulate it, while at the other extreme they are standing fully in not-knowing. The model gives rise to four types of contract that allow not only the therapist but also the client to respond to 'what is'—according to the client's perceived and experienced needs and wants, his personality, or psychological awareness.

The *behavioural change contract* (top right) requires of the client a high level of clarity about their problem and desired goals as well as an ability to describe those goals in behavioural terms. Clients who come to psychotherapy with a clear aim—and perhaps a time limited frame—may find these contracts most useful.

Types of Contracts

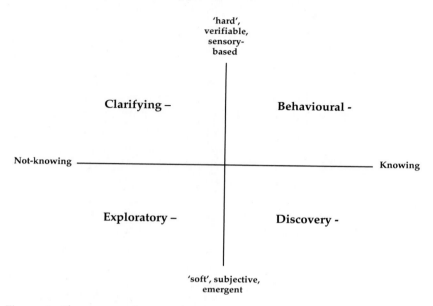

Figure 6. The contracting matrix.

The *clarifying contract* (top left) is one offered to the client when he knows broadly where he wants to be, or at least that he wants clearly definable change, but he does not understand what the problem is and what he needs to do.

At the bottom of the matrix lie two types of contract for a subjective internal change or development, not an externally defined one. The *exploratory contract* may be suitable when clients have neither understanding nor clarity other than a need to feel better; they need to go on an inner journey in a relationship with a trusted other.

Finally, there is what in TA may be called the *autonomy contract* (with the particular meaning that autonomy has in TA, see e.g., Berne, 1964, pp. 158–160)—sometimes called the *discovery contract*. The contract provides the container for the journey, which might be exemplified by the opening quotation from Goethe's *Faust*: "No paths. Into untrodden ways". At the centre of the matrix is the point between known and unknown and between rationality and subjectivity. This is the place of bounded instability where the relational psychotherapist can be attentive moment by moment to both uncertainty and structure as the work unfolds.

Conclusion

The desire for truth leads us to embrace facts and knowledge as if they were unchanging. However, if we search for certainty in therapy we are denying the changeability of truth and the possibility of having a new conversation there—or anywhere. In order to work in the creative area of bounded instability, both therapist and client must hold the balance of knowing and uncertainty. We need to make sure that our TA theories are allies in this therapeutic endeavour, finding an honoured place for uncertainty in the moment.

Predictably, although I did not predict it when I started this chapter, saying anything interesting about the importance of uncertainty is hard if you want to come across as not being too certain about things! I would have liked to write with what Gestaltists call "creative indifference", without investment in the outcome. But that is difficult because I am in a one-sided relationship with you, the reader. My views cannot be changed by our meeting, only by my imagination of our meeting. Nevertheless, there is a way in which putting our words out to an unseen reader is the essence of uncertainty …

Principle 7

The importance of curiosity, criticism, and creativity

CHAPTER THIRTEEN

Fighting for a mind of one's own

William F. Cornell

*Among the ways of being that I value in the analytic setting … is the effort
on the part of the analyst and the patient to face the truth, to be as honest
with themselves in the face of disturbing emotional experience. Doing so
is one of the most difficult of human tasks.*

—(Ogden, 2005, p. 21)

I had given many professional talks over the years, but this one was of
particular importance to me. I was co-presenting a paper with Lore
Reich Rubin, Wilhelm Reich's daughter, "Wilhelm Reich and the
Corruption of Ideals: Idealization and Ideology" (2006). It was Lore's
first public presentation as Reich's daughter. She had never allowed
her parents to become part of her professional identity, and now she
was reflecting professionally on Reich's work and personality. Lore and
I had spent many hours discussing her life with her father and mother,
Annie Reich. Hers was not an easy childhood, and her feelings towards
her father were those of tremendous ambivalence. She listened to my
respect for her father's work, rereading much of his writing with fresh
eyes. The preparation for our talk was deeply personal and emotional
for each of us.

141

As I sat on the stage watching the audience gathering, I was shocked to see my therapist (my second analyst) sitting in the centre of the auditorium. He had not told me he was planning to come. Still more unsettling was that he was seated with my supervisor, and it was clear in the way they were talking that they knew each other well. I had not known they knew each other at all, other than as occasional professional acquaintances. I felt suddenly speechless, panicked, dismayed, and then furious. I decided to create a kind of black hole in the centre of the audience, disappearing them from my line of vision. Lore and I gave our talks, which were often quite emotional, and had a question and answer period with the audience. I had pulled it off (no thanks to my fucking analyst as I thought to myself afterwards).

In my next session, I was furious, "Did it ever occur to you to at least *mention* the fact that you were planning to come, or maybe even *ask* me if it was OK? Like that it might be the sort of thing that we should have talked about in advance?!" "*No*," was his reply. "*No*?!" I said, "*No*? That's it, like there isn't anything else to say?" "Well, you seem to think I should have something more to say." "Yeah, like why did you come?" "I wanted to hear what you had to say, and I know Lore and wanted to hear what she had to say." I was not the least bit satisfied, so on I went, "But you are my therapist, my *analyst* [trying to suggest that being an analyst was a higher order of something or other]. So isn't this the sort of outside the frame bit that we're supposed to avoid, or at least talk about?" "Well, no, it didn't occur to me in that fashion." "So how did it fucking occur to you?" "Well, like you're a big guy, you give talks all over the world. It was a public lecture, so why shouldn't I be able to attend? Do you screen people at your lectures and papers to be sure no one gets in who might upset you?" This response slowed me down. He did have a point, I had to reluctantly admit to myself. But I hated like hell to give him any points at that moment.

"I think you should have told me." "Why? What difference would it have made?" "I could have been prepared." "Prepared for what exactly?" Good question, but I couldn't answer it. "So what did you do when you saw us sitting there?" "I put a big, black hole in the centre of the auditorium and refused to see you." "And if you had seen me?" "I would have cried." "So what the hell is wrong with that? Why would your first and lasting impulse be to create a dead space? What is so dreadful about letting your loves and vulnerability show in public? That is what we need to be talking about, not why I didn't think I needed your permission."

I have long believed that my clients pay me to have and keep a different mind from theirs, even as they press me to only see things from their frame of reference. In this encounter with my analyst, I became fully aware of the fact that he held a very similar point of view. I felt my own wish for some sort of empathic comment or countertransference confession on his part to get me off the hook (or keep him on the hook, as was my original intention). My therapist kept the responsibility for my reactions on the stage that night, and in his office, squarely in my seat, and I felt squarely put back upon myself.

As I write, I am reminded of a recent session with a client, who ended his passionate and furious account of his most recent fight with his wife as I sat in private anguish, thinking I couldn't bear yet another one of these stories. "So what do you think of that?" he asked as he wound up his rendition. "Do you really want to know?" I asked. "That's what I pay you for!" Is it?, I wondered silently. But I guess that's a contract of sorts, I thought to myself, so I said, "I think it's a breathtakingly mindless way for two people to treat each other." "Ugh. Well. I see. Yeah. So ... [long pause] If this isn't too personal a question, I wonder if you were out sick when they were doing the classes on empathy in grad school?" "Not out sick," I said, "I skipped empathy and statistics because I thought they were both over-rated." "Well, would you consider a little reading, brushing up on the topic a bit?" "So you prefer that I enter into the same fused mess with you that you have with your wife, under the guise of empathy and caring? You don't have to like what I say or agree with it, but you might at least consider my point of view." Long pause. "I'm beginning to see what you mean, but I can't say that I like your way of going at it." "I have absolutely no investment in your liking it. I only ask that you consider the meaning of what I'm saying."

It has not been an easy road between this fellow and me, but he has gradually discovered a profound pleasure in having his own mind (and a lively, independent sex life).

Both of these clinical moments are what, I suspect, Rollo May (1983) would have characterized as "encounters". My analyst and I did not take up his attending my talk as some sort of countertransference enactment, or my upsets and demand as transference reactions. My client and I did not discuss his transference wishes towards me, nor did I disclose how badly I wished he would just get the fuck out of his miserable marriage and find somebody with whom he could have good sex. These were face-to-face encounters in which the therapist refused to give up his own mind, and in so doing opened a passage (or cleavage) in the client's mind. May (1983) challenges the over-use of transference interpretations, arguing for the importance of authentic encounter:

> In the first place, transference can be a handy and ever-useful defense for the therapist ...; the therapist can hide behind it to protect himself from the anxiety of direct encounter. Second, the concept of transference can undermine the whole experience and sense of reality in therapy; the two persons in the consulting room become "shadows," and everyone else in the world does, too. It can erode the patient's sense of responsibility, and rob the therapy of much of the dynamic for the patient's change (p. 19).

May's words foreshadowed Bollas's articulation of what he calls "the dialectics of difference" (1989, p. 64), arguing that:

> **By endeavouring to introduce the factor of difference, we slowly establish the dialectics of difference**. I want to be free to differ with my analysand. I want him to be free to differ with me (1989, p. 65, emphasis in the original).

In so doing, Bollas seeks to underscore the centrality of separate subjectivities and of the essential right and responsibility for both therapist and client to correct one another. His is a powerful invitation to think together in the present, often as a means of interrupting the over-determining forces of transference and countertransference, which can rapidly diminish the potentialities that seem possible within the therapeutic dyad. It has always been of particular interest to me that Bollas suggests that this process of establishing difference right from the beginning of treatment is particularly important in working with more disturbed clients, the corrective force of this freedom of independent minds being something that I have seen validated over and over again in my work with deeply troubled clients.

Of course, the freedom for encounter and difference goes in both directions. In recent sessions with Ruth, deep in the midst of our long-term work together, I have had tremendous difficulty tolerating her levels of intense anxiety, disorientation, and vulnerability as she has been undertaking a series of major, risky changes in her way of life. The level of upset between us became so intense that neither of us felt we could speak freely in our face-to-face sessions, so we used email to supplement our communications, hoping to find it easier to write what we could not speak. I had written a frustrated email telling Ruth that I felt that my words and actions repeatedly felt hollow to me in the face of (my experience) that her history kept wiping out the present between us. This interchange occurred over three days' time during the holidays when we were not seeing each other:

Ruth: I don't know what you mean by your words ringing hollow. that is pretty shallow if it means what i think ... leaving me to believe i have to shed my own history over the years ... only to believe whatever it is you meant there ... i am getting your process.

Bill: What I mean by hollow, "pretty shallow" as you say it here, is that I often feel my words, my hopes, my actions don't stand up to your history. I don't believe we can ever shed our histories, but we do need to step away from them, confront them, not allow them to define reality and the future. I think that is absolutely necessary to create a present that is real, alive, and satisfying. I'm not sure you agree with that. Maybe you feel like it's impossible to do or it's a stupid thing for me to say. "You don't get it," as you wrote earlier. Maybe I don't get it. Or maybe you don't get it. You sure as hell don't get my process.

Ruth: I think that "i" am the one you are speaking about as being shallow and that is the life i have had so when you have expectations instead of suggestions as if i am supposed to know things of tremendous value such as memory building holidays you believe that i have what you have can you see how such a simple thing is now fucking up my head ... better to NEVER HAVE A DESIRE!!!

Bill: I certainly do not think you are shallow. Hurting deeply, often hiding, untrusting, defined by your past, determined, strong, struggling, always on the edge of giving up but never quite giving up. That's how I see you. Getting to know you, even as I feel constantly on the edge of getting it wrong, doing it wrong, as you say in all your writings here, has not been easy. But there have been times for you and for me that have been very sweet, heartfelt, important, and very enjoyable. Then they just seem to evaporate. That is very hard.

It is NEVER better to never have a desire. I believe that with my whole being. That doesn't mean you should believe it. You probably think it's stupid and more evidence that I just don't get it.

Ruth: You say you have to stand outside my history if anything is going to change. you do stand outside my history in a way that to me has no feeling when i m trying to break out of the horror i feel inside. we agree that it would be helpful if you could understand that i am in that place of confusion (fight or flight), and not react to it which sends me back, crawling on my stomach, into my own mind. but, standing outside my history feels like standing far enough away from me that you become an onlooker and i think that is your point.

When i try to write about my anger and pain in the messed up way i do ... you stand outside of it. yes, and then you stand up to my history and accuse me of not doing so and hurting you ... and, the relationship ... and causing frustration ... and putting you on the edge ... all the things you have said that i do to us. you blame me every time, saying i sure as hell don't get your process. well, i get that one ... loud and clear. you say you won't be defined by my history. i have said in the past that when i get angry, you back up ... nearly off the porch if you had been outside the house i lived in. then, you get definite about how you have to be ... and, you feel far away. so, i go, too. stand outside all you want. i will, too.

Before reading on, take a few moments and put yourself in my place: what might you have been thinking and feeling? As Ruth's therapist what might you have said or done? What if you were my consultant? Take a few more moments to put yourself in Ruth's place: what might you have been thinking and feeling? What might you have said or done?

Perhaps as you read this interchange, you could sense the ways in which my deep commitment to Ruth's well-being (or *my* version of *her* well-being) interfered with my capacity to "get" her worldview. Perhaps, also, as you read these passages, you could sense how

Ruth's version of me interfered with her being able to "get" me and what I was doing in the way I wanted to be understood. Perhaps all sorts of transferential and countertransferential interpretations come to mind.

Ruth could have adapted to me. I could have adapted to her. She could have quit. I could have become agreeable on the surface in some form of pseudo empathy, while being silently resigned in my being. I admired her ruthlessness, and her writing threw me back on myself. She gave me a great deal to think about. She struggled to respect and understand my frame of reference, even as she spelled out its confusing and disturbing impact on her. Each of us, in our own inelegant ways, held on to our own minds. Our work together came back to life with a quality of intimacy that could not be considered particularly empathic or cuddly but was enlivened by our willingness to be ruthlessly real in the face of what seemed like a severe, and possibly terminal, rupture.

Our email exchanges occurred just a couple of weeks before I began writing this chapter. As I was writing, our interchange kept coming back to me. So I asked Ruth if I could quote part of our exchange in the article I was working on, sending her the first draft of the article so that she could see what I wanted to quote in the context of what I was writing. Reading the chapter gave her further, concrete evidence of how seriously I took what we were struggling with and the thought that I brought to it. She gave me her permission, and our subsequent discussion of the chapter has become part of our work.

Could any of these clinical incidents described here be examined and understood as a transference/countertransference dynamics enactment? Without a doubt. Would such a discussion have enriched the understandings that began to emerge? I don't think so, at least not at the point in time that each of these encounters occurred. I think it is more accurate to see these as incidents of frank encounter in the here and now. While each of these therapies has involved times of transference and countertransference interpretation and rumination, it is not the style of working that has been the primary mode of the treatment in any of these three cases.

There is no doubt that contemporary transactional analysis has been profoundly enriched by the varying perspectives subsumed under the umbrella of "relationality": the integrative work of Clarkson (1992), the processes of inquiry/attunement/involvement emphasized by

Erskine, Moursund, and Trautmann (1999), the model of co-creative TA articulated by Summers and Tudor (2000), and the landmark volume by Hargarden and Sills (2002). From the 1991 issues of the *Transactional Analysis Journal* focused on transference (Friedlander), to the 2005/06 issues focused on the interface of transactional analysis with contemporary psychoanalytic models (Hargaden, 2005; Cornell & Hargaden, 2006), and the 2008 issue devoted to "The Relevance of the Unconscious for Transactional Analysis Today" (Tosi & Cornell), we have witnessed a deepening understanding of the power of unconscious communication, the transference-countertransference matrix, and intersubjectivity within therapeutic relations.

Nonetheless, when our theories privilege and idealize mutuality or co-construction, we may risk missing the richness and disturbance of separateness, privacy, and personal encounter, and lose the opportunity to develop the capacity and responsibility to know, articulate, and keep one's own mind. There are crucial periods when the therapeutic relationship emerges from the shadows of the past into the bright and often unsettling light of the present in which two adults face themselves and their differences, each in the other's presence. I have chosen these vignettes to vividly illustrate the fierceness of encounters between two differing minds with the richness of self-realization and the vitality that can then be generated.

CHAPTER FOURTEEN

Where do we dwell?

Steff Oates

S amantha arrives in my consulting room. Her opening line is, "I've been told that you're a person in the area who works relationally." Her friend, who has contacts in the local transactional analysis community, had given her my number. My internal response was one of discomfort. I felt put on the spot and under demand to deliver in a prescribed way. I also felt defiant and had no idea at this stage whether my responses stemmed from my history and/or was more in response to Samantha. I will return to this later.

The above episode is not uncommon; I receive many referrals from people within the profession who see me as working relationally. "How so?", I wonder when I am still in the process of finding out what relational transactional analysis means to me? In the next few pages, I hope to share my curiosity with you, offer some critique with regard to assumed definitions, and share some case examples linking Berne's (1964/2010) concept of autonomy, i.e. awareness, spontaneity, and intimacy, to some current thinking about relational transactional analysis.

In 2002, Hargaden and Sills described a relational model of transactional analysis as a coherent system of psychotherapy for "deconfusion of the Child ego state" (p. 1). They contrasted their approach with transactional analysts at that time who appeared to valorize the process of facilitating the strengthening of their clients' Adult ego state. I was inspired and comforted by the book. I had felt challenged in particular by some approaches in TA that, in my mind, over-emphasized the clients' responsibility in the therapeutic process and discounted what might be sometimes a genuine lack of skill. In these cases I felt TA theory was being used as a cosh to supposedly provoke clients from passivity (Schiff & Schiff, 1971) into action and in response I often kept quiet about my empathic feelings towards the clients. Hargaden and Sills's work (2002) helped me come out of the "empathy closet" (2002, p. 3), which may provide one answer as to why I am considered to work relationally.

My discomfort at Samantha's description of me revolved around the fact that I felt pulled into working on one side of a dichotomy—I had to be relational or something else, classical maybe? I had entered into transactional analysis training because I did not want to be either a cognitive behavioural therapist or a psychodynamic therapist. I felt the potential for another straightjacket.

In actuality what Samantha was asking for was that I accompany her in finding her own way without imposing my idea of what was best for her. At this early stage of the therapy she really did not know what she wanted. Her request for relational work was in fact what her friend had told her she needed. At an interim stage, she described our work much to my disillusionment as "Tea and Sympathy". When I looked surprised at her description of my style she contrasted my approach to another psychotherapist (whom she had interviewed), who had wanted a clear explicit contract about what they would achieve together over the course of their work. I let go of my somewhat superior investment in her understanding more fully my intention of providing "evenly suspended attention" (Freud, 1912, p. 111). Samantha was clearly benefiting from the work, however she described it.

My discomfort at Samantha's opening line has, I believe, two strands. The first stems from the challenge of describing and doing justice to the complexities of what may go on in the therapeutic relationship. In other words, how can we make explicit the intricate and unpredictable experience of two people willing to examine themselves, symbolize and use what may be held deeply in their unconscious? The other lies in how a particular approach may be defined in terms of a theory and may become reified, as "This is the way!". I took heart from

Emmanuel Ghent (2002) in his opening speech at the first conference of the International Association of Relational Psychoanalysis and Psychotherapy in New York.

> There is no such thing as relational theory but there is such a thing as a relational point of view, a relational way of thinking, a relational sensibility.

With regard to Samantha in particular, I was aware that often what a client presents as wanting in the early stages often transpires to be a desire for a repeated and familiar experience. Samantha's request on the surface appeared to make sense. I think Samantha both "longed" for a relational approach and "feared" it (Fowlie, 2005). What transpired, in fact, was that the transformative process between Samantha and me more often than not required me to be an objective observer. I sensed really early in our work that any participation on my part would likely result in a repeated and familiar experience for Samantha. As the therapy progressed, and Samantha felt more able to be honest with me, she told me that any comment that I made, for example if I shared my views on how I received what she had spoken, felt like a criticism or as a direction that she should be experiencing or doing something different.

Samantha's family system of a highly intrusive, narcissistic mother and violent father meant that she was remarkably astute at adapting, more often than not in the form of rebelling, to the subjective world of the other whether that was made explicit or not. Although I was of course a participant observer, any interest, excitement, or involvement on my part needed to be kept well under wraps. Helen Rowland (2011, personal communication) engaged my thinking about the possibility of working in the intersubjective space while not explicitly working in the realm of the interpersonal or working in the transference. At the beginning of the work, it might have appeared that I was not working in or even with the transference, yet my feelings of defiance and a compelling need to allow Samantha space and time were indeed a process akin to metabolization that I now consider an attuned response to the intersubjective.

At the beginning of the therapy, Samantha's lifestyle was precarious—she was abusing alcohol, she would often turn up for sessions with a hangover, she was out of a job, and following a second divorce she was now in a violent relationship.

I began to understand how the therapist that Samantha had interviewed prior to me would have felt pulled towards behavioural change as the goal. I also felt anxiously pulled towards doing something to effect change. What became clear to me was that although my subjective experience in response to Samantha was intense, the therapy in the early years required a more impersonal response. I (as a person in the room) needed to stay clearly out of the way. I convinced myself that my job was akin to that of a surgeon. I held an attitude of hope and appropriate concern while putting aside any investment in this relationship making a difference. I made few interpretations and gave Samantha the requested information regarding ego states, transactions, scripts (Berne, 1961), and strokes (Berne, 1964), as if I was teaching an introduction to TA, a 101. I used supervision to explore whether this was a defensive act on my part, i.e. part of my needing to do something, to soothe myself, to have some effect at least, or a fear of being truthful with Samantha regarding my concern about her safety. With this reflection, I concluded that my using theory was not born out of my anxiety, in fact more out of a feeling of patience; I truly believed Samantha would engage more personally when she was ready. For now, her curiosity about psychological processes and how these might be understood in TA appeared to be enough. It was as if Samantha could only allow herself to reflect in the third person and to my mind this was as good a starting place as any.

I have often considered that there are clients for whom it is beneficial for us to "get in the way" and those for whom it is beneficial for us to "get out of the way". My subjective experience with Samantha was one of needing to be watchful and patient. Whenever I made an intervention that was more personally directed I would see Samantha flinch and move away from her own experience. Other clients are assisted more by the interpersonal. They learn to bring meaning to their experience through being with another person who can help them. Samantha's early years meant that her mother, instead of helping her bring meaning to her experience, had taken it over.

I began to understand this process more fully on reading Margaret Crastnopol's (2002) article, The Dwelling Places of Self-Experience. Crastnopol argues against the "dichotomizing of psychic life as either intrapsychic or interpersonal", and suggests we think in terms of a "continuum of self-experience from the most private or interior to the most public or exterior".

Crastnopol describes four domains of self-experience (p. 267) without prizing one over the other. The Phenomologic is comprised of a person's unformulated, lived experience. The second is the Intrapersonal, which she describes as generalized internal voices including I (me), and my version of you in an indiscriminate form. The Interpsychic describes more specific relations between myself and my version of the other including my fantasy of their experience of me, and finally the Interpersonal domain is comprised of the self in process with others and things, that is, the self relating interpersonally. In the example below Crastnopol elegantly describes how inflexibility in one domain might hinder a client's felt sense of an internal shift.

She describes a client who achieves "a certain level of insight without feeling a thoroughgoing internal shift". Crastnopol's patient says, "So my negative image of myself doesn't mesh with others' perceptions of me. I get that. But why doesn't this translate into me liking myself more?" (p. 274). Crastnopol's view is that the patient may have a "pervasive inhibition of the ability to make a transition from the interpsychic to the intrapersonal realm of the self", and states that this "might well have to do with an avoidance of the troubling internal relations present at that more private level" (p. 274).

Crastnopol advocates a degree of flexibility between the domains as essential for good enough psychic functioning.

In my view, Samantha spent a great deal of time in the intrapersonal domain. That is, she privately reflected a great deal about herself in relation to generalized others; she also would access the interpsychic—developing fantasies about specific others and what they might feel or think in relation to her. Samantha's limitations were, I believe, in the phenomologic and the interpersonal domains, that is, she quickly moved to interpret her experiences at the intrapersonal and interpsychic level without staying long enough with her very personal and private lived experience. For example, during the sessions Samantha would often slip into silence and I would watch and wait. If Samantha, however, became conscious of herself doing this she would quickly shift into asking me a question about what I was thinking. The drama in Samantha's family with her hysteric mother and violent father had left her little time to be with her own experience. If she did not join in with mother's latest madcap project, then she would be bounced off the walls of the family home. My "staying out of the way" enabled Samantha to find more of herself, discover her personal experience, and eventually bring that into relationship with me.

In the early years, any exchange that I might have considered interpersonal would be translated in Samantha's mind into an interpsychic process where Samantha would be the one who decided and often distorted my intention. In my view, as Samantha accessed the phenomologic domain she would be able to hang onto enough of her own experience to approach the interpersonal.

As I reflect I am reminded of a paragraph in *The Little Prince* by Antoine de Saint-Exupéry (1943).

The fox says to the little prince. "If you want a friend, tame me."

"What do I have to do?" asked the little prince. "You have to be very patient," the fox answered. "First you'll sit down a little away from me, over there in the grass. I'll watch you out of the corner of my eye, and you won't say anything. Language is the source of misunderstandings. But day by day, you'll be able to sit closer" (p. 60).

I discussed with my colleague Laurie Hawkes that the translation of the French word, *apprivoise* (to tame) has a subtle but important nuance. It means to approach slowly so that the other is no longer afraid.

As the work proceeded and Samantha became more trusting of her own experiences, I found there to be more space for me to become involved. For instance, she would share her difficulty with knowing how to protect herself from her violent partner, and more recently she told me about her naïveté in relation to a tender intimate relationship she had began to develop. At these times I considered that she needed (and she appreciatively received) my input to help her develop new skills (i.e. calling the police, obtaining injunctions, etc.). I felt genuinely engaged in providing knowledge, experience, and engagement at a level that felt more interpersonal. In the later stages of our work together Samantha and I were inevitably drawn into shared experiences that would prove to be enactments reminiscent of each of our backgrounds, including threats from Samantha to end the therapy prematurely. At these times, I would be thrown back into feeling like the one who got things wrong, messed things up, suffering the consequences of my defiance against what I considered a regular therapist would have done. What was different for Samantha and for myself of course was by this time we shared a commitment to working things through, to using the painful process of our disappointments in each other to find a powerful, mutual, and transformative experience.

At the end of our work together Samantha was in a close, loving relationship, running a successful business, and had no dependence on alcohol. These behavioural changes were not made explicit in our work, yet Samantha acknowledged the improvement in the quality of her life.

I have described the process between Samantha and me as if it were a consciously graduated approach through Crastnopol's (2002) domains. She describes these as "domains that lend a specific quality to one's internal life, and together (but in varying proportions) they constitute the psychic dwelling place unique to a given individual" (p. 259). The fact is, the process was not a conscious treatment plan and I remain intrigued as to what informed the varied therapeutic process and particularly my discomfort at being expected to work in a particular way. As I ponder this I am reminded of Berne's writings on autonomy, both in terms of its attainment (1964/2010) and the illusion of it (1972).

Samantha's defiant behaviours towards her parents and my felt defiance in response to her request for me to work relationally have some similarities. Defying the wishes of others in a thoughtless way is not autonomy. Yet there was wisdom in my discomfort, and a genuine curiosity and willingness to examine why I would feel so strongly defiant. My thoroughness in thinking and talking this through helped me confirm that at the beginning of the work Samantha did need me to work in a way that certainly would not appear relational. In fact it might be judged as the very approach that I resolved to get away from. I have recently become curious as to whether the theorists that I have railed against and defied have in fact been more relational that I have given them credit for. Carol Solomon, who knew Eric Berne personally, attended a workshop that I co-facilitated at the International Transactional Analysis conference (2010) comparing the lives of Eric Berne and Leonard Cohen, the Canadian bard. Carol remarked, "It may not be obvious in his writings but Eric Berne touched my soul much in the way that Leonard Cohen does today." While much of Berne's later writing appeared to promote a more cognitive behavioural approach with emphasis on strengthening the Adult ego state, in practice he was not afraid to involve himself and affect his clients.

In conclusion, as I ponder on my own relational sensibilities, I think about the flexibility required if therapists are to be aware of their own and their clients' preferred dwelling places.

In this, there is ideally an awareness of the subtleties of each dyad and the danger of imposing technique. Alongside this, therapists may experience uncertainty and vulnerability if they step out of their familiar role or dwelling place and allow for surprises or spontaneity. In my mind, the recovery of intimacy in the therapeutic dyad involves a willingness to remain as curious and flexible as possible, to notice what the client brings of themselves, to notice how this impacts on us, and to use our skills and knowledge in the service of the work.

Principle 8

Working with adults

CHAPTER FIFTEEN

The reality of the functioning and changing adult

Carole Shadbolt

Introduction

This chapter is about treating clients as the chronological adults they are rather than as pseudo children, a principle embodied in the reality of the functioning and changing adult. I draw on the work of Cornell and Bonds-White (2005) and their article "The Truth of Love or the Love of Truth". I describe what adult intimacy might mean, reflect on its complex dynamics, and propose that its attainment is one of the primary goals of relational therapy. I go on to suggest that the manner of facing the psychic realities of life with clients, in order to reach adult intimacy, inevitably involves engaging in a kind of loving and I argue that there can be no distinction between the two powerful statements contained in the title of Cornell and Bonds-White's article; I suggest, instead, that they are intrinsically interlinked.

Time changes everything

This Christmas holiday (2010), in a rural part of the UK we have been snowed in. We could not get out easily and our loved ones could not get to us. So the usual Christmas round of visiting did not happen, and we stayed put for the entire two-week holiday. Everything stopped. My partner and I decided that this was a marvellous opportunity to have a good clear out of collected paper, cards, unwanted presents, and worn-out clothes. We sent ten plastic sacks of old unwanted stuff to the charity shop.

I am not good at throwing things away—especially if they are connected with a part of me in my past that is significant. They are meaningful symbols and relics of a lost attachment or person or time that has gone forever in reality but never forgotten or let go. Consequently any process of clearing out is potentially painful and I sift every last birthday card, postcard, love note, restaurant bill, museum guide, bus or entrance ticket to check I am not inadvertently tossing away a treasured memento.

I discover a postcard written by a friend. I instantly attach to her particular writing hand, her distinctly recognizable way with words, where she has put the date on the card, and the diminutive for me that only she uses and that jars if someone else does.

She is not having a good time thirty years ago, I read; she is on a long holiday on the other side of the world. I then read a phrase which is imbued with a type of past redundancy, "My kid has had enough and wants to come home".

"My kid"?

Now as I read that phrase I physically squirm at what it engenders in me; it has a rebarbative, almost revolting, embarrassing quality to it. As the past rushed up to meet the present I can clearly see in the long-ago words of my still beloved friend how our thinking as psychotherapists has developed, our practice deepened. We have ceased to infantalize ourselves both as clients and as therapists. We no longer grandiosely elevate ourselves into Parent or parents who can make up for the losses or unmet relational needs of an unsatisfactory childhood. Instead, we now face the losses and inevitable disappointments of life with our clients as they meet themselves and us, in our consulting rooms. If we do our job well, we face with them our shortcomings and ordinariness as human beings and make it possible for them to do the same.

We respect and engage with them and in so doing we help them to live through shame, losses, and yearnings which have converted, through lack of truth, unhelpfully into shameless narcissistic entitlements. For example, that they have a right to be recognized, their unmet wants to be met by others. In coming to their heart's knowing that no such thing is possible, we deal with the loss of that fantasy and deal instead with real life in all its facets, good and bad, loving and hating, peaceful and disturbing, jealous and generous, faithful and betraying.

In their article, Cornell and Bonds-White (2005) critique the maternal/corrective/relational model of therapy so familiar to transactional analysis and other modalities of the last decade. They suggest that "There has always been a tendency within transactional analysis psychotherapy to focus on personal change and management of emotions rather than to struggle for a deeper understanding of the ambivalences of love and hate that motivate all human relationships" (p. 136). They make an impassioned plea to transactional analysts to disengage from the type of therapy that seeks to replicate a parent child dynamic—the type of therapy that believes it is possible to make up for past parental failures. Instead they advocate facing with clients the "less than palatable and more turbulent side of relations" (p. 137). They encourage us as therapists not to postpone or calm the "struggles and distress that are necessary for characterological change and psychological mastery" (p. 137) by engaging in what they describe as a therapy that is a "temporary, mutually gratifying, narcissistic merger" which "envelops a client in empathic and attuned mirroring where nothing is changed in the client's psychological structure" (p. 137).

They carefully bring to their scholarly thesis a comparison between theories of child development and "Child" as made concrete in the consulting room to show the very real differences between the two. Cornell and Bonds-White model what they describe by showing how to engage with truth rather than with fantasy. They show with devastating effect, to my mind, that "the adult therapeutic relationship is not and cannot be a mirror or re-creation of the mother/infant relationship" (p. 140) and as such cannot bring about lasting change. They quote researchers Slochower, D. N. Stern, Bowlby, Winnicott, Tronick, Modell, Lachman and Beebe, Emde, Ainsworth, and Main, among others, whose work demonstrates the differences between the biologically determined relationship of the mother child dyad and the adult therapeutic relationship. For example, they quote Modell, (2005):

"The analogy between adult and infant dyads breaks down at several points. One is that the adult therapeutic dyad, unlike the mother-infant dyad is not a biologically determined process; second, in the adult therapeutic dyad both participants are encumbered with the weight of their affective memories of the past, the infant's past is just beginning" (p. 140).

Primitive preverbal and developmental experiences and motivations for reworking in psychotherapy are powerful. Consequently, echoes of a particular mother/infant relationship will perhaps be sought and felt in transferences such as projective identifications. Powerful and present as these unconscious processes are between therapist and client, they are nevertheless still a reaching back into a past already experienced by our now adult clients. Cornell and Bonds White again quote Modell, "This is not the infant's agenda" (2005, p. 140), for the infant has not yet had a past to re-experience and reach back into.

So, though useful, attractive and compelling as theories, the Child and Parent ego states (Berne, 1961) are only theories and, as such, not *the truth*. Berne's original point that "Parent, Adult and Child represent real people who now exist or who once existed, who have legal names and civic identities" (p. 32) and which gave rise to the story that one could look up a Parent ego state in the New York phone book (Clarkson, 1984, personal communication), is now not taken literally in the therapeutic encounter. They are ideas, metaphors. Distinguishing between the two in our consulting rooms and not conflating them into what Cornell and Bonds-White call "a hash" (p. 142) of developmental theory is central to the principle of the reality of the functioning adult.

Barnes (2004) suggests that these traditional theories of Adult, Parent, and Child have been introjected into the Parent ego states of many therapists. In his seminal work, *Homosexuality in the First Three Decades of Transactional Analysis* (for which he was awarded the Eric Berne Scientific Award in 2004) he showed how early TA theory dealt with homosexuality by viewing the very real struggles that gay, lesbian, and bisexual people faced, as personal pathology and signs of unresolved Child material. He sets the blueprint perhaps for naming and challenging how uncomfortable life truths can be disastrously missed and reframed by the therapist (and TA theory) from an ill-informed, patronizing position.

With the emergence of these relational re-examinations, we can now envisage a therapeutic stance and practice that takes into account the problems of understanding and working with what we call deep unconscious communications and attachment styles, and that also honours and respects those problems, if problems they be, from a place of adult engagement as described above.

To my mind, engaging with these processes as adults, rather than "adult babies", translates and maybe demands that we forge a rigorous and meaningful therapeutic relationship, which matches the passion, desires, and disturbances that clients bring to the consulting room. I call a commitment to this type of engagement with our clients love, though it is a love that is worlds away from the re-parenting models of TA as described in part by the Cathexis School and Schiff and colleagues (1975) which, though well intentioned, and some would say effective as technique, is entirely different in character from the love I am suggesting.

It is a vigorous, edgy loving, which is both the truth of love and the love of truth; a balance of both, which acknowledges life's truths in a loving way rather than believing that we can exclusively love or re-parent our clients into characterological change. Neither is it a love that in its vigour withholds support or gratuitously speaks truths in an unkind manner to a client. It is a love that provides a "vital rather than a secure base" Cornell (2005, pp. 213–224) which is low on reassurance and high on holding the tension and waiting for the client to find their own space for engagement with and resolution to what is worrying them: a love that I understand as adult intimacy.

I can find a place for this kind of loving easily in relational practice; since love or intimacy in all its complexities, paradoxes, and contradictions is what clients bring to us in the first place, is it not? To get close to these complexities I include a quotation from the work of novelist John Dufresne (1999). In his extraordinary and poetic novel *Love Warps the Mind a Little*, he is dealing with the fundamental and complex nature of love through a fictional character who is a writer. Here, he is drawing differences between fantasy and love—fantasy which seeks to pretend that all things are possible and colludes with the attainment of a future that can never be, and love:

> "… which is different … love is anticipation and memory, uncertainty and longing. It's unreasonable of course. Nothing begins with so much excitement and hope and pleasure as love, except maybe writing a story. And nothing fails as often, except writing stories. And like a story, love must be troubled to be interesting. We crave love, can't live without its intimacy though it pains us. Judi [his love and a therapist] told me that every person in therapy has a love disorder; never felt love, can't find love, trapped by love, unraveled by love, thinks love is lust, or love is loss, fears love, loves too

much, uses love for profit, is jealous in love, lost in love, love affairs, unrequited love, love sick, doesn't love mum, won't love dad, can't love the kids, can't love self, hopeless love, self-absorbed love, love as a crutch, love as a truncheon, love in ruins, crazy love, love that eats the heart, love that dare not speak its name, blind love, consuming love, obsessive love, conditional love, dangerous love, first love, last love, fickle love, love and marriage, borrowed love, love lost, secret love, thief of love, love in embers, love in vain, love in shackles, love maligned ... love that warps the mind a little"

(1999, p. 227).

Dufresne describes love as disturbing and having many faces. To me he brilliantly portrays struggles that we regularly meet in the consulting room. These most intimate of human inner turmoils, many of which have their infantile antecedents, now reside within the adult client and to clinically dodge our client's right to learn how to bear these as adults, by infantilizing them, is to steal their power to transform them.

By implication and by naming them as meaningful and troubling truths, Dufresne makes them real and perhaps by so doing he also provides the loving, therapeutic response to those turmoils. Empathy (when misunderstood as something that offers no rigorous confrontation), constant reassurance, soothing, defensively "cooling out" clients, as I call it, instead of collaboratively entering into their disturbances, does not cut the mustard. Withstanding, without retaliation if possible, surviving aggression and anger, accepting and encouraging a client's capacity for "curiosity and differentiation" as Cornell and Bonds-White (2005, p. 151) say, does. The freedom to develop a capacity to struggle and deal with the psychic realities of loving, adult intimacy, and living as portrayed through fiction by John Dufresne is, to my mind, the central goal implied by the principle of the functioning and changing adult in relationship.

Love changes everything?

If it is love that hurts then perhaps we might say it will be love that heals, for us as therapists, through a therapy that warps the mind a little—a therapy where we are willing to be impacted personally by our clients, affected and troubled by them. Somewhere, I cannot remember now where, it has been said that we need to go a little crazy with our clients. If this rather startling statement has any therapeutic validity rather than cliché, the challenge it brings is to develop a personal robustness, where we can both enter into our clients' experience, and yet keep our own minds. We need to strive for a personal emotional strength which allows us to ultimately say, if necessary, in a timely and respectful manner, that the real reason our clients came to therapy is to have their worst fears confirmed about themselves. By this I mean, when they are faced with themselves and their ordinariness, we are part of that facing and naming. When this topsy-turvy, counter-intuitive logic becomes a joint therapeutic journey, such self-realization makes the knowing not only bearable or survivable but character changing. Often, from my experience, in the end it comes down to this truth, one way or another.

Actual examples are difficult, but many times I notice that buried in a throw-away remark made by a client is a truthful knowing about themselves and a yearning for self-acceptance. I might have previously understood and perhaps confronted this as a discount of themselves or their potential. When close to self-realization and acceptance, a client might smuggle a half-known truth into a session in an anecdote told about someone else who is critical and shaming of them. Wrapped up in the story is a shame, and dreading that we might agree with the criticism, perhaps they may say, "I knew you wouldn't agree, you know me better than that!" When we reach this point of agreeing or rather not disagreeing with what feels like an attack, both internal and external, on themselves, a robust loving and adult intimacy is called forth from us. Keeping our own mind in what feels like a crazy-making process is a challenge indeed.

As I hope I have shown, this is not a therapy of techniques, so I have no "how to's". Additionally, it is much easier to write about what this kind of therapy does not look like than what it does look like. It is rather similar to asking a client what they want to change about their life in a classical behavioural TA contracting style when they can scarcely glimpse their own internal world let alone know what change they want. However, I offer the following guiding and working principles in relation to the reality of the functioning and changing adult. They are of course not concrete truths, because each therapy is different, each client a unique individual. True to humanistic and TA ethical principles I place respect, mutuality, and authenticity at the heart.

Strive for a non-pathologizing view of human nature

Most behaviours and emotions are relationally understandable when all the facts are known. By relationally I mean culturally, personally, and socially mediated. This is not to say that there is no such thing as craziness, psychosis, or deep psychic pain. But as Richard Bentall (2009) dismally re-reminds us, the cultural and social roots of psychiatric illness are far more convincing than the myths of mental illness being genetic in origin or it having its roots in brain disease. Similarly, in clinical practice it is all too easy to diagnose as pathological the cause of an uncomfortable rupture as coming from inside a client or our-self, rather than between us. A caveat, though, about co-creative processes. Just as it is easy to diagnose and pathologize, so it is easy to think that all rupture, mistakes, and struggles are co-created. To do this is to dogmatize and distort the complex theory of intersubjectivity and co-creativity as intended by Summers and Tudor (2000). It is axiomatic that we will have independent histories, characters, stages of awareness, unconscious process. It is what we do about these processes that is perhaps the point about co-creation.

Request descriptions rather than definitions or explanations

By this I mean that to define another rather than to describe the impact of them upon us runs the risk of infantilizing them and setting ourselves up as experts. Likewise, inviting descriptions from a client of their experience rather than asking them to explain themselves has the effect of empowering them.

Strong emotions are about progression not regression

By this I mean that within this framework, emotions can be understood as a client reaching forward for mastery and for expression of a yet unformed self which is about to come into being, rather than automatically viewing this as a re-living of past developmental states. For an elaboration of this notion, see Oates (2003).

Reflect on self disclosure

Little (2010) and Maroda (2010) have observed that good practice uses self disclosure judicially and that relentless self disclosure is counter-therapeutic. Spontaneous self disclosure, defensively used, for example continually apologizing, can result in a loss of confidence in the therapist's ability to contain and manage strong emotions, as will be a contrived holding back. Being responsive in the moment to our clients is a mixture of judgement and skill.

Conclusion

This chapter has been a reflection on the principle of the functioning and changing adult. I have not written it as a standalone piece but as one axis among the others in this volume and elsewhere from which to view relational TA theory and practice.

CHAPTER SIXTEEN

The development of Adult capacities through relationship

Brian Fenton

A relational approach situates the therapeutic relationship at the centre of client transformation. It also challenges the parental paradigm and maternal metaphor, where the practitioner acts as a temporary replacement for unsatisfactory parents. This chapter reflects on some ways in which the therapeutic relationship does provide for the client, and how these experiences relate to the development of Adult functioning (Berne, 1961) in both the client and the therapist. In doing so, I will refer to a client presentation where, after not gratifying the client's repeated request to be physically held, the subsequent experience and co-reflection on this process was provision of a different nature. This chapter argues that reflective function underlies integrating Adult.

Presentation

Catherine presented for therapy as an intelligent, professional forty-four-year-old woman. Though dyslexic, she had carved out a successful career. She had also maintained a long-term marriage and had raised a family. Despite these successes, in her felt sense, she suffered a range of psychological concerns and engaged in self-harming behaviours, stemming from experiencing developmental, emotional, and psychological neglect and multiple traumas. Her childhood was plagued by sexual abuse. In short, she was left to make meaning of herself and others and to find ways to contain and hide her more real selves (Winnicott, 1960). She had been in therapy on and off before coming for treatment with me, and while she had made progress, she felt stuck. Catherine's therapy with me is in its seventh year.

From the beginning, Catherine pushed and tested my ability to understand her process, leading me repeatedly to my own therapy and supervision, attempting to decode what was happening between us. With hindsight, even our beginnings, from a brief period of my being her supervisor in the public sector, to becoming her therapist in my private practice, had an air of transgression. While this initially escaped my mind, it was not long before I experienced her as pushing at the boundaries of the therapy in an attempt to move me to become the safe container (Bion, 1967) she required. Over this period, we negotiated the boundaries of our roles and from this, formed our (overt) contract to reflect together on what emerged between us. One important element was that Catherine wanted to reclaim her sexuality as her own, which pointed to a need to develop her identity in a wider sense. From this, we began formulating how we might best work together, and through a combination of considering procedure (theory and method) and situation (the unique presentation and our mix), we embarked in what I hoped would be a fruitful developmental direction. Central to this was a belief that Catherine needed to find her own mind and to do this she would need mine.

Theoretical comment: the development of adult capacities through relationship

Cornell and Hargaden (2005) suggest that a relational perspective denotes a shift away from "a focus on the observing ego and cognitive insight as the primary means of psychological change, to the importance of unconscious, affective and relational interactions as a primary means of growth" (p. 5). This statement situates the dynamic between therapist and client (the relationship) as the primary organizer of development.

Vygotsky (1962) considers that the capacity of the infant to develop an organizing subjective perspective about self and others is dependent on the mother's empathic involvement in her infant. In this way, he implies that the origin of mind is first dyadic and interpersonal, then personal (intrapsychic), situating the mind of the other in the development of the self, and situating experiential learning as of particular importance. The psychodynamics of relating can then be seen to be the origins of our sense of self and other. While one of the central tenets of transactional analysis is that we are born with the capacity to think (see Berne, 1961), in part this capacity is developed within relationships (see Stern, 1985; Trevarthen, 1992).

Tudor (2003) describes the integrating Adult as "the individual's capacity to reflect upon and integrate their own archaic states as well as past introjects, and to draw on them in the service of present centred relating" (p. 202). In addition, Hargaden and Fenton (2005) propose Adult processing as constituting "an integration of conscious, unconscious, verbal, and nonverbal experience and relating in the here and now", which extends the Adult ego state to allow for a norm of unconscious, bi-directional relating. Thus, temporary losses of self/other boundary (see Sandler, 1993) are not necessarily Script (Berne, 1966) but can be part of normal identification processes and relational development. This accommodates intersubjectivity (Stern, 1985; Trevarthan, 1992) where phenomenological experience includes being taken beyond ourselves, and into self/other phenomenological experience such as in "we-ness" (Summers & Tudor, 2000), including notions of where self (and mind) can be found in other (projective identification: see Klein, 1975). From this we can see that the ongoing location of experience within and between selves is a key Adult function.

As a relational psychotherapist, I have become interested in the Adult ego state as reflective capacity derived from thinking specifically about relationships. Fonagy and Target (1997) define reflective function as "the developmental acquisition that permits the child to respond not only to other people's behaviour but to his conception of their beliefs, feelings and hopes, pretences, plans and so on. Reflective function enables children to 'read' other people's minds" (p. 1). Reading minds suggests that one is able to make accurate enough assumptions on such things as the intention of others. Implicit in reflective function is the capacity to tell self from other, and to identify whose mind is whose. Through relational experiences we construct a range of implicit and explicit abilities to relationally discern, both within ourselves and in relationship to others (see Diamond & Marrone, 2003, for a list of reflective functions).

To my mind these reflective functions include ulterior relating (Berne, 1964) and underlie integrating Adult (Erskine, 1988; Tudor, 2003).

Reflective function is vulnerable to context in various ways and to varying degree. When in close relationships it may be enhanced or impaired. It can be globally underdeveloped as in disorders of the self, or temporarily lost, for example in a game (Berne, 1964) or racket (English, 1971). There can be particular disengagement of reflective functions such as in trauma-related processes (see Gildebrand, 2003) and stress, where our minds can be taken by pre-reflective modes of functioning (See Fonagy & Target, 1998).

Catherine

> Catherine functioned well enough within the social matrix and arrived for therapy with a developed use of language and symbolism (her use of poetry conveyed very poignantly the pain and loss and injustice she had suffered). However, she had historically struggled with and was disturbed by intimate relationships. The therapeutic relationship with its boundaries and asymmetry triggered a maelstrom of experiences which were projected into the dyad for us to consider together.
>
> For a period during the work, she seemed to lose her ability of reflective function altogether, to the point where she was unable to hold a representation of my face between sessions. This process brought to mind the work of Beebe (2004) who describes a process of holding in mind, primary intersubjectivity (Trevarthen, 1979), and nonverbal interaction (mirroring, mimicry, and identification processes). We negotiated a way through this to the point where Catherine seemed to gain or regain some basis for reflection. Much of the overt work was reflective, both in the sense of reflecting back feelings and thoughts to her that she was expressing, and reflective in the sense of me noticing feelings within me (potential countertransference), and tentatively sharing these feelings, intuitively assuming she might be experiencing them too.
>
> During this period, I made many mistakes (for example, offering complex interpretations), but fortunately these were inconsequential. Catherine seemed fixated in an idealizing process (see Hargaden & Sills, 2002) and was quite determined in how she was going to experience me. At times, this must have required "gymnastics of

the mind" but given the way she had to silence herself in the family, "gymnastics of the mind" were indeed her forte. Powerful motivational processes released within the idealizing itself seemed to be keeping her on developmental track.

Changes in how she needed me indicated internal reorganizing had taken place and that "the required relationship" (Little, 2011) was changing. From the idealizing process, she moved into more overt ambivalence of the longed-for and feared relationship (Fowlie, 2005), and then began to want me to hold her physically. This request felt distinctly teleological, where only a physical act would change her subjective state. I worked with Catherine to make meaning of her request. As a result, she would perceive me as withholding, cruel, and uncaring. She would be left to cry with grief in the car after sessions, just as she had cried alone in her bathroom as a child. Angry, Catherine would push me away and chastise herself for needing me. Meanings made from all this led to her becoming more self-aware, and simultaneously more aware of me.

This process was a combination of me taking on the attributed role projected out from Catherine such as in relational units (Little, 2004), and me denying myself to Catherine in our here and now relationship. While the pain in longing for (m)other seemed lost to her, the pain in the longing for me at different levels was real enough. Working through this loss using empathic transactions (Clark, 1991; Hargaden & Sills, 2002) allowed Catherine over time to develop an internal working model (Bowlby, 1969) where she could notice and manage this loss, and for us to return to an exploration of (m)other and make fuller meaning of Catherine's previously fragmented experiences. In these ways, her reflective function was being co-constructed directly between us.

Further, Catherine was prone to repression. Her initial attack aged five was remembered only at twenty-eight. Within the safety of the developing empathic bond (Clark, 1991), including, I believe, the security she felt from my decision not to hold her physically, unprocessed images began to emerge from other attacks she had suffered. From these memories, she could come to new meaning of experiences she had in her body, and with this, experience relief as a sense of control emerged. She reported that she felt more space within her which I link to her having freed up reflective function capacity previously bound by repression.

During one enactment where I had been curt regarding a mix up about a telephone session, I emphasized in the post-match analysis Catherine's directing fury at me, as the most beneficial element of what had occurred. This was, to my mind, progress from her lateness for sessions, her dangerous driving, and other subversive expressions of aggression. However, her insistence on another level of meaning led to me noticing and owning my aggression toward her—not of taking on the role of her mother who did not want to hold her, but me, Brian. On close reflection, I had been unwilling to hold this element of myself. I relate this experience to a paper by Jody Messler-Davies (2002), where there is confusion between the analyst and her client in relation to just whose bad object was in the room. By Messler-Davies revealing and owning a nastier element in herself, there seemed to be a healing sense of togetherness between them. I sensed a relief in Catherine not only in her success in moving my mind to meet hers but in recognizing that I was, at times, like her. This situating of feelings within our experience pushed me to reflect further in my therapy on my own anxieties regarding aggression, and how these might be impacting on this therapeutic work. Thus, while the focus of the therapy is generally joint attention on Catherine's process, this turning towards my process led to us both being changed, and the therapy expanded.

While elements of relationship and intersubjectivity do play a central role in organizing our minds, it is important to recognize also the intrapsychic one-person organizational element at work within us (see Gill, 1994b). Silverman (1995) reminds us, one- and two-person modes function simultaneously. An example of this can be seen in a significant shift in Catherine's therapy, which seems to me to have come from her own internal resourcefulness, from what I can only describe as her intelligent unconscious. After much inquiry and working through loss between us, Catherine still had a desire to be held. Not being versed in body therapy I felt stuck. The relational tension from my not physically holding her seemed to be having a detrimental effect in that she began to feel masochistic. Catherine then had a very powerful dream, where in a session I walked over to her and held her. This dream was profound in the sense that while the holding felt gratifying, it was followed by a sense of loss of the idealizing relationship and the understanding that others can never make her whole and that she can never be understood fully by me. This insight followed her into her conscious life. Meanings from dreams are multiple, and a rich source of material for reflection. However, for now, I feel it is more illuminating to point to a dialectical situation, where relational development is both one- and two-person and that these seem inextricably bound.

From this point on, we seemed in a more real relationship, and Catherine was increasingly able to view me and my mind as separate from her. By coming to know herself as separate from me, she became able to take me as I am. Before this if I were not as she had wanted, she perceived me as overwhelmingly intrusive. Through these last two years and due to a combination of factors including Catherine's adopted sister dying tragically and her mother entering a residential home, Catherine has changed considerably, to the point where it has become obvious to us both that our collaboration is more symmetrical. Catherine currently takes more self-care. She has very little road rage, wears her seat belt, and her eating concerns have dissipated. She experiences much improved relationships and, importantly, feels in control of her sex life. She reports feeling more "together" and is not nearly so captured by projective experiences. Though not completely resolved, her not being held by me is now experienced as irritating as opposed to life threatening. Significantly, she knows that I have been holding and continue to hold her emotionally and psychologically.

Theoretical comment: what initiated the changes in Catherine's reflective capacity?

The initial treatment direction in not providing the physical holding was crucial. While the holding may have provided comfort and some (potentially risky) direct assaults on injunctions (Goulding, 1979) such as not to be close, the departure from a reparative Parental stance led into different ways of using the therapeutic relationship in the service of Catherine's development of her sense of self and other, and ultimately her reflective function capacity. Various factors were involved. Initially there was a co-constructing of a sense of self (and other) through the reflective work, and also a freeing up of existing psychic energy and reflective functions through locating and engaging with repressed experiences as they emerged between us. Open communication, realness, and congruence (Rogers, 1959) played a significant role. Cornell and Bonds-White (2001) cite "Love of truth", where willingness and capacity to acknowledge reality about the self is viewed as essential to therapeutic outcome. Indeed Catherine's push for me to acknowledge a truth about myself led to "our truth of it", and from these types of exchange we were both more fully understood, and our ability to recognize and situate emotions enhanced.

However, finding the truth about ourselves (knowing our own mind) requires at times engaging with a different tact, involving a holding of boundary, as opposed to transparency. While intersubjectivity makes sharing minds in part inevitable, open self disclosure is distinct and needs to be thought through (see Benjamin, 2002). I intuitively chose when to refrain from self disclosing, and to persist with inquiry, supporting Catherine to make meaning of her experience of being with me. Working through these projections led to her finding her own mind, and simultaneously enhanced her capacity to tell self from other at differing levels of relatedness. Additionally, in the working through of relational units, there is the effect of us co-constructing new reflective function capacity through self possibilities acquired directly in our interaction (i.e. in the alternative possibilities experienced in my responding differently to Catherine's unconscious expectations).

The experiences above are complex and bi-directional. Collectively they support development and recalibration of our understandings of inner and outer, self from other, and ultimately our capacity for reflective function itself. For me all this points to an innate search for experiences in psychic truth, from which we can develop our capacity to predict human relations. This truth about ourselves and others includes recognition that we are all flawed, that we are all vulnerable to primitive process, and there is an understanding that inner and outer reality do not necessarily match (i.e. we consciously and unconsciously mislead each other).

It seems pertinent then to suggest that reflective function emerges from a range of relational experiences. Indeed Fonagy (1999) acknowledges that while secure attachment is central to the emergence of reflective function, there is no one causal reason for it. Rather, he cites the challenges over time to the client's frame of reference, stimulating a need to develop new ways of perceiving, and he emphasizes "the active engagement of one mind with another" (p. 9) as the crucial element in therapeutic change. This accords with the emphasis in the relational approach on the "activity of relatedness" (Cornell & Bonds-White, 2001), where relationality is the central protocol for self-development.

While Catherine's demand to be held was grounded in the physical, her capacity to reflect and symbolize emerged, not from physically gratifying this need, but in working through and making meaning of her dilemma. Self transformation seems best placed away from the therapist as a provider of need, towards therapist as a provider of mind. What we can hold in mind, our ability to be flexible, and our capacity to be authentic while mindful of how we share our minds, all seem central to the development of Adult ego state in our clients. This development is seen to be in part achieved through relational experiences (one and two person), and is akin to the development of reflective functions. Framing Adult in this way emphasizes relational knowings as pertaining to self-organization and self-other discernment, with a view to supporting clients to develop their capacity to make personal meaning of experience.

To conclude, when I asked Catherine what she felt had worked she said that, despite the difficulties, the therapy had always felt collaborative. A crucial element towards this sense of collaboration was Catherine's attitude, both in terms of her motivation to work through her concerns and in terms of her goodwill at times where the relationship felt overwhelming to her.

PART II

RELATIONAL TRANSACTIONAL ANALYSIS IN CONTEXT

CHAPTER SEVENTEEN

Working with difference relationally

Phil Lapworth

Despite this title, I am going, paradoxically, to emphasize similarity: a specific similarity in a specific context in which I believe the relationship between therapist and client can be supportive, facilitative, and effective in addressing the needs of a particular group of clients. But that will come later. Intrinsically this piece is concerned with difference as I hope will be apparent.

Difference, the quality of being unlike, may sometimes be exciting, it may sometimes be frightening, it may often be both. It is always relational in the sense of involving an/other for discrimination from and comparison to. Calling round at a friend's house on my way to junior school one day, I was given a slice of fried bread spread with tomato ketchup. Compared to my bowl of porridge, this seemed the most delicious and exotic breakfast I had ever had. I felt excited at the taste of it but also anxious. This different breakfast raised an uncomfortable thought: maybe this was what most, perhaps *all*, other families had for breakfast. If so, why did my family not have it? Was my family boring, strange, restricted, poor, or simply ignorant of such delights? Beneath these anxious questions, I felt some fear and shame: I was different. I came from a different family.

I suspect I did not mention this incident to my parents because I knew their dismissive response would pertain to some judgement as to the class of my friend's family, along with other value judgements of right or wrong, better or worse, healthy or unhealthy, the done thing or the not done thing. At the same time, I did not tell them because at some level I knew they might have heard it as a criticism and, feeling shamed, might have vented their anger on me. Or was this my shame and my anger projected onto them? For shame and anger was what I was left feeling later in the day: my initial excitement had become subsumed by anxiety and shame and, in turn, transformed into anger in a defensive reaction formation. I did not walk home with my friend that day.

This may seem an insignificant and trivial story and, in the grand scheme of things, it is. But if a difference in breakfast food can engender such thoughts, fantasies, feelings, and behaviour, how much more so the existential differences between us all—geographical culture, socio-political culture, ethnicity, gender, age, sexuality, even our innate physical, temperamental, and characterological differences? It is sadly evident that, far from giving rise to excitement (though thankfully this sometimes happens), our fear of difference plays out on the world stage in devastating ways. We defend against our anxiety and shame in the face of difference with anger and aggression (albeit sometimes with the passive aggression of the bystander) as manifested in our discrimination, violence, and oppression. The themes and underlying dynamics of my comparatively innocuous childhood story become writ large both locally and globally. Fear of difference transforms into prejudice and hatred.

In the consulting room our clients come to us with their difference—often with concomitant archaic fears and fantasies in their Child ego state (Berne, 1961)—and with others' responses and attitudes to their difference—often internalized in their Parent ego state (ibid.) as self-limiting and self-oppressive beliefs (see Shadbolt, 2004). Their experiences may range from a lack of self-esteem and self-confidence due to parental disappointment in their gender to extremes of physical, sexual, and psychological abuse both within the family and society at large in response to their difference, whatever that may be. And, as therapists, of course we come with our own experience of difference and our own attitudes and struggles with it, both external and internal. These differences of therapist and client with their potential for both excitement and fear will be engaged with, attuned to, explored, tussled with, understood, mutually confronted, and challenged within a TA relational approach, undoubtedly with many misattunements, disturbances, and enactments en route to a reparative understanding and experience. I am sure that many of the chapters in this book will refer to these aspects of relational work and will be very relevant to working with difference.

However, I want to focus on a particular group of people of difference who may require (at a specific time and in a specific context) a specific aspect of a relational approach. This group of people cannot be recognized for their difference at birth. Their difference only emerges later, and their adjustment to, and acceptance of, their difference (which instantly places them in a minority group in society) is known as "coming out", a phrase that could be synonymous with being born. These are lesbian, gay, and bisexual clients in the specific context of addressing their sexual identity.

Before I describe this specific relational aspect, I want to make it clear that I am not precluding any other clients from this way of working relationally, nor am I precluding lesbian, gay, or bisexual clients from other ways of working relationally. Whatever our differences, I believe any effective psychotherapy will call upon us to explore a variety of relational styles such as those described in this book. Here I am specifically addressing clients in the unique context of "coming out".

My hypothesis draws mainly on the work of Kohut (1971/1984), Hargaden and Sills (2002), and my own personal and clinical experience. Hargaden and Sills (2002) use the term "introjective transference" to describe the process by which clients seek to meet their unmet developmental needs and longings through the internalization of a healing relationship with the therapist. In my understanding, this process is described as transference because it refers to our early need of a parent's attention being transferred onto the therapist—and introjective because of the developmental need to take in the qualities of this attention in order to develop the Self and its self-regulating functions. This type of transference was first identified by the Self psychologist Heinz Kohut (1971/1984) who called it "selfobject transference".

Arguably, lesbian, gay, and bisexual clients' relational needs, like any clients' needs in therapy, require their therapist's empathic inquiry, attunement, and involvement (Erskine, 1997). Some of these needs may be the early, relational needs and longings identified and described by Kohut as mirroring, idealizing, and twinship. In brief, *mirroring* is the baby's healthy exhibitionistic need of unconditional positive regard—the need to be reflected, accepted, and confirmed for simply being who they are which, if met adequately enough, can lead to a secure sense of self and to healthy self-esteem. The *need to idealize* is the need the child has of a powerful, calm, and knowledgeable other to identify with and gradually internalize into a self-soothing, self-containing, self-confident Self. And *twinship* is the need a growing child has to be like others, to share important aspects of those around them and not to be too different from the world in which they find themselves—twinship can engender a secure sense of belonging.

If not met adequately in early childhood, these needs may emerge forcefully, often unhelpfully, in later relationships and, inevitably (and hopefully more usefully), within the therapeutic relationship itself. This is not to deny that these needs are ongoing throughout our lives, but to say that the intensity of these needs, if not met well enough in those early years, may be disproportionate to our adult needs of mirroring, idealizing, and twinship. Getting these early unmet needs met later in life, either in therapy or in other relationships, may be a potential task for many of us. But I wonder if lesbian, gay, and bisexual clients may require these three types of need to be responded to specifically in relation to their sexuality—a sexuality which was not apparent at birth and which, for most, was not apparent in very early childhood, and in puberty and adolescence received only the sort of negative and homophobic responses to difference to which I have referred earlier.

If someone, say Susan, is fortunate as a baby, her gender, her ethnicity, her physicality, her feelings, thoughts, and behaviours will not only be received positively by her parents but also be encouraged and fostered by them. This is likely to lead her to have a secure sense of her self, good self-esteem, and creative self-confidence. But Susan's parents, having been brought up in a homophobic family and society themselves, may well later respond to Susan's emerging lesbian sexuality, however unwittingly, with a less than positive welcome. Nonetheless, it is my guess that Susan, because her early relational needs were well met, may well navigate the journey of her sexuality with some confidence. It is a bit like Berne's (1961) analogy of (excuse the unintentional pun) the "bent pennies": if the pennies at the bottom of the pile are flat and well aligned, any later bent ones will not topple the whole pile. However, I still think that Susan, at some point early in her sexual development within our hetero-normative society, will need to meet people who will mirror her and twin her and provide positive role models for her to idealize (in the sense of admiring, trusting, and depending on) and integrate in relation to her sexuality.

Imagine then, someone else who in childhood did not receive the attunement necessary to meet those early needs of mirroring, idealizing, and twinship. How much more then might be the need of lesbian, gay, and bisexual people, not just for attention to that early deficit, but for attention to a later deficit in response to their sexuality? I think heterosexual men's sexuality is mirrored, twinned, and validated all the way from the cradle to the grave—not just by parents and families, but by the wider culture, the media, the church, the state—the world. Most of them do not need their heterosexuality affirming. On the other hand, I think, at some point, many heterosexual women and the majority of lesbian, gay, and bisexual people probably do. Few of my clients tell me coming out stories that involve positive mirroring, idealizing, or twinship experiences. In fact, even in this 21st century, just the opposite. My client Simon tells me of violent bullying at school, Magda tells me of being disowned by her family, and Jonathan tells me of his fear of losing his job if his sexuality became known.

So how might therapists helpfully address what I am seeing as the specific needs of lesbian, gay, and bisexual clients in relation to these three possible introjective transference needs? First and foremost, I think an important part of making sure we work as well as possible with our lesbian, gay, and bisexual clients is to use our personal therapy and supervision to explore the homophobia we may still be carrying in our Parent and Child ego states. We are then less likely to humiliate and shame our clients and can more fully meet, from our Adult ego state, early relational needs as well as later ones specific to our clients' sexuality. This self-reflection and decontamination of our prejudices and oppressive attitudes would apply to our work with all clients of any difference.

So what might it mean to meet the *mirroring* needs of our gay, lesbian, and bisexual clients? Kohut suggests that mirroring is showing how welcome the child is, what a pleasure it is to have that child around, how unique they are, how their very being and most basic identity is seen and reflected positively. This may well be what our clients need from us as therapists regarding their sexuality: literally *regarding* their sexuality. It is not that we necessarily need to do or say anything specific in this respect. It is more an attitude of acceptance that is reflected in our facial expression, our tone of voice, our body posture, and the holding gaze of our eyes. As mirrors, we need to reflect the essence of our clients back to themselves as uncontaminated as possible by our own issues, assumptions, and prejudices. However different our clients may be from us, and in whatever ways, including sexuality, we need to mirror *their* difference in an accepting and confirming way. Our clients may deeply need this authentic response to their sexuality from their therapist: to feel truly met as a lesbian, gay, or bisexual person.

In order to be mirrored, although it may be helpful, it may not be essential for the therapist to be the same gender or sexuality as the client. I believe it is possible for a straight, bisexual, or lesbian therapist to authentically mirror and welcome a gay man's sexuality and vice versa. I think the core message of the mirror transference is: you and your sexuality are OK with me.

This leads on to *the need to idealize*. As I wrote earlier, this is a need of a powerful, calm, and knowledgeable other to identify with and gradually internalize into a self-soothing, self-containing, self-confident self. And here I come to the similarity I mentioned right at the start. Specifically in relation to sexuality and the need for idealizing, it may be essential to have a therapist of the same sexuality, someone who can demonstrate the power, calm, and experiential knowledge of being lesbian, gay, or bisexual. Later in therapy, even when, perhaps, still dealing with issues of sexuality, this may not matter so much—I think what would be important then would be for the client to feel that the therapist is confident and assured in their own sexuality, whatever it is. Thus, a lesbian client may have an erotic transference with a straight female therapist without feeling that the therapist is threatened by her, overpowered by her—or seduced into an acted-upon sexual enactment by her. This is obviously essential whatever the sexuality of the therapist.

But for clients in the process of coming to terms with their sexuality, it may be vital to be inspired, nurtured, and protected by another of the same sexuality who can be gradually internalized and developed into that part of the self which, as Kohut saw it, has a fourfold purpose—as the repository of the ideals which guide our lives, the part of our self that controls our impulses, the part that can soothe ourselves in times of hurt or stress and, lastly, is the source of humour, empathy, creativity, and wisdom. So this idealized parental imago, as Kohut put it (and which Lapworth and Sills (2011) refer to as the "Good-enough Parent Mode"), has a lot to answer for! I think the core message of the idealizing transference is: you have the right to be the sexuality you are and you can rely on me to support you.

Again, in the third type of introjective transference I emphasize similarity. Unlike mirroring, in order to respond to their need for *twinship*, it seems to me by definition essential that lesbian, gay, and bisexual clients know that their therapist is of the same sexuality. I believe this need to be like others, to belong, to share common ground in respect of sexuality can only be met by the therapist disclosing their similar sexuality and sharing their own experience of being lesbian, gay, or bisexual. I once worked with a man in his twenties who was referred to me via a gay switchboard service. He was struggling with accepting that he was gay and the work we did was slow and ponderous and, though we seemed to have a good working alliance, we seemed not to connect very well. I worked on the assumption that this was some very early issue of basic trust and that it might take some time to build a closer relationship. However, some six months later, there was still a lack of connection between us. One day, he was explaining how he felt about not being "out" in his work situation and he said in frustration, "You know, this would be so much easier if you were gay. Then you'd know what it's like!" I'd wrongly assumed that because he came to me through a gay switchboard service he knew that I was gay. In response I said, "You know, I do know what it's like. I'm gay too." It was a delightful moment of meeting and, through my disclosure and now knowing his sexuality was "twinned", my client's trust in me and our work together profoundly changed and his therapy took off from that point.

Hargaden and Sills (2002, p. 55) write about twinship: "The therapist will need to show how she is like the client, provide the client with an affirming sense of essential sameness and validate her sense of belonging and connectedness." Here they are referring to the potential need of every client to feel that link. I would add here … so that she can experience and accept her true sexual self for herself and in relation to others.

It almost goes without saying that, in order to be effective within this twinship transference, the therapist will need to be accepting of, and positive about, their own sexuality. I think the core message of the twinship transference is: you are not alone being the sexuality you are.

This may all seem like a very tall order. Can we possibly provide all this for our lesbian, gay, and bisexual clients? Can we always be the perfect mirror, the protective idealized other, the potent twin? Of course we cannot. However, while these developmental needs may require a merged relationship in order to be met, no growth or development will take place if the merger is total and permanent. Indeed, if not worked through, such merging could lead to a very damaging and infantilizing dependency. It is only through the experience of failures that healthy introjection (what Kohut called "transmuting internalization") and independent growth will occur. Like parents, we need to strive to be good enough and to accept that, at times, we will fail our clients. Whether we are dealing with early introjective transference needs or what I am identifying here as later introjective needs specific to coming out, we will sometimes inevitably miss our clients, we will get it wrong, we will disappoint them. However, at such times when we do get it wrong and are open to acknowledging that we have, if there have been enough previous occasions when we got it right near enough, the client will be able to use the opportunity of the failure to draw upon those accumulated positive experiences and will learn that they can mirror, support, moderate, protect, and motivate themselves. They will discover their own power, calmness, and knowledge in and of their difference.

It is not surprising that the process of "coming out" is difficult for many when the wider social and political reality is as it is; when the UN General Assembly votes (as it did recently) to remove "sexual orientation" from a resolution protecting persons from extrajudicial, summary or arbitrary executions, or, closer to home, Sharia law classes in the UK and Ireland (teaching the Saudi national curriculum) use textbooks which tell children that the penalty for gay sex is execution (Panorama, November 2010). Religious and State discrimination and oppression regarding lesbian, gay and bisexual people (despite legal changes in some countries) is still a worldwide phenomenon. The personal is very much political and I believe no psychotherapy should focus solely on intra-psychic processes or exclusively on the co-created relationship without reference to the world outside the therapy room. However, as part of addressing this wider context, I hope the relational approach I have described here might equip and strengthen them to challenge and transform the prejudice and oppression they—we—still sadly face.

CHAPTER EIGHTEEN

Cross-cultural transactional analysis

Marco Mazzetti

> *The writer has had the privilege of visiting mental hospitals in about thirty different countries in Europe, Asia, Africa, and the islands of the Atlantic and Pacific, and has taken the opportunity of testing the principles of structural analysis in various racial and cultural settings. Their precision and predictive value have stood up rather well under particularly rigorous conditions requiring the services of interpreters to reach people of very exotic mentalities*

—(Berne, 1961, p. 11).

This extract from the preface of *Transactional Analysis in Psychotherapy*, Eric Berne's first book (1961), bears witness to the fact that, since its very beginning, transactional analysis was intended, by its founder, as a cross-cultural instrument. According to his biographers (Cheney, 1971; Cranmer, 1971; Jorgensen & Jorgensen, 1984; Stewart, 1992), he visited psychiatric institutions in India, Singapore, Fiji, Tahiti, Papua New Guinea, Thailand, Sri Lanka, Hong Kong, The Philippines, Syria, Lebanon, Guatemala, Turkey, Bulgaria, and several other countries. He was curious about different ways of treating people in various cultural environments, and in his books and articles we meet people from all over the world as he developed and tested his ideas.

In my opinion, Berne was right: transactional analysis does seem to be effective cross-culturally (Mazzetti, 2007, 2010a). The success it enjoys all around the world seems to confirm its effectiveness in working with what Berne, from his white Western ethnocentric perspective, called the "very exotic mentalities". I think that its strength lies in the fact that Berne seemed to understand people and what "made them tick".

First of all, transactional analysis is deeply rooted in neuroscience, as evidenced by several references that Berne made to the work of the neuroscientists of his time such as the neurosurgeon Penfield, and to the psychodynamics of phenomena as described by Paul Federn, Berne's first analyst, and by Edoardo Weiss, the chief exponent of Federn's school (Berne, 1961). Indeed, most of Berne's theoretical constructs have been confirmed by recent advancements in neuroscience (see below). Secondly, Berne's sense of what he called "life positions" (1962, 1966, 1972), which in some ways anticipated the studies on attachment, and other concepts, such as his motivational theory, appear species-specific (of humankind) rather than culture-specific.

I started experimenting with TA in cross-cultural setting very early on in my career as a doctor. During the 1980s, before I became a psychiatrist, I worked as a paediatrician in Africa, Asia, and South America. In order to promote my patients' trust in the prescriptions I gave them, I found that I needed to be an effective "complementary counsellor", as well as a doctor. I found TA concepts extremely useful in helping me with the second of these roles.

When I came back to my own country of Italy, at the end of the '80s, I decided to move into psychiatry and to the clinical use of TA in psychotherapy. As a part of this, I started to work in agencies dedicated to supporting refugees and victims of intentional violence. During these years, I experimented with using transactional analysis in the clinical setting, and at times in counselling and educational settings as well (with, for example, teams of educators who were working with the refugees' children). As a result of my various experiences, I have arrived at some conclusions very similar to Berne's own findings.

I think that the effectiveness and strength of the approach lies in the fact that Berne's theories, while theoretically sound, arose out of his intuitive sense of what people needed. As a result, much of TA theory is transferable to a number of contexts and situations, and their relational dynamics (Hargaden & Sills, 2002). In other words, in all relationships we can observe primary and secondary intersubjectivity (Hargaden & Fenton, 2005). There are transactions, and there is transactional analysis.

I outline below—amongst others—these aspects of TA theory:

1. *Ego States*: At the end of his life Berne (1970) stated that ego states, and what he called structural analysis, were the real core and foundation stones of transactional analysis. I share Allen's (2003) opinion that the "delineation of ego states as actual and, in particular, of the Parent ego state as something different from the theoretical construct of the superego were major contributions to the understanding of human beings" (p. 127). While describing ego states, Berne hypothesized three physio-anatomical structures (archepsyche, neopsyche, and exteropsyche), the "psychic organs" as he called them, underlying what was observed. Fifty years later, advancements in neuroscience are offering us evidence that the human mind works as Berne hypothesized, with different neural networks and specific anatomic structures corresponding the psychic organs (Allen & Allen, 1989; Allen, 1999, 2000, 2003, 2009; Cornell, 2003; Gildebrand, 2003; Hine, 1997). Across cultures, there is evidence that all human beings have neural structures and networks incorporating or introjecting from the external world (exteropsyche), reacting and memorizing (both implicitly and explicitly) from the internal (archeopsyche), and reflecting and organizing all the data to produce new adaptations and new cognitive options and patterns (neopsyche). As Berne (1961) said, "the principles of structural analysis in various racial and cultural settings ... have stood up rather well"(p. 11).

2. *The Contract*: Transactional analysis is a contractual psychotherapy. This means that every phase of the therapeutic journey is discussed and agreed between therapist and patient, on the basis of the transparency of thinking and the equality of the relationship, in order "that the therapist and client have a shared idea of why they are in the consulting room together" (Hargaden & Sills, 2002, p. 32). The contract is an effective tool in a transcultural setting. It is based on the basic values inherent in TA (Stewart & Joines, 1987) that: "People are OK; everyone has the capacity to think; people decide their own destiny and these decisions can be changed" (p. 6). The need for a sense of agency in contracting and in taking decisions about

themselves seems—in my experience—to be present substantially in all human beings and all cultures.

3. *OKness*: Closely connected with the contract is the concept of *OKness*. This philosophical principle leads us to honour the cultural world-view of the client, their understanding of their problems, their causes, and their explanation for their situation. It can be surprisingly useful to enquire into and legitimate the patients' opinions about their suffering and to support their strategies of self-care. The table (Figure 7), below, offers a useful tool for investigating the subjective perception of the patient's condition, which I have adapted for clinical practice (Mazzetti, 2003, 2007) from the work of medical anthropologist, Helman (1981).

1. What happened?
Description of the symptoms and the accompanying emotions

2. Why did it happen?
Enquiry into the possible causes of the illness, even of non-naturalistic type (magic, etc.).

3. Why did it happen to this person?
Explore the possible explanations, either of a naturalistic (diet, behaviour, hygiene rules observed or neglected), psychological (personality elements), or non-naturalistic origin (for example violation of taboo, influential phenomena or possession, etc.)

4. Why now?
Onset (progressive or sudden), temporal connection with other events.

5. What are the consequences?
The "physiopathology" of the disturbance, how does it cause the problems it creates in the client?, etc.

6. What would happen if nothing were done?
Prognosis, possible danger, and complications.

7. What should be done?
Treatments available to the client, according to the context (self-care, allopathic medicine, alternative medicine, etc.), and also their compatibility with "our" approach.

Figure 7. Outline for the enquiry of the subjective perception of illness (Helman, 1981; Mazzetti, 2003).

Recognition of the client's explanatory system is particularly relevant. For example, I would not be able to take care of some African clients if I did not get into the logic of magic and the phenomenon of possession that they propose to me. The therapeutic strategies that I employ in this situation must include ways to protect against danger. Even if this danger looks quite different from the ones most European psychotherapists usually deal with, it is possible to think in terms of protection (Crossman, 1966) and employ TA tools to effect this. It is also a way of validating the "OKness" of the patient's point of view. This attitude embodies an important principle of relational therapy in that it enquires into, recognizes, and respects multiple truths. It has a direct bearing on the issues of culture-related transference/countertransference dynamics (Hargaden & Sills, 2002; Shivanath & Hiremath, 2003), and the necessary attention to cultural references and/or prejudices.

Linked to the concept of OKness are the "life positions" described by Berne (1962): I'm OK—You're OK; I'm OK—You're not OK; I'm not OK—You're OK; I'm not OK—You're not OK. Berne's sense that these implicit relational patterns heavily influence human relationships was confirmed, twenty years later, by the first studies on attachment (Ainsworth et al., 1978). Secure attachment (Bartholomew & Horowitz, 1991; Hazan & Shaver, 1987; Simpson, 1990), which Mary Main and her collaborators refer to as "autonomous" attachment (Main, Kaplan & Cassidy, 1985), was effectively shown to be correlated with the Life Losition I'm OK—You're OK (Boholst, Boholst & Mende, 2005).

Attachment—and consequently life positions—is thus proved valid in the transcultural sphere. Attachment is developed and consolidated in a substantially similar way wherever it takes place in the human species (Schaffer, 1998). Human beings are able to see beyond cultural and linguistic differences, and can sense if they are in relationship with a person who is open to them, welcoming and acting from an I'm OK—You're OK attitude.

4. *Strokes*: This is the result of another of Eric Berne's "revolutions", his motivational system that appears to be species-specific (of humankind) rather than culture-specific. He described human beings as driven (amongst other "psychobiological hungers") by a deep need for recognition, and he defined a "stroke" as one unit of it. It is easy to connect strokes (Berne, 1972) too with attachment theory, and Allen (1989) identifies the neurological basis for this. Human beings need recognition from others, and this is true all around the world, because this need is rooted in anatomy and physiology. The effect of strokes is the same because we have similar amygdala and limbic lobes, acting in the same way.

   In my work with refugees and immigrants, I notice that the action of strokes appears to be stronger and goes deeper than their biological effects: it seems to be an important part of helping people to restore a positive sense of personal identity. When migrants leave their country, they are aware that they are leaving their homeland and their nearest and dearest, but it is only on arrival that they realize that they have said goodbye to something else: to the person they were before their departure. The migratory experience has a profound effect on the perception of identity. One of the most significant therapeutic challenges is to help the person reconstruct a sense of continuity between the self *before* and the self *after* the migration (Mazzetti, 2008). In particular, it is quite commonly a severe loss of social status. This situation—with a pathogenic effect—is the general rule particularly among refugees. Many leave high standards of living and high professional status (as health professionals, teachers, journalists, politicians, and so forth), and it is difficult for them to have their qualifications recognized in the host country. The use of positive strokes in therapy can be extremely valuable in helping our patients to recognize themselves as worthwhile and positive persons.

5. *The script*: Berne (1972) defined the script as "a life plan based on a decision made in childhood, reinforced by the parents, justified by

subsequent events, and culminating in a chosen alternative" (p. 445). Even if he underlined the rigid and limiting characteristics of it, subsequent authors (Cornell, 1988; English, 1988; Summers & Tudor, 2000; Heiller & Sills, 2010; Mazzetti, 2010b) also viewed the script as a creative life project that could be flexible, dynamic, and open to the future. It is creative in that it represents a solution to often difficult existential events. In my experience, it is an effective mechanism, and the more powerful the more it is used in its positive, dynamic way, as an identificatory story of the life of the person. I have not yet met anyone, from any part of the world, who was not able to tell the story of their life, its crucial turning points, to make sense out of it, and, if necessary, change it.

6. *Physis*: Berne's first book *A Layman's Guide to Psychiatry and Psychoanalysis* (1968), first published in 1947 as *The Mind in Action*, was re-edited and revised in 1968, when transactional analysis theory was a solid and well defined theory. Berne speaks about "some force which drives people to grow, progress, and do better .... The psychiatrists and psychologists know little or nothing about this part. Religious people might say it was the soul" (Berne, 1968, p. 88). These words echo Hippocrates (the father of medicine), who noticed that the majority of illnesses tend to heal spontaneously. He discovered that according to the principle of the *Vis Medicatrix Naturae* (Latin translation of *physis* in ancient Greek) living beings naturally drive spontaneously towards well-being, suggesting that "the organism is the doctor of our illnesses". Berne referred to the philosopher Zeno, who suggested that "*physis* was the force of Nature which eternally strives to make things grow and to make growing things more perfect" (Berne, 1968, p. 89). Linking this with the Freudian drives of libido and mortido, Berne hypothesized that *physis* could be considered as libido that is "inwardly directed" (p. 90).

Again in his last book (1972), Berne refers to physis (nature), this time as having constructive parental programming, in contrast to a destructive one (the demon). Thus, he suggests that physis is one of the forces that influence human destiny (the other two being fate and independent aspiration).

My experience with clients, particularly in the transcultural sphere, convinces me that we can trust physis and that it can function well in all those who belong to the human species. It is simply a question of finding effective ways to form an alliance with it.

7. *The ethical dimension*: Transactional analysts have a tradition in this sense. The most recent Code of Ethics (EATA, 2006) is broad, rich, and attentive in reminding practitioners of their responsibilities to themselves, clients, trainees, colleagues, and the environment—and is an important container for the relational psychotherapist. Based on the Universal Declaration of Human Rights, proclaimed by the General Assembly of the United Nations in 1948, it is representative of virtually the whole of humankind. This code functions very well in the transcultural sphere; it has value and utility in a changing world.

Probably the most challenging aspect of working in a context where the practitioner and the client are from quite different cultural environments is to find a balance between what are called "universalism" and "cultural relativism". A universalistic attitude means to believe that all human beings are the same, and the way to understand and heal them must, obviously, be the same too. The implicit risk is ethnocentrism: in this case "our" (whoever "we" may be) system appears as "the" system. A relativistic attitude can lead to a general legitimizing of cultural differences, including such things as gender inequality or dangerous traditional habits (female genital mutilations, for example). Transactional analysis appears to be universalistic enough to function in quite different cultural environments, because it is deeply rooted in common biology, and it is relativistic enough to accept—thanks to the concept of OKness—to be accepted—or inculturated into different systems. I offer as an example of this balance the concepts of strokes. They are essential to everybody, based on biology (universalistic dimension). Yet if I wish to give a stroke to a client who comes from the individualistic Western world, I might say, "You certainly know your stuff!", while a patient from a more social-oriented culture (like several African ones) would appreciate a stroke such as, "Your father, and the father of your father, are proud of you!" (relativistic dimension).

Implications for relational transactional analysis practice

In summary, fifty years on, Berne's intuition looks as if it is sound: many of the tools of transactional analysis are heuristically both applicable and effective in cross-cultural settings.

Their relevance in relational practice is founded on the basis that transactional analysis is born (and takes its name) from the "unit of social intercourse" (Berne, 1964, p. 28), the transaction. It is essentially relational. The relationship is central to the cross-cultural encounter; the co-created relational field can be effectively explored and transformed using the concepts of primary and secondary intersubjectivity, the relational contract, as well as the fundamental use of empathy, transference and countertransference (enriched by the cultural component), and the availability of the therapist to be transformed inside the therapeutic relationship.

From this perspective all the concepts we have considered find their potential: ego states as flexible entities transformable by the cross-cultural relationship, the contract as a co-created goal and reason to stay together, OKness with its legitimation of all the possible worlds (of the patient, the therapist, and others), strokes with their cultural sensitiveness, script as life-story that therapists and patients modify and co-create together, allied with physis, and the protection of the ethical code.

CHAPTER NINETEEN

Lost and found in translation: therapy and the bilingual self

Marit Lyngra

Introduction

As a counselling and psychotherapy trainee, I heard it said that: "Type II impasses (Goulding & Goulding, 1976; K. Mellor, 1980) can only be resolved in the first language," and "The Child ego state, or certain aspects of the Child ego state, will be excluded when using a second language in therapy." Although not intended as such, I remember experiencing this as rather insulting.

I had moved from Norway to London a few years previously and my experience of living with and "in" two languages did not quite match the assumption made in the statements that speaking a second language is a mainly Adult (Berne, 1961) activity. If that were true, then having therapy in a second language would mean that certain depths, such as those involved in deconfusion (Berne, 1961) could not be reached or explored fully.

Norwegian and English feel different to me, and the experience of having therapy in Norwegian is different to therapy in English. In my own practice, I work with clients who also have English as a second language, and in this situation a third language seems to develop. Mispronunciations, incorrect and lost words emerge and find a new meaning. I think a third language develops in most therapeutic relationships, but I am particularly curious about what emerges when working with the bilingual self.

This chapter is an enquiry into what can be lost as well as found from having therapy in a second language. After having thought of the title for this chapter, I discovered it already existed in the book *Lost Childhood and the Language of Exile* (Szekacs-Weisz & Ward, 2004). I chose to keep it, however, but added my own sub-heading to clarify the context.

Language and the brain

Research into this area is not extensive but seems to suggest that while first and second languages are located in different places in the brain, the overlap is extensive and very complex particularly in proficient speakers of a second language(s) "… proficient bilinguals activate the same brain regions irrespective of which language being tested" (Crinion et al., 2006, p. 1537). In a similar vein Thierry and Wu (2007) suggest "… that two languages mastered by one individual are constantly coactivated and interactive …" (p. 12530). In other words, polyglots, or bilinguals, are unconsciously translating into their first language while simultaneously processing their second.

I am intrigued by the idea that languages are co-active and interactive, even within the brain. In a comment to this chapter, Charlotte Sills (2011) described this as feeling like a "real relational internal experience". She offered the example of a friend who speaks three languages fluently, as does her husband. In their conversation, they move freely between the languages, because it allows them to express (and think) things in one language that perhaps does not have words in the others. Also, "Studies have shown that bilinguals change how they see the world depending on which language they are speaking … even something as fundamental as who you like and do not like depends on the language in which you are asked" (Boroditsky, 2011, p. 45).

Language, culture, and identity

Learning a second language is a complex process: in addition to it being an expression of individual experience, language is inevitably also a reflection of the society and culture where the language was developed. Attempting to express culture and individuality using a language where the implicit cultural assumptions are different from your own language can be challenging. This is why direct translation is often problematic, and seems to sometimes clash culturally. For example, in Norwegian, there is no word for "please". The closest is a phrase that directly translates to "be so kind" but this phrase is not used in the same context as the English "please".

Although I regard myself as a fluent English speaker, I will still mispronounce and create odd sentences at times. This creative use of English is common amongst UK immigrants, and it requires a willingness of the native English speaker to be interested in the meaning behind accents, mispronunciations, and wrong sentences.

I believe it is also important to consider that in some parts of the world English has a history of being the "language of colonizers". This means that in some countries English can be seen as a language of opportunity as well as a language of oppression, creating a sense of the native language as inferior or under threat. In the therapeutic relationship it is then important to consider what the different languages mean to the client and in what context the second language was acquired. Put simply and for the purpose of this chapter: is a client's second language (often English) experienced as a language of opportunity or oppression? Does the client experience herself in her first language(s) with shame or with pride?

For example, a Greek-Cypriot client, Elena (not her real name) was born in the UK and learnt English when she started school at four. Because Elena's parents did not speak English very well they were unable to support her in her learning. Partly in response, she developed individual as well as cultural script beliefs (Berne, 1961; James, 1973) such as "I'm not good enough" and "I'm stupid". These beliefs were confirmed and reinforced when, for example at school, if she did not understand something, she would keep quiet and tell herself how stupid she was.

In the therapy sessions, Elena would often feel "ashamed and stupid" because she believed she did not speak "proper" English. She also had feelings of shame, connected to her mother tongue because it represented the language of "poor uneducated immigrants". Elena's script beliefs were also reinforced at home when she was ridiculed and punished for not being able to speak either English or Cypriot Greek "properly". Elena would also talk about how Cypriot Greek had a lower status than modern Greek. I believe Elena's parents may have felt shame at being non-English speakers and for speaking a "low status" language before they came to the UK. This might have been reinforced further as they struggled to integrate in the UK as well as into a community where immigrants from mainland Greece and Cyprus lived together. By ridiculing Elena at home, they "dumped" their own script belief "I'm stupid" onto her.

With my Norwegian background I have no feelings of shame connected to my mother tongue. Nor do I feel inferior because of my accent or sometimes incorrect use of English. The context in which I learnt English was also very different from Elena. I started to learn English at school when I was ten years old and I remember the enjoyment of finding alternative words for things, experiences, thoughts, and emotions. (This is not to say I don't feel shame, I do, but speaking English or Norwegian does not itself trigger feelings of shame.)

The cultural differences between Elena and me were obvious, and our experience of speaking and learning English were very different. In the therapeutic relationship, Elena criticized herself for mispronouncing words and described her vocabulary as unsophisticated; she wondered if she had a speech impediment or a learning disability. Although she knew English was my second language, she perceived my use of English as "proper" and more sophisticated. In this situation I became part of the wider white society (Hiremath & Shivanath, 2003) and there was a risk that the therapeutic relationship might reinforce her individual and cultural script belief and her life position "I'm not OK—You're OK" (Berne, 1961). Much of the work involved finding words and expressions that helped her to feel understood and enabled her to self soothe when she felt distressed and confused.

Language and therapy, what happens?

Perez Foster (1998) gives several instances of therapists working with clients across languages. For example she wrote about the work of Ralph Greenson, whose bilingual client refused to speak in her native tongue because she claimed, "I have the feeling that talking in German I shall have to remember something I wanted to forget" (p. 47). Also, "Kraph, a multilingual analyst working in Argentina reported several examples of patients shifting to the language which aroused the least amount of emotional intensity and disruption" (p. 10).

I can certainly relate to the quotations above but I also believe that a second language can make it possible for a client to begin talking about "what has been forgotten, or suppressed". If we consider the previous quote by Thierry and Wu (2007), that languages are "coactivated and interactive", and that bilinguals are unconsciously translating into their first language while simultaneously processing their second, then it is perhaps likely that whatever is spoken about in a second language can "filter through" into the client's first language.

Rosenblum (2003) suggests that clients presenting with trauma can benefit from talking about the experience in a second language or in the third person, because it provides a sense of distance, while being involved in a way that is tolerable. "A man confronted with unbearable memories is better able to confront them when he speaks [of] them in the words of others" (p. 195).

My thinking at the moment is that when we acquire a second language we go through a process very similar to when we learn our first language—or mother tongue. The language starts off as the language of other (or mother) and will either gradually be integrated into our self and "made our own" or remain separate as "the language of others". In the first it is integrated into the self in a way that allows for a full range of creative self-expression from all ego states; in the second it remains an introjection of something that is other than us.

Second language as a buffer

The very act of speaking a second language can effectively create a buffer between the internal dialogue that the client experiences between their Parent and Child ego states (Berne, 1961). The therapist, by responding in a language that the client has to partly digest through the Adult (Figure 8) creates a relational sphere where the Parent and Child ego states have become temporarily silenced, or where the volume has been turned down, so to speak.

For example, a Be Perfect or Try Hard Driver (Kahler, 1974) can be challenged quite effectively in a second language as it might allow justification for asking "stupid" questions. Because the dialogue between therapist and client is conducted in a different language from the internal dialogue, the client might gradually start to experience a sense of relief. On the other hand, the same process can also emphasize a feeling of alienation (or defence), and where the client can feel excluded from the relationship in some way (Figure 9).

It is not hard to imagine how this can happen if you have been forced to move countries and where learning another language is an

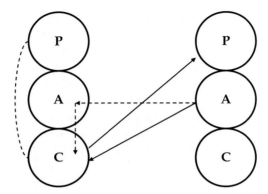

Figure 8. Second language as a buffer between the client's Parent and Child.

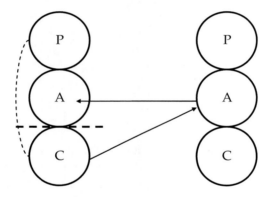

Figure 9. Second language excludes aspects of the client's Child, reinforcing a "Don't Belong" injunction.

act of adaptation, as opposed to creative expression, reinforcing a Don't Belong injunction (Goulding & Goulding, 1976).

Second language and the Child ego state

A second language can also function as a buffer between the client's experiencing of P_1 and C_1, by for example translating the words of a vicious P_1 attack into something that is experienced as more bearable for a traumatized self (C_1). However, if the second language remains an introject of something other than me, integration becomes problematic. In other words, the client's experiencing of P_1 and C_1 is so shame laden that feelings of alienation are increased and therefore prevent impasse resolution.

On the other hand, if the second language can become more integrated, it becomes possible for the client's experiencing to be included in the therapeutic relationship in a way that supports impasse resolution by, for example, creatively playing around with the dialogue between P_1 and C_1. This will often include invented words, and a mix of languages, which allows the client to express thoughts and feelings in one language that cannot be expressed in another.

As a therapist it is important to be aware of and curious about how the functions of the client's languages are played out in the therapeutic relationship. For example, does the therapist feel an urge to correct the client's English, or is she able to engage with the words and expressions that emerge and to find the meaning behind these?

If both the therapist and client are able to play around with the different languages in an open way, a new kind of relationship seems possible, a relationship where the internal P_1 and C_1 feel less overwhelming and where type II impasses can be explored (Figure 10).

For example, at times, Elena experienced her mother's words as unbearable and she remembers being scolded and ridiculed in Greek at home. Elena's mother used to call her "Aubergine" in Greek, to emphasize her stupidity. In English Aubergine is not a term for

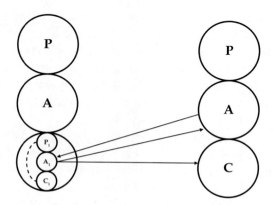

Figure 10. A creative dialogue between client and therapist, using both/all client's languages. Supports a "dilution" of the impasse.

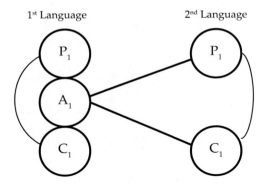

Figure 11. Client's internal dialogue is moving between languages; internal dialogue with co-active languages.

stupidity. By saying Aubergine in English, and hearing my clumsy attempt at saying this word in Greek, Elena was able to move back and forth between Greek and English and in a way dilute the impact (see Figure 11).

This process enabled Elena to soften the type II impasse and explore her feelings without feeling too overwhelmed, contributing to the gradual process of impasse resolution. This example is somewhat simplistic as the overall process was more complex, but it illustrates one aspect of how to work with a bilingual process.

Again, this process can reinforce injunctions as opposed to challenging or loosening them, and will depend on what sort of impasse the client is struggling with and why the client is using a second language.

For example, Ana (not her real name) found it difficult to verbalize her emotions in any other way than labelling them as "anxiety". As we gradually uncovered what was underneath what was in effect a racket feeling (English, 1971), she discovered that she could express anger in her mother tongue, but not sadness and grief.

In the therapeutic relationship, Ana is discovering English words for feelings that were forbidden in her mother tongue. Although this "feels right" she is not able to "really feel the feelings"; it is as if her mother tongue self is split off from her English self.

In the example of Ana, there is a risk of English remaining the language of others in order to maintain the split and defend against what might have been experienced as unbearable pain in C_1.

Transitional space and integration

Winnicott (1953) suggested that therapy involves the creation of a "transitional space". Within TA this space is often thought of as one in which integration and impasse resolution can take place.

I believe that conducting therapy through the use of a second language can impact positively upon this process, as the following example shows. In his article "Samuel Beckett's relationship to his mother tongue", Casement (1982) refers to Beckett's complicated relationship with his mother, and also to his mother tongue, as rather strained and intrusive. He suggests that Beckett "solved" this problem by moving to France and learning to speak and then write his major plays in French, before translating them into English. Casement writes, "We might consider whether Beckett uses his writing, and in particular his writing in French, as a 'potential space' (Winnicott, 1971) in which he is able to play out something of his own unresolved internal relationship to his mother alongside the new phenomenon of the 're-created' mother of his literary art" (p. 101).

I see this as a way of Beckett reclaiming the mother tongue, but without (or with less of) "the mother"—less of the internalized conflict and symbiosis (Schiff et al., 1975) involved in his relationship with his mother.

Integration and resolution

For any impasse to be worked through successfully, integration of old and new material is necessary. In terms of TA and the therapeutic relationship, I think of the transitional space as a Child ego state phenomenon where the client and therapist are engaged in a similar process to that of Samuel Beckett.

Through using a second language, the client is able to "write a few plays" and create a different or different sounding dialogue between P_1 and C_1 (Figure 11). This is then reinforced in the relationship with the therapist, who is an active participant in this dialogue (Figure 10). This enables the client to be involved in the impasse and the relationship with the therapist, but without being so overwhelmed as to be rendered inarticulate.

I also think the bilingual process is useful particularly when working with symbiosis (Schiff et al., 1975). Through developing the language of other not mother a sense of separation and individuation can start to occur. By a gradual process of translation, it becomes possible to re-integrate the mother tongue while remaining separate.

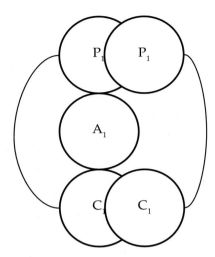

Figure 12. Language integration supporting impasse resolution.

I believe the relationship to the first language will also change in this process, particularly if languages are co-active and interactive as the research I quoted above suggests. The integration can then be illustrated as in Figure 12 above.

Having a space to play around with language enabled Elena to develop her English and Cypriot Greek speaking self. As the work progressed, Elena started to understand her English pronunciation as her accent, as opposed to a speech impediment. She started to incorporate Greek-Cypriot words in the sessions, both as a way to express certain feelings as well as acknowledging her ability to think.

In time, I also hope to find a way to engage with Ana in a way that will allow her to access and work with forbidden feelings. Perhaps this will develop following a period of time of expressing what is forbidden in a foreign tongue.

Conclusion: co-creation and finding new language

Not being understood and not belonging are familiar experiences for most people, and whether we share a common language or not, with clients we will at times miss as well as understand them. I think the process of therapy can be thought of as an individual's attempt to find a new language to express and make sense of her self. An attempt to re-frame our experience and to express and be ourselves more fully will inevitably require a new language. In the co-created relationship between therapist and client a new language develops. Or at least a new way of experiencing the language and the meaning it holds for us. I think about the relationship between the therapist and client as an inter-subjective space, a place where the client and therapist meet. In this space a new language is created, a language that is influenced by the therapist and client and the differences between them. The implications in terms of culture and language can of course be many and complex. For some clients who use as a second language in therapy, it will represent liberation and integration, for others alienation.

CHAPTER TWENTY

Transactional analysis and the wider world: the politics and psychology of alienation

Karen Minikin

A lienation as a description of the dynamics of social organization is a theme for politics, economics, and sociology. Additionally, as a way of defining human disconnection, it is a theme for psychotherapy. However, perhaps definitions are not always so distinct and so, in this chapter, I move between the social, cultural, political, personal, and the psychological. Drawing on principles and ideas from relational psychotherapy and radical psychiatry, (Steiner et al., 1975), I describe and discuss my work with a black Jamaican woman, whom I call Colleen.

Colleen was referred by her GP for depression following work-related stress provoked partly by "explicit" and "implicit" racism (Batts, 1982). She had also acquired diabetes, complicated in some ways by self-neglect. Historically, Colleen's maternal grandmother had been her main carer She left Jamaica for England when Colleen was six, and for the next five years, different relations cared for Colleen. When Colleen was eleven, her grandmother "sent for her" and she came to England.

Like Colleen, I spent six years of my childhood in a foreign country. I was in West Africa, in a country torn by civil war and ongoing political unrest. Where I had experienced Africa directly as a child, Colleen carried something of this continent in her ancestral unconscious. I had an Asian father and a white English mother and had witnessed the tension that partly arose from their differing assumptions and expectations of each other. Colleen too had struggled with conflict in her marriage to a white British man. However, a significant difference between us was that I had belonged to a socially and economically dominant group in Africa as part of the white and more privileged community there. In addition, I had not experienced the same kind of generational oppression that she had.

In the first session, Colleen asked about my cultural and racial background and stated how important it was that I was a woman of colour. I asked whether she might prefer to see a black therapist but she said that she would feel ashamed to speak of her feelings to a black woman. This hinted at the stoicism she felt was culturally required of her and was an indication of her having had too little opportunity for emotional relating. So it seemed that both my difference and similarity helped Colleen make initial contact with me. It was as if in seeing both my whiteness and my blackness, she felt encouraged to speak about the racism she had experienced and later, her feelings of shame for being black in Britain. These struggles represented a sense of social and personal alienation that on occasion I too had experienced:

> Everyone internalizes the dominant culture, both consciously and unconsciously up to a degree. When the culture does not mirror our identity or, worse, devalues it, then essentially, we internalize a sense of rejection of ourselves (Hargaden & Sills, 2002, p. 98).

Radical psychiatry

In response to these experiences, I thought about alienation in terms of Steiner and Wycoff's (1975) writing on radical psychiatry. They suggest that all mental difficulties are forms of psychological alienation created through oppression. By alienation, they refer to a felt sense of isolation and not being right with the rest of the world; as if something is wrong with you. A key aspect is that the oppression is not understood by the oppressed because the oppressed are lied to about their oppression. Mystification is key in establishing a process whereby people remain isolated and unable to claim their power. Their definition is:

$$\text{Alienation} = \text{Oppression} + \text{Mystification}$$

They then go on to discuss the importance of people becoming aware of how they are oppressed. As people realize how oppression has affected their deep sense of not OKness, they start to recover. As a result, they will become appropriately angry.

$$\text{Oppression} + \text{Awareness} = \text{Anger}$$

For Steiner and Wycoff, anger is a useful motivator leading to a desire for action and change. If anger is met with support and impetus from others, in other words "contact", people can liberate themselves from oppression. Politically, this gives rise to action against oppressive systems. Examples of this include the wave of action in 2011 within countries across North Africa and the Middle East, and the peace marches in Britain during 2002 and 2003 against the Iraq war. At the more personal level, this awareness describes a movement away from psychological enslavement towards autonomy.

$$\text{Awareness} + \text{Contact} = \text{Action} + \text{Liberation}$$

In relational psychotherapy there is a greater focus on the importance of intersubjectivity. This influences the quality of contact and meaning therapists make with clients. In the case of Colleen and myself, this included the importance that Steiner and Wycoff place on having contact with others who are in a similar position.

Case example: Colleen

An example of the above arose when Colleen spoke of her sense of isolation when she moved from London to the north of England. In London she had enjoyed the company of other black women, who like herself were married to white men. On moving, she was in a predominately white community and in more direct contact with her white husband's family. Furthermore, she felt guilty that she had imposed her blackness on her children. She described wanting to hide in social situations; I thought then of the internalized racism shared between us. Her naming this spoke to my own experiences of feeling shamed about my colour and I felt a strong identification with her. Almost simultaneously, I felt ashamed of my shame and experienced a pull to distance myself and avoid feeling the magnitude of how debilitating my visibility felt. Unconsciously,

I connected with her disempowerment as a mother who could not protect her children from racism, just as I had struggled to protect my siblings or myself at school. As I reflected on this, Colleen continued reminiscing on her experiences as a younger mother:

C: It was difficult for me to go by myself at their school … because of the possibility of my children not wanting to see me there … as the black half in the partnership … whether they would … you know … [looks down]

T: … feel ashamed.

C: Quite often, I didn't turn up and … I've neglected a lot of their schooling because of that …. And the first time I saw my son at school with his friend, I was prepared to walk past him … when he saw me and introduced me … and that was the proudest moment of my life … [crying]

T: So, you wanted to protect your son from the shame he might feel by having a black mother.

Colleen nods

I considered it important that Colleen should be conscious of me feeling moved by her experience. Indeed, I could not but feel deeply sad. She had sensed that I might relate to her story and had felt encouraged to speak. In defining herself as the black half, she simultaneously suggested black was not OK. Over time, her telling of this and other similar stories deepened her awareness of her willingness to devalue herself.

As I got to know more about Colleen, I thought about the significance of our social, racial, and cultural heritage and how our mutual and differing experiences of alienation affected the dynamics between us, as well as our more general relating in the wider world. I noticed how I sometimes felt disempowered and deadened and would lose my connection to her and myself. Initially, my countertransference was difficult to make sense of because, on the face of it, Colleen seemed available for contact. Overtime, I thought of this experience as a shared sense of helplessness and dissociation between us that was connected to both personal and cultural trauma.

On a personal level, I thought of Colleen's experience of isolation, caused by her separation from her mother and grandmother.

Socially, she was also separated from her people and homeland. At the personal and social level these experiences were familiar and conscious to Colleen. Her coping strategy was to establish herself as the "independent one" who could be depended upon. Hence, she took up a number of jobs and did all she could to provide for both her British and Jamaican families.

Colleen's independence was paradoxically linked to a deadening passivity, however, which suggested that it was more than an individual adaptation and response to modelling from her grandmother. It seemed instead to hold an ironic flavour of enslavement and so I began to reflect on her ancestral history of slavery. I hypothesized that something of the psychological process of slavery had been unconsciously passed down for generations via the maternal line. It seemed that for Colleen and the many women before her, independence was a facade and key to the mystifying process of slavery. What emerged through our work was that even after hundreds of years, the trauma and oppression of slavery was evident in Colleen's presentation. For example, often Colleen's voice deadened, her face glazed over, and her expression became blank. Listening, I often felt enormously drowsy. When this was paralleled in supervision, I became more aware of the powerful capacity for both of us to kill our energy and to quite literally do nothing (Schiff & Schiff, 1971) in response to each other. It was as if Colleen's schizoid process would also evoke my capacity to freeze in the face of aggressive primitive processes.

Slavery and gender politics

> Keep the body and take the mind. In other words break the will to resist (Willie Lynch, 1712).

The history of slavery included creating an enforced dependence so that slaves experienced their survival as reliant on their masters. During the eighteenth century, Willie Lynch, a plantation owner in Jamaica and slave consultant across the Americas, recognized that control was not feasible through guns and whips alone. His strategy was to eradicate the main threat (rebellion from black men) in a way that would be passed down for generations. According to him, black women were key to this process. The following quotations are taken from a speech he gave to plantation owners in 1712.

"… you must keep your eye focused on the female …. Pay little attention to the generation of original breaking, but concentrate on future generations."

It seems that Lynch understood the process of scripting (Berne, 1961), which can be thought of as a process whereby a person's sense of self becomes alienated. What feels particularly sinister and sadistic here is the conscious use of oppressive power to control women in order to guarantee future generations of slaves. According to Lynch, it was essential for women to witness and experience violent and degrading acts. Emasculating the men in their presence and legitimizing rape added to the apparent omnipotence of white men and was further recipe for the psychological traumas already experienced since capture.

"By her being left alone, unprotected, with male image destroyed, the ordeal caused her to move … to a frozen independent state. In this frozen psychological state of independence, she will raise her male and female offspring in reversed roles."

Such terror provoked a survival strategy among the women and coerced them into meeting the needs of their white masters. Here, I am reminded of Gramsci's (1971) idea of "spontaneous consent". Following in the Marxist tradition that economic control is embedded in ideology, he described how the less powerful in society are unconsciously coerced to align their needs with those that oppress them. Thus consent is offered, seemingly willingly by the oppressed to be oppressed. I think there is opportunity for this mystifying dynamic in most societies, and in the case of slavery it created an enforced dependence, helping to maintain the plantation system for hundreds of years.

Case example: Colleen, continued

Recognizing my countertransference to Colleen's passive self enabled me to monitor my energy levels and notice when Colleen's power seemed diminished. As I awakened, instead of feeling sleepy I sometimes felt frustrated, wishing she would fight back. Yet Colleen remained impassive. She seemed to personify Lynch's words, "without the will to resist" (ibid.) as if constantly reliving the very real threat that complaining within that system would have held. In response it was I who often held her unexpressed rage, which manifested in an aggressive desire within me to see her fight. In response, I was reminded of the influence of Colleen's ancestral and cultural containers, which I explain below.

I believe our identities and psychological processes are affected on many levels and are shaped by different containers, which I illustrate at Figure 13. This builds on Hargaden and Sills's (2002) model of the cultural sense of self. The individual (C_2 placed at the heart of A_2) is in relationship with different Parent containers. Together A_2 and C_2 hold identity and responsiveness to daily life. A_2 mediates, moderates, and makes sense of processes in C_2, and both A_2 and C_2 are affected by dynamics and influences from the Parent containers.

P_2 is portrayed as the family container and PC represents the connections to ancestors and with society, which are also portrayed as influencing containers. And $P \infty$ represents the existential realities of being in this world such as wanting life to have meaning. I have drawn the containers with dotted lines to illustrate the permeability

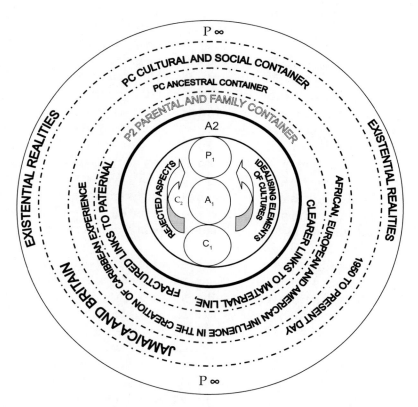

Figure 13. Colleen's self in relational to her cultural parents (adapted from Hargaden and Sills, 2002).

of the boundaries. Hence, conscious and unconscious communications ebb and flow from the environment to the individual and from the individual to the environment. Whilst I have used Colleen as an illustration here, I think that for all of us the chain of conscious and unconscious thoughts and feelings can be tracked back hundreds of years.

For Colleen, deeply held within her C_1 self there is likely to be what Morgan-Jones (2009), drawing on the work of Bion (1962) and Miller (1998), describes as a primitive fear. A fear that exists in an individual or a group, in terms of not surviving because of not belonging, which often results in an individual or group being driven to find ways in which they can belong. Socially, for Colleen and myself, our tendency was to adapt through pleasing others, or deferring to authority in order to survive.

This dynamic of adapting (A_1), including to oppressive others, in order to maintain relationship, is an outwardly expressed defence against isolation. Simultaneously, our capacity to be the oppressive master (P_1) is turned in on ourselves, in an attempt to diminish and isolate us from our feelings (C_1). When these processes were active between Colleen and me, I often felt impotent and lost, then later on aggressive. However, paradoxically this reflected a connection between us and created the possibility for emerging awareness and eventually insight.

Internalized oppression continues to be something the two of us wrestle with in the work. However, over the years we have been able to reflect much more on the impact of Colleen's history and her race. A behavioural outcome of this work is Colleen's deeper involvement with black groups in her home town, where she is an active member of a voluntary organization for parents and children of dual heritage. She is involved with events for black communities and organizes a number of social activities for families in the town.

These connections have been vitally important in helping Colleen to recover aspects of herself. The contact with others in similar situations to herself has been the antithesis to her sense of isolation and has validated many of her experiences, allowing her to grieve for some of her early and cultural losses. In engaging in this way, a change has taken place between us. While I still occasionally enact Andre Green's concept of the "dead" mother (2001), now it is often she who wakes me up, demanding that I should hear her. In sharing this in supervision, I described a chick I once reared. It had been a wet spring and her mother had become cold and ill while brooding her. Having hatched her egg, the mother was indeed dying, and I watched this small chick peck her mother to keep her alive. Her efforts won her warmth and protection for three weeks and though brief, it was important.

In this chapter, I considered how Colleen and I shared early social and cultural experiences of isolation. For Colleen, this provoked terror of separation and an independence interlocked with passivity. Both she and I had experienced a sense of worthlessness and shame with regard to our colour, which was a powerful script response to the devaluing we experienced in Britain. Colleen's cultural scripting added complexity to her personal difficulties, as did mine, and led to a recycling of familiar themes in the therapy. However, our willingness, albeit difficult at times, to engage at many levels, including the social, cultural, political, and personal—provided opportunities for powerful connections. Through this, Colleen awakened somewhat from a state of passivity and has been able to contact her rejecting thoughts and feelings on many levels. My writing has illustrated and suggested how deeply some of these themes speak to me and how essential I believe it is to hold the significance of the personal, political, and cultural dynamics in this work.

CHAPTER TWENTY ONE

Relational practices and interventions: neuroscience underpinnings

James R. Allen

Recent developments in neuroscience research have opened up new and exciting possibilities for studying the process and effects of psychotherapy. This chapter explores some of them and their practical implications for the relationally-sensitive practitioner. It focuses on the following question: what is the biology subserving psychological integration, attachment, attunement, intersubjectivity, mindfulness, and mentalizing? The first part summarizes some key research findings. The second suggests implications.

Biology

Stress and security systems

Like other creatures whose early survival is dependent on a caregiver, humans are hard-wired to seek security and comfort. We are also hard-wired to respond to stressors. Vast bodies of literature attest to how both are moulded by experience. For both, the orbitofrontal cortex just behind the eyes, the amygdala, and other mid-line structures of the brain have special importance.

Attachment is a biological process. It manifests in seeking comfort and safety, and in the importance of social support and communities of belonging. It has subserved our species' survival and it is the foundation of psychological functions important for the therapist:

1. "Internal working models" of self and others (Bowlby, 1991), variously termed "RIGs" (Stern, 1985), "relational units" (Little, 2006; Zvelc, 2009), "emotional schema" (Bucci, 1997), and "early organizing principles" (Allen, 1991);
2. Later attachment relationships;
3. Early ego states;
4. Availability of and style of processing early experiences in our life-narratives (Main, 1995);
5. Ability to understand our own mental states and those of others (Fonagy et al., 2002; Allen, 2003).

Responding to threat by fight or flight, or by dissociation and withdrawal is also hard-wired. The best worked-out of our emotional responses, fear involves the amygdala, hypothalamus, pituitary-adrenal axis, and sympathetic nervous system (Le Doux, 2002). When action is not possible, we collapse into parasympathetic activities associated with collapse or dissociation (Porges, 1995).

Trauma increases the power and size of the amygdalae, recalibrating them to be more sensitive. It also decreases the functioning of the speech centre, the hippocampal circuits important for encoding declarative memory, and the dorsal-lateral frontal cortical areas involved in working memory, action planning, and separating past from present.

Threat of rejection shares neural circuitry with those for physical pain. This helps explain why a negative emotional signal, especially from an intimate, can trigger primal pathways of rage, fear and demand, or withdrawal. On the other hand, the relationship provided by another can change responses to pain and danger. Neurochemically, spurts of oxytocin associated with a warm relationship deactivate the amygdala, the brain's threat detector.

In short, attachment is a survival behaviour for the young, and a stress-relief behaviour for those who are older. The importance of attunement and relational repair can be seen to arise from this basic need to connect.

Autonomic regulation

Porges (1995) has traced how components of autonomic nervous system regulation have appeared in stages of increasing sophistication during our evolution. The earliest (chromatic tissue and dorsal motor nucleus of the vagus nerve) created a parasympathetic metabolic baseline. The sympathetic system widened our range of responses, as is evident in expressions of fear and anger. The most recent development (the "smart vagus"), appeared in mammals. It is an inhibitory system with contributions from various cranial nerves. Through the activation of muscles of the eyelids, turning of the head (social gestures), and laryngeal and pharyngeal muscles (prosody) it can rapidly cue others as to safety or danger. This is important in the transmission of nonverbal signals from caregivers to young children. Inhibiting ones coming from an angry or frightened parental Child ego state have an important role in injunctions (Gouldings, 1972) and the formation of scripts and episcripts (Berne, 1961; English, 1969; Allen, 2003). It also activates the muscles of mastication (ingestion) and middle-ear muscles which extract the human voice from background noise.

Memory systems

Depending on their content, memories are subserved by different neural networks. Two have recently become very well-known: (1) implicit (procedural) and (2) explicit. Their differences can be schematized in this very simplified table (Figure 14):

Memories may be expressed with or without the conscious awareness that they are memories. Indeed, much of what we consider

Implicit	Explicit
Involves: Behaviours, sensations, and affect	**Involves:** Facts and autobiography
Qualities: No sense of time No sense of space	**Qualities:** Sense of time Sense of place
Neurological Amygdala, prefrontal cortex **Underpinning:** basal ganglia, cerebellum	**Neurological** Hippocampus and **Underpinning:** thalamus
Subjective experience No sense that one is remembering	**Subjective experience** Sense that one is remembering
Attention Attention at time of event not necessary	**Attention** Attention necessary at time of event
Appearance Present at birth	**Appearance** Comes on line between two and three years

Figure 14. Memory neural networks.

nonconscious is a manifestation of the implicit system, such as we find in nonverbal behaviours and transferences, including enactments of early experience.

Many transactional analysts have treated the script primarily as an explicit verbalizable extended autobiographical memory. This type of memory begins during the second year, and includes specific decisions. As other chapters explain, we have now come better to appreciate the importance of the early nonverbalizable experiences which Berne has referred to as "protocol" (1963), and that interpretive work needs to be complemented by working with procedural/implicit/preverbal levels in the intersubjective crucible of co-created transference-countertransference.

Interaction between these memory systems is both more powerful and more complicated than previously realized. Much of it seems to take place in the cerebellum and its connections. Levin (2009) has proposed that these systems may even take "snapshots" of each other. Explicit memory snapshots of the implicit system, for example, manifest in aspects of transferences, dreams, enactments, and paraphrases.

Plasticity and neural networks

The term "neuroplasticity" means that repeated experiences influence the number and strength of cell connections. As experiences are repeated, the neural connections they stimulate become stronger. Kandel's groundbreaking work (2001) demonstrated that short-term memory storage involved the modification of existing proteins, and that the formation of long-term memory involves the syntheses of new proteins. These are striking examples of brain structure changing secondary to experience.

The idea that neural networks subserve psychological processes has a long history, but the formulation that has most directly stimulated cognitive science is found in Hebb (1949). Put in simple terms, neurons that fire together wire together and are more likely to fire together again. Helping patients connect thoughts and feelings and thoughts and actions, we facilitate the expansion and integration of the subserving neural networks.

Levin (2009) has aggregated evidence that the cerebellum can operate in two separate modes, one using copies and updates it has made of other brain systems. These two modes are undergirded by two different types of neural networks which, in turn, may underlie two different ego state manifestations: separate modular networks manifesting as Parent, Adult, and Child in times of stress, and integrating neural networks manifesting as integrating Adult in periods of empathic relatedness (Fowlie, 2005).

A state of mind can be conceptualized as the total of neural activations at a given point in time: thinking, memory, feelings, sensations, perceptions, and internal models. It is a neural network. Ego states are really frequently occurring states of mind. They should not be conceptualized as fixed, but rather as potentials for reactivation, and capable of being expanded, shrunk, or modified by later experiences, including psychotherapy. Indeed, Allen (2003) has suggested that transactional analytic understandings which include consideration of the creation of structural changes in the brain through the development, maintenance, modification, and integration of such neural networks might well be called neuroconstructivist transactional analysis.

Cortical structures and mindfulness

Much of the cerebral cortex has six layers, the lower ones involved in sensory processing. Mindfulness, the paying attention to one's experiences of the moment without judgement, would seem to activate these deeper levels and weaken the effects of energy/information flowing from higher ones, such as that associated with preconceptions and memories. As an example, a middle-class friend could no longer enjoy the food she enjoyed when she was less affluent because it reminded her of when she was poor. Mindfulness practice allowed her not to get inhibited by associations so that she could enjoy the sensory experience directly.

Mirror neurons

Located throughout the brain, mirror neurons allow us to have the experience of another. The original discovery (Rizzolatti & Fadega, 1998), that they fire in the same patterns whether one makes an intentional gesture or sees someone else make it, suggested a basis for many forms of learning by modelling. Such neurons and their circuits, including those of the insula, seem to underpin intuition, somatic resonance, empathy, and the Little Professor of the tripartite model of ego states (Berne, 1977). Most important for this chapter is their role in the internalization of others, including the development of various Parental ego states, and patients' internalizations of the therapist.

Medial prefrontal lobe

The prefrontal lobe continues to develop into adulthood. Its medial area has been associated with several functions. Siegel (1999) summarized some of them as: affect regulation, impulse control, empathy, sensitive communications, autobiography, mentalizing, and attachment. There is now a growing body of literature that both mindful meditation and good-enough attachment experiences enhance its development.

It is important to note that there are neural connections between the medial prefrontal area and the amygdalae and mid-line brain structures, but not between the amygdalae and the speech area or the area of working memory. In fact, during trauma (or retraumatization in therapy), the speech area may shut down, as does the dorsolateral cortex which normally links past and present. This makes verbal reconstruction of a trauma narrative difficult.

In discussing her rape twenty years previously, a middle-aged woman suddenly began to stutter, clutched her chest, and felt nauseated. She needed not to tell stories about the event but to go inside and find the areas of tension in the mid-line of her body where she held the trauma. Much of this involves activation of the insula, a major player in interoception. Her nausea was probably secondary to the release of endogenous opioids.

Neuroscience documents how the non-dominant (right) hemisphere is fundamentally involved in the unconscious processing of emotional stimuli, including activation of relational schemas, the early principles we use to organize experience and which manifest both in interpersonal relationships and in our beliefs about ourselves, others, and the world. This non-dominant hemisphere is also more active than the other in activating arousal systems, whether the hyperarousal associated with the sympathetic nervous system or the parasympathetic hypoarousal associated with shame, disgust, or hopeless despair. Both can take us out of the window of tolerance necessary for optimal cognitive functioning.

Meaning, integration, and narrative

Meanings are made in many different brain networks simultaneously. Some are known and verbalizable. Some are implicit but can become known. Some emerge in the interaction between individuals. Some may be unknowable. These flows are assembled in a process that carries with it a sense of expansion of coherence. *Life Scripts: A Transactional Analysis of Unconscious Relational Patterns* (2010, edited by Erskine) outlines a variety of current understandings of how we make meaning of our life by forming the stories we tell ourselves and others.

These stories impact others. They are part of verbal communications. As such, they depend on the neurological processes subserving communication and language (dominant hemisphere) and social practices involving cultural forms of rhetoric and conversation (both implicit and explicit memory). They include senses of self that are nonverbal and associated with the non-dominant hemisphere and the mid-line structures of the brain where we find the innate motivational emotional systems of seeking/well-being, fear, rage, lust, care, panic, grief/distress, and playfulness (Panksepp, 2009). These preverbal senses of self and early Child ego states are activated in intimate relationships—as in therapy. It is important to note that the non-dominant hemisphere is the hemisphere most active during the first years of life.

Therapeutic practices and interventions

For the relationally-sensitive therapist, what are the practical implications of such neuroscientific findings? While they overlap, five seem especially relevant.

Complementarity in engagement

Complementarity is a kind of agreement between people as to how each is to act. Nonconscious aspects of this process seem to develop early in life, arising out of the back-and-forth circles of communication between mother and infant (Greenspan, 1989). These are encoded in implicit memory. Short (2010) points out that it encompasses five domains:

a. Attunement
Attunement is the sensing into and sharing of what another is experiencing, without losing one's own boundaries. This can occur at the level of feeling, thinking, or doing. Indeed, motor mimicry occurs automatically in close relationships. An easy check to see if one is in rapport with another is to observe the extent to which movements match.

Therapists do well to recognize that a patient's apparent opposition to the flow of treatment (resistance) may be a communication about aspects of her experience she finds difficult to communicate verbally. Noticing that therapy with Marjorie seemed stuck, I consulted her, asking if she had noticed this and what sense she made of it. She replied that she did not know. At the next session, however, she presented a dream which depicted my recent lack of mirroring and emotional distancing.

b. Attachment

Increasing proximity in times of distress increases the chance of survival for the young. Attachment provides security and a safe haven from which to explore, whether this be the physical world for the toddler or interpersonal and intrapsychic worlds for the adult. A good fit occurs when one person shows distress and another offers support and availability—communicating that she is affected by it, can understand it and the intention behind it, and can both tolerate and help deal with it.

Over the long term, insecure patterns of attachment may be changed. This is a manifestation of modified neural networks. Such changes are accompanied by less problematic relational units and therefore less pathogenic transferences, a greater availability for and ease in processing early relational experiences, and an enhanced ability to elaborate more detailed verbalizable life-narratives.

c. Reciprocity

Reciprocity involves the negotiation of matched benefits among equals—fairness. This concept opens the option for therapists deliberately to disclose some of their thinking and feeling—if it is relevant and they are not using patients as friends, or depriving them of free choice, but helping them recognize and own previously disavowed or dissociated aspects of themselves. Such self-disclosure may be particularly useful when the therapist finds himself in a cognitive or emotional straight-jacket—a possible sign of being in the grip of a (co-created) enactment.

d. Acknowledgement

Acknowledgement is an intellectual task. We need to acknowledge both the existence and the significance of a person's beliefs and values about themselves, others, and the world—not that we necessarily agree. Especially important is a patient's belief in her own value, her self-esteem—as the unwary therapist who is too complimentary to a patient who believes she is not worthy is likely to discover.

e. Leading and following

Within a few seconds after meeting, we determine who will lead and who will follow. Presumably, this dance is a manifestation of the smart vagus, mirror neurons and their connections, and early circles of communication encoded in implicit memory. Such an understanding can change how we think of passive behaviours.

Mentalizing

The ability to understand one's own internal states (emotions, dynamics, thoughts, and motivations) and those of others—and to use this information in actual situations is termed mentalizing or reflective functioning. Its explicit aspects involve the dominant hemisphere; its implicit aspects, the non-dominant. Fonagy et al. (2002) suggest that it is subserved by the medial prefrontal lobe and related circuits, and facilitated by attachment. A vital element of successful relationships, it is modelled and explicitly supported by verbal therapies which encourage exploration.

Desomatization

Self states and ego states that are not integrated into a person's current sense of self may be expressed in her body—as in a closing of the throat, a vocal catch, or a gesture out of context. Such manifestations may be handled, Gestalt fashion (Perls, 1951/1984), by encouraging the patient to give them a voice, exaggerate them, or simply become mindful of the experience and wait for more information to emerge. Some therapists may just raise awareness of these somatic manifestations and the possibility of other ways of organizing the present moment (e.g., emotion, cognition), so that it gets integrated.

Transforming enactments

Enactments involve the recreation of early behaviours encoded in implicit memory. Usually, they are accompanied by projection of a complementary role onto another. The therapist's countertransference, role-responsiveness and curiosity can lead to their transformation from implicit presymbolic levels to verbalizable symbolic ones, and the patient's integration of them into her conscious awareness. In this process, the therapist supports and models mentalizing and mindfulness. Both interventions free us from embeddedness in enactment. Simultaneously, the therapist is likely to become aware of a similar transformation of his/her own implicit presymbolic levels of experience to verbalizable understandings.

Schore (2009) has pointed out that the sensitive therapist "allows the patient to experience dysregulating affects in affectively tolerable doses in the context of a safe environment, so that overwhelmingly traumatic feelings can be regulated and integrated into the patient's emotional life" (p. 130). This would include both sympathetic arousal and its parasympathetic opposite.

Such a conceptualization of therapy differs from approaches that seek to minimize or avoid rather than titrate emotional arousal and its potential for brain integration. It involves the therapist becoming entangled in and then clarifying and working to facilitate the processing of enactments. The goal is to increase the patient's integration of dissociated aspects of his experiences, and to increase his affect tolerance and ability to mentalize. Becoming part of the patient's world through enactments, the therapist can gain direct access to unverbalized and unverbalizable aspects of patients' experiences, their past struggles in abusive, oppressive, enmeshed, or superficial relations, the effects of their resultant disconnection and isolation, and the protection strategies they have developed.

Dealing with this material while it is in working memory facilitates its later storage in an altered form in long-term explicit memory. As a result, it later can be remembered consciously (explicit memory) but in a modified form—a good reason to work within the transference. When repeated several times, the process is called "working through".

Conversations about the conversation

In his study of psychotherapy outcomes, Wampold (2001) noted that about 60% of effectiveness was due to the therapeutic alliance and another 30% was due to allegiance factors. Only about 8% was due to therapeutic model and technique.

A key feature of relational approaches is the examination of the therapeutic relationship. For both patient and therapist, this is an opportunity for mindfulness, mentalizing, keeping the other's mind in mind, and for the repair of attachment disruptions. Having a relational model such as that outlined in the introduction of this book may provide the therapist with a secure base from which to do so with curiosity and flexibility.

We encourage mindfulness in both our patients and ourselves when we examine the flow of the therapeutic relationship, the ever-shifting turning towards, away from, and against each other, and then reconnecting. Indeed, ongoing awareness of ourselves, the other, and the relationship flow can be a kind of co-created mindfulness meditation.

There is a growing literature on the therapeutic benefits and improved patient satisfaction resulting from therapists' receiving ongoing feedback from their patients—and the inaccuracy of therapists' own evaluations (Norcross, 2010). Quite apart from the opportunity it offers the therapist, inviting the patient to be a consultant supports mutuality in the relationship and the patient's sense of self-efficacy and internal locus of control. All are major components of a sense of self and self-esteem (Allen, 2010).

Conclusion: presence

The notion of presence encapsulates the effects of the preceding practices. They facilitate the therapist becoming real and felt, someone who provides a concrete response to the provocative question articulated in a recent keynote speech by Johnson (2010), "ARE you there for me—accessible, responsive, and engaged?" (emphasis in original, used as an acronym for accessible, responsive, and engaged).

CHAPTER TWENTY TWO

The erotic relational matrix revisited

Helena Hargaden

The subject of erotic transference and countertransference is rarely addressed in our training, supervision, or journals. In this article I propose that by underestimating the significance of these dynamics we are doing ourselves, our clients, and our profession, a considerable disservice. At the very least we will miss valuable clinical opportunities for change and at the very worst we are discounting the potential for psychological damage to those who come to us in a vulnerable state, seeking help. I begin this article with some personal experiences to highlight how and why the erotic seems to be so threatening. I set the notion of the erotic transference in its historical context and, drawing on the work of Gabbard (1997), explore the most likely reasons for sexual transgressions. I conclude with the importance of recognizing the inherent transformational potential of the erotic and finally suggest a model I have developed, based on relational methodology and techniques.

Personal, clinical experiences

When I first wrote about the erotic transference (Hargaden, 2001), and presented my chapter at two different conferences, I was surprised, perhaps rather naïvely, by the type of responses I met with. It may seem strange now to hear about these responses, as I think the TA community has become more familiar with and knowledgeable about this subject, but at the time the responses ranged from titters, innuendo, and gossip to a widespread resistance to understanding the erotic as anything other than concrete. For example, there was speculation about me, that maybe my having such feelings indicated that there must be something unsatisfactory in my own life. Another perspective put forward—and published—was that I had misunderstood the feelings to be psychological rather than a straightforward social case of my client fancying me or vice versa. I became—perhaps understandably—defensive about these reactions, but my research into this subject, and subsequent reflections, helped me to understand that there were complex reasons for the feelings of shame and aggression unleashed by my attempts to start a discussion about the erotic transferential matrix; these feelings were linked to the topic and not actually about me at all!

A compelling reason for the type of attitudes I encountered is unequivocally identified by Dimen (2003), who links the emergence of the erotic with the feelings of shame and hatred. She humorously captures the complex feelings aroused by referring to them as the "eew" factor. The source of this "eew" factor has an archetypal echo in the story of Adam and Eve when the emergence of consciousness brings with it painful feelings of shame and fear of exposure and judgement. This goes some way to accounting for the collective experience of "eew" I experienced. But this collective disavowal of the erotic costs us dear (Gabbard, 1997) as I will explain below.

Another reason for the aggression elicited by this subject is the threat posed by engaging with symbolic reflection which takes us into an intellectually more complex and uncertain world of meaning than the easier, more comforting one offered by concrete explanations. Concrete understanding reduces anxiety, is less intellectually demanding, and sometimes is appropriate, as in Freud's oft-quoted maxim that sometimes a cigar is just a cigar. A problem occurs when we use our theories to reduce meaning to the lowest common denominator of our understanding, a sinister consequence of which being that it inevitably includes our own biases and allows for envy and aggression to be couched in shallow explanations and interpretations. Naturally we all feel threatened by such judgements. These fears can silence us and keep us on the surface of relatedness. Recently a supervisee feared she would be stigmatized because she was a single woman and she feared that her subjective experience of the erotic would be used to judge her situation rather than used to understand the complexity of relatedness she was engaged in with her client. It is crucial that we go beyond our prejudices to allow for a deeper experience of relatedness. Erotic feelings are never simple but potentially provide opportunities—as demonstrated in the following brief case history.

I first became aware of erotic feelings in the therapeutic relationship when I had a dramatic dream which informed me, or maybe it would be more accurate to say warned me, that there were sexual feelings between me and my client whom I called Jonathon (Hargaden & Sills, 2002). I initially denied my feelings; they only came into my consciousness through the dream. When I recognized their erotic nature I felt threatened by them. I wondered if I was a bad therapist because I found my client sexually attractive. When I began to realize that my feelings could be useful to the therapy I started to ponder the significance of them and wonder about what my client might be trying to communicate to me through this unconscious process. Jonathon's deepest yearnings and needs emerged in our relationship. By acknowledging our sexual feelings, we explored his deepest fear that we would enact them, coupled with a strong hope that we would. There is a direct parallel here with incest in the family. The child seeks adoration, love, attunement and, as we know, strokes of any sort, and because children are also sexual beings, sexuality is part of this. They may sit playfully on our knee, and even turn us on, but our job is both to avoid rejecting or humiliating that child and to contain our own aroused desires.

In my case, the client needed me to fall in love with him. Initially nothing could have been further from my thoughts or feelings as I had not found him remotely attractive and indeed had been rather repulsed by him. Interestingly, and significantly, it turned out that Jonathon's mother had been deeply depressed at his birth, in love with another man, not the father. It seemed that my client had never aroused that primal love which also contains the erotic (Kraemer, 1999) and which he so cleverly, unconsciously elicited in me in order to move towards psychological health. Another way of understanding this process is to recognize that the client is attempting to find the "new, developmentally needed object in order to address a primitive longing" (Little, 2007, personal communication).

The shadow of the erotic

It is understandable that psychotherapists are instinctively and appropriately cautious of the erotic, which is why I am inclined to have some sympathy with the defensive reactions that I have encountered. Nevertheless, in order to protect ourselves, our clients, and our profession, it is important to overcome our resistances, initially by acknowledging the significant role the erotic plays in our work. Knowledge gives us power and supports the developing maturity of the therapist, whereas denial keeps us in the primary school of neat circles, pretty colours where everything makes sense, allowing us to remain youthful, naïve and even encouraging stupidity by denying our power. Guggenbuhl-Craig (1971) suggests that power is the shadow of the helping professions. When we deny the power contained in the erotic then it hovers in the shadows and comes out of the blue when we least expect it. Yet, as psychotherapists, we know that once we begin talking about the forbidden, it loses some of its power over us. This power is not always for ill; Mann (1999) describes the erotic as psychically binding—bringing individuals into deep relationship with each other. For those psychotherapists who are willing and able to enter into relationships of depth with their clients, they need to be conscious of the erotic and know how to work with it.

Without this awareness, relational TA psychotherapists at worst are making themselves unnecessarily vulnerable, and at the very least they could be missing signals that the client is striving towards psychological health, vitality, and growth that are often suggested by this type of transference. Moreover, it is arguable that those psychotherapists who stay in what appear to be the less risky waters of cognitive behavioural therapy are also at risk of enactment, maybe even more so, because of the tendency to work more with the concrete than the symbolic (see below).

History of the erotic countertransference

In his article, "Sexual Attraction and Phobic Dread in the Countertransference", Tansey (1994) describes a history of confusion and enactments in relation to the erotic matrix. He tells us that the first documented erotic countertransference was the well-known analysis of Anna O. by Breuer in 1880. Tansey describes how Breuer was obsessed by his beautiful young patient to the extent that his wife began to get jealous.

Ending the treatment out of fear, his final session with Anna found her "confused and writhing with abdominal cramps" (p. 142). She cried, "Now comes Dr B.'s child" (p. 142). It is not hard to imagine how terrifying this would have felt for Breuer. He left immediately, later referring her on to another colleague. Breuer's is the first documented case of erotic transference and countertransference, although this was not how they saw it at the time. In the light of our collective disavowal of the erotic transference in psychotherapy it is quite sobering, even amazing, to consider that this erotically charged therapeutic relationship launched the original talking cure, psychoanalysis, in 1880 with Breuer and Freud's book *Studies in Hysteria*. Freud's relationship with Jung was marred by Jung's sexual involvement with his patient Sabina Spielrein of which Freud disapproved. He attempted to dissuade Jung from his actions but to no avail. Writing to Jung in 1909 Freud uses the term countertransference for the first time, in relationship to Jung's and Breuer's erotic enactments (Tansey, 1994, p. 143).

> Such experiences [in the countertransference], though painful, are necessary and hard to avoid. Without them we cannot really know life and what we are dealing with. I myself have never been taken in quite so badly, but I have come very close to it a number of times and had a narrow escape. I believe that only grim necessities weighing on my work and the fact that I was ten years older than yourself when I came to psychoanalysis have saved me from such experiences. But no lasting harm is done. They help us to develop the thick skin we need and to dominate the "countertransference", which is after all a permanent problem for us; they teach us to displace our own affects to best advantage. They are a blessing in disguise. The way these women manage to charm us with every conceivable psychic perfection until they have attained their purpose is one of nature's greatest spectacles (Freud, quoted in Tansey, 1994, p. 143).

Although Freud disapproved of Jung and later Ferenczi, who married one of his patients, even he betrayed his principles when he encouraged a patient, one of his training analysts, to divorce his wife and marry his patient. The consequences were catastrophic for everyone: the wife died, the analyst became psychotic, and the new marriage collapsed. Such disastrous consequences, including the break-up of collegial relations (Freud's breaks with Breuer, Jung, and Ferenczi were, amongst other matters, all connected to their erotic enactments), are reasons why the erotic was repressed because it was seen as a very negative influence. It is also significant that Breuer, Freud, and Jung blame the women for what happens and do not take responsibility for their own actions.

It is difficult to find a history of the erotic in transactional analysis. Eric Berne's view was characteristically pragmatic. For instance, in *Games People Play* (1968) and in *Sex in Human Loving* (1973), he identifies the elements of seduction, guilt, hostility, excitement, pleasure, and other factors aroused by erotic situations. However, he tends to focus on a rational exposition of the psychological, social, and existential gains of such behaviour. While this understanding is useful it easily becomes defensive rather than containing for a therapist who has not explored her internal world sufficiently to hold and contain complex projections.

Cornell (2001) wrote a critique of my article making links with Bollas's work on hysteria (Bollas, 2000). Since then little else has been written on the subject in TA journals or books. The original article, as well as the responses from the original discussants (Cornell, 2001; Erskine, 2001; Sills, 2001), provide an opportunity within transactional analysis to learn about the development of relational TA thinking as it pertains to the erotic (Cornell & Hargaden, 2005).

Sexual transgressions and the organizational shadow

Gabbard's excellent work on this subject is mostly concentrated on psychoanalysts, but is relevant for psychotherapists of whatever ilk. His conclusions make interesting reading for all of us in the talking profession. It seems that it is much more prevalent than we think.

Gabbard (1997, p. 2) argues that one of the primary ways the analytic profession deals with the phenomenon of therapy sexual abuse is through projective disavowal such as the following type of statement: "Sexual boundary violations only occur in a small and marginal group of psychopathic analysts who have nothing in common with me." Gabbard (ibid., p. 2) says the facts are otherwise and that he has repeatedly received requests to evaluate people of whom it has been said, "This is the last person we ever thought would be involved in an ethical transgression. He has been a pillar of the analytic community. He has been a valued teacher and supervisor of all of us." I know several cases where sexual transgressions have ended careers, damaged marriages, and generally wreaked havoc on people's lives. Curiously, I have also known some people to remain unscathed even though they have broken this sacred taboo. They are usually those who occupy powerful positions in the profession and seem to go unchallenged. Some people think the rules do not apply to them. They are exceptions who can get away with things that others cannot. Gabbard (ibid., p. 3) distinguishes four areas in which therapists are most likely to enact out their sexual countertransference:

1. When the therapist is psychotic.
2. When the therapist has a predatory form of psychopathy and/or perversions.
3. When the therapist is lovesick.
4. When the therapist is involved in a masochistic surrender.

Psychosis in psychotherapists is rare. Predatory psychopathy, which is also rare, describes a group that includes persons with severe narcissistic personality disorders. These therapists have a grandiose sense of entitlement that enables them to exploit patients for their own needs. I think we need to ask ourselves, as a profession, certain telling questions. Why and how does our collective implicitly support such behaviour, especially by people in powerful positions? Is it because our profession prefers the safer liberal ground of moral relativism, which enables us to avoid the moral dilemma of saying something is either right or wrong? This is a rather benign interpretation which could have some truth in it and is perhaps linked to fear of moral absolutism. However, it does not account for the paradox that trainees or those fairly low down the professional hierarchy are, quite rightly, often suspended and required to do more therapy, but sometimes quite harshly treated. Could they be the scapegoats who are punished for the sins of others while the powerful who transgress are ignored by the same collective? It is an acknowledged fact that public institutions and organizations often have a pathological shadow side such as we have seen recently with devastating consequences for the Catholic Church as well as those that were abused within it. Gabbard's analysis must lead us to ask: are our psychological organizations suffering from a form of pathological narcissism as do those religious institutions, where those in power protect each other, where the metaphorical elephant, slap bang in the middle of the organization, is denied or ignored for fear of unsettling the status quo and vested interests?

At the IARTA conference in December, 2010, I used this article as the basis of my workshop. Diana Shmukler and Ray Little articulated their belief that it was *always* wrong to turn a therapeutic relationship into a sexual one. Diana Shmukler reminded us of the clinical reasons for keeping this most sacred of boundaries: the client must be allowed the opportunity to work through Oedipal conflicts, which are those developmental conflicts, deficits, disorders, and disturbances that comprise the work of psychotherapy. I elaborate on the clinical aspects of the Oedipal process later. This working through is never really completed, as we know, but effective therapeutic work leaves the client engaged with an internal sense of evolving maturity and autonomy in which the internalized object of the therapist plays an ongoing part, even when—some might say especially when—the therapy has ended.

Such unequivocal statements made by psychological leaders in our community will perhaps go some way towards countering the collective disavowal. We may feel more encouraged, as a community, to explicitly champion the client's right to be protected by the therapist from any sexual enactment, no matter who initiates it, and make it less possible for us to tolerate transgressive behaviour within our community.

Recently I taught a workshop on the erotic transference and countertransference. With a strange synchronicity, the following week, in the therapy group I run, the first client to speak told us that family friends had gone to therapy because their marriage was in trouble. He went on to say that the husband had stopped going and the wife had begun an affair with the therapist. Before I had a chance to respond another man piped up to say that he too knew of a case where the therapist had apparently fallen in love with her client. He told us in a rather sarcastic tone that the client had been a wealthy man. Three other members then recounted personal experiences of when a therapist had behaved in a sexually suspicious way and betrayed their therapy. I had not said anything at this point and by the time they had all spoken I was rather inclined to hide under my chair in embarrassment at the evidence of such pervasive misconduct in my profession. I was struck by the coincidence of these transgressions emerging in the therapy group so soon after my teaching the subject, almost as if they had unconsciously picked up my receptivity to hearing about these transgressions. The reported incidents seemed to confirm Gabbard's assertion that sexual enactments were far more common than it was customary to acknowledge. I wondered, too, in the case of the therapist and the wealthy client, if this might be one of the rare examples of psychopathy. Money has long been known for its aphrodisiac qualities and a cynical part of me can see how the therapist may have exploited her position to abuse her client in this way. I am not so sure training or supervision would make much difference to this group of therapists, which is depressing but at least realistic. What can be said, however, is that perhaps training institutes need to be more rigorous in responding to narcissistic defences observed during a person's training, in order to protect the public (Little, 2007, personal communication).

Gabbard emphasizes that under certain life stressors, such as divorce, loss, and other personal misfortunes, any of us may become vulnerable to using patients as objects to gratify our emotional needs. According to Gabbard, virtually all sexual involvement between analyst and patient begins with subtle breaks in the frame that lead progressively to the final denouement. In one case that was brought to my attention, the therapist whose marriage had recently failed allowed the boundaries to gradually be broken—through email, mobile phone usage, and texting.

Most of us will more easily recognize our vulnerability to be in the last two categories within which the majority of sexual transgressions take place. The lovesick group refer to those analysts who are in some type of life crisis, such as the illness of a child or spouse, the death of a family member, or profound marital problems. This group are inclined towards narcissistic injury rather than personality disorder. As we get older these life events become more likely and it is perhaps useful to consider our vulnerability to these issues and events while we are strong enough to think about how we may deal with it if the time ever comes. According to Gabbard, masochistic surrender describes the dynamic when therapists take pride in treating the so-called "impossible" or "difficult" patient.

> These analysts appear to pursue humiliation and victimization in their work and often in their private lives as well. A common scenario involves a male analyst who is treating a female patient with a history of incest. The patient demands demonstrations of the analyst's caring, and the analyst uses reaction formation to defend against

growing resentment and hatred towards the patient. The analyst attempts to demonstrate genuine "caring" for the patient (with an increasing disregard for professional boundaries) by holding the patient, extending the hour, and meeting the patient outside the office. They re-create an internal object relationship involving a tormentor and a tormented victim. This group of therapists distinguish themselves through their suffering and their willingness to "run the extra mile" with the patient (Gabbard, 1997, p. 3).

I imagine some of us recognize elements of ourselves in this description—perhaps prior to deeper explorations in our personal therapy about why we have chosen and what we are doing in this profession. Probably, many of us are familiar with clients who complain that we do not care enough, that because they pay for the therapy it is not real, and who make demands upon us to demonstrate our genuineness. It may make us uncomfortable to feel the extent of our hostility towards someone who deserves compassion and we may resist knowing our real feelings while trying to keep a relational alliance with the client. A therapist can find himself in an untenable position, having broken boundaries and getting into deeper waters, until there feels to be a point of no return. Although these are exactly the dynamics Berne (1964) warns us about, I know of two cases where the therapist had thought he was protected by the contract and did not recognize what was happening to him until it was too late. In one case the therapist allowed the boundaries to gradually be broken by text messages and email contact until eventually there was virtually ongoing daily contact which led to the therapist finding himself in an uncompromising position. The unconscious process had tricked the logical mind into a state of complacency because it thought it was in control.

Importantly, one of the major causes of enactment relates to my earlier point about acknowledgement and reflection. It is when the symbolic is understood in a concrete way. For example, when erotic feelings emerge, the therapist and the client may feel that the only way to deal with them is to act them out. For instance, psychotherapists will argue that "this is the real thing" and forget the transferential aspects of the relationship. Gabbard refers to this (ibid.) as a collapse of the analytic play space and argues that men in particular are vulnerable to this error of judgement. Indeed, most transgressions involve a male analyst and a female patient, about 20 per cent of cases involve female therapists, and about 20 per cent involve same-sex dyads.

Transformational potential

While this article focuses upon the betrayal of the erotic when this is acted upon and acted out, I want to acknowledge the power for good inherent in this transference when betrayal is avoided. It is not, however, without its dangers. We can find ourselves navigating the psychic waters between Scylla and Charybdis, fearing we will fall victim to either the serpent or the whirlpool.

Such danger also brings with it the creative aspect of the erotic turning our attention towards life instinct and energy. Mann (1997) links the universality of the erotic unconscious to the presence of incestuous desire. My intuitive sense is that people often come into therapy feeling bad about themselves and that it is only love that can change this around. From this perspective, the question is not whether we feel erotic love for a client but rather why do we not feel this love in relation to a particular client? Tudor (2007, personal communication), points out that in ancient Greek, whose language is generally more nuanced than English, there are four words to describe different kinds of love: *agape* (self-giving), *philia* (friendship), *epithymia* (sexual desire) and *eros*, meaning the quest for fulfilment. This makes clear the importance of the erotic in relationship; indeed one may say that, by definition, relationship is erotic.

This subject raises our deepest fears and because of this we need to feel contained theoretically. I propose the following model as a guide for the clinician to work with the erotic transference. This model is grounded in TA literature on the transferential relationship—see for example Moiso (1984), Novellino (1984/1990), Hargaden and Sills (2002), and Little (2006). The model relies upon a willingness by the therapist to engage with depth psychotherapy so that she is not a stranger to her own desires and yearnings and how this emerges in her own therapy.

Relational methodology and technique

These principles of relational psychotherapy (see introduction) form the basic model which identifies the type of techniques to consider when thinking about the erotic transference:

1. An acknowledgement of the existence of erotic feelings.
   Through use of associations, dreams, and an analysis of our emotional and behavioural responses to our clients, we can begin to recognize any elements of the erotic in our countertransference.

2. An analysis and reflection of countertransference for possible meanings.
   It is important to learn to play with possibilities, and not to get fixed on just one meaning.
3. An awareness of the distinction between the erotic as an attack on the relationship and the erotic as a means towards transformation.
   These are not mutually exclusive processes but sometimes the client may try to sexualize the therapy as a way of avoiding emotional connection. This will be experienced as a narcissistic attack on relationship (Little, 2006) rather than an attempt to emotionally connect.
4. An appreciation of the erotic as symbolic.
   It is important to recognize the erotic as symbolic and not concrete. When a therapist starts to give her clients objects, to speak with the client outside the therapy hour, or to accept clients' comments as concrete expressions without any attempt at interpretations, she could be heading towards trouble!
5. An understanding of projective identification and inter-penetration (bi-directionality).
   In matters of the erotic, it is very useful to have an understanding of this type of transference and its overpowering effect. Indeed, falling in love could be said to be a projective, inter-penetrative experience. We are hopefully all familiar with the sensations associated with this process. It can feel as though one is in a delirious state of being, fevered, with rapid heart-beats, a dry mouth, and a feeling that one has been taken over by one's deepest yearnings and longings. This state amounts to an alteration of consciousness in which our usual judgements are skewed. Yet we may convince ourselves that we are completely Adult and thinking sensibly. It is essential to understand this type of projective identification and seek help through consultation immediately. The novel and recent film *Notes on a Scandal* (Marber, 2006) demonstrates this process very well, in which a young female teacher loses all sense of appropriateness and is literally taken over by the senses and desires of not only her self, but the other, in a love which is shown to be fundamentally exploitative on both sides.
6. The use of self-disclosure.

The question here is how to engage with these issues in a sensitive manner. How do we translate our countertransference into an emotionally connecting and relevant transaction? It may be that we alter our attitude or behaviour in some subtle way or it may be necessary to raise the matter verbally. In the case where I had my dream, I decided to raise the matter explicitly with the client, by saying "I think there are sexual feelings between us." This proved to be useful; by finding a way to refer to my countertransference, I intuitively enabled us to make the sexual feelings in the dream into what Ogden (1991) calls an object of knowledge for reflection. In this instance my self-disclosure meant the client was able to reflect on the feelings and come to recognize that he could feel both affection and sexual feelings with the same person. Until then his sexuality had been expressed in a "Madonna versus whore" type split.

Because of the traditional cultural gender relationship, a particular question arises about disclosure when the situation involves a male therapist with a female client. How do they reflect matters of sex and sexuality in a way which is not gratuitous on the one hand, yet shows they are taking the feelings seriously on the other? When a female client referred to something "down there" the male therapist knew it was significant but was also terribly conscious of the potential for shaming. He was able to deal with it in a very sensitive way, without ignoring it; he picked up her confusion and shame and responded to it empathically whilst offering her the sensitive interpretation that she wished to explore something sexual with him and at the same time this felt frightening and shameful. As therapists we must always be asking ourselves the question of how to have a conversation about these things. We need to be conscious too of the client's state of mind. A client in a concrete state of mind, functioning at a primitive level, may hear our interpretation or comments, not as a metaphor, but as an intention. The question here is: when and how to say something and perhaps when to delay saying something (Little, 2007, personal communication).

The use of the erotic to trace the evolution and development of the therapeutic relationship

Sometimes it feels as if the erotic has you in its grip. For example, I was alerted to the developmental needs inherent in the erotic when, in my dream, I saw the client leaning over to give me a kiss in an erotically charged moment, only to morph into an eighteen-month-old baby at the point of contact. I realized that this client was manifesting erotically a profound need for mirroring, acceptance, and containment. When a client stares at us adoringly, and tells us all about their life, without wanting too much input from us, we can recognize the idealized transference and know that the therapy is in its early stages. Guntrip (1962) said that as he drew towards the end of each analysis he experienced warmth and affectionate feelings towards his patient and would happily have married them (men or women). This feels to me to be a useful measurement of knowing when therapy is moving towards its end because there is a sense of a more mature type of love, where there is mutual respect, affection, liking, and closeness which can often include sexual feelings in the knowledge, sometimes sadly, that nothing will ever happen between you.

A contemporary understanding of the Oedipus complex

Freud drew on the Sophocles myth of Oedipus in order to understand incestuous longings. He has been criticized about this for, among other things, using it to disguise the fact that his patients had been sexually abused by their fathers (Masson, 1990). However, revisiting the Oedipus complex from a contemporary perspective (Britton, 1998; Mann, 1997), clinicians may find it useful to consider several aspects of it when working with the erotic.

Perhaps the most important aspect is to consider the significance of the third in the psychological development towards maturity. Traditionally this was thought to be the "father" but contemporary thinkers (Aron, 2006) interpret the third as anything that forces the child/client to recognize that he or she is not the sole focus of the mother's/therapist's benevolent attention. This recognition is essential if the client is to be helped to individuate from an idealized notion of mother. Britton (1998) describes how his patient cries out to him, "Stop that fucking thinking." His patient feels abandoned by the therapist because the therapist is involved with his own internal object, which represents a type of third in the relationship: as when the mother has a relationship with the father, the analyst is having a relationship in his head. In this example, thinking is an Oedipal object; it is like an internal intercourse. This view challenges a relational sense that we should always be attuned to our clients and available to hear their every word, which of course creates a rather contrived relationship. At some point, in order to grow, the client needs to recognize the therapist's separateness. This can be very difficult for some clients who have deeper narcissistic injuries than others. For example, when I broke my foot some years ago, thereby bringing indisputable evidence of my vulnerable and separate self into therapeutic relationships, one client sat in such a way as to avoid seeing my plaster cast. It was an Oedipal object. Our reflections on this intrusion into the therapy have raised the painful consciousness of how much the client had denied my separateness and of the resistance to psychological growth contained in that denial.

I have concentrated on the therapeutic relationship in this discussion but all relationships which are inherently asymmetrical, such as the training and supervisory relationships, can also create the emergence of these dynamics and again discussion seems taboo (Napper, 2007, personal communication). It would be odd indeed if most if not all our relationships did not hold aspects of the erotic. Gerrard (1999), in a lovely article, asks her therapist the following question, recounting the therapist's oh so wise response:

> "When will I know that you love me?"
> "When you come to feel loved by me, then you will know"

> (Gerrard, 1999, p. 29).

CHAPTER TWENTY THREE

Relational transactional analysis and group work

Geoff Hopping and Gun Isaksson Hurst

T he purpose of this chapter is to share some of our personal experiences as they parallel the history and development of transactional analysis towards relational principles and practice. We aim to illustrate how our professional journey has been formed by our engagement with unconscious group processes, both in theory and practice.

The early years

Geoff

My first experience of group work was in the mid-1980s as a participant, then as a facilitator of the experiential workshops known as "Life and Death and Transition" founded by Elisabeth Kubler Ross (1926–2004). They were intended for people with life-threatening illness, their families, and their carers. The primary focus in these large groups was to help people express their feelings about their situation and thus free up essential energy for the here and now. The thinking that underpinned the work was that people would often be burdened by isolation and unexpressed emotion which could lead to poor problem solving and burn out. I learned about the importance of clear contracting and agreed boundaries, such as confidentiality and mutually respectful behaviour. I also learned first-hand about the potential problems and pitfalls with the use of touch. It was only through the creation of a safe space that emotions could be expressed and validated. By listening to other people's experiences, participants could begin to own their emotional history. With the use of psychodrama techniques (Moreno, 1964), individuals would take turns to work within the group. It was apparent that although the individual work was important, the large group process was also fundamental and enduring. Participants began the five days as strangers, often fearful and isolated, then ended with a celebration of their connectedness.

Gun

My initial encounter with group work was also in the mid-1980s, while I was training and becoming a counsellor within a residential addictions treatment centre. The main focus of the treatment was group therapy through process groups, psychodrama, and family therapy as well as structured psycho-educational groups. The aim of these groups was to create an environment that aided and supported the patients to become part of a community that provided them with the internal resources to become functioning members of society, and to find a way out of the isolation and alienation that the experience of living with active addiction ultimately brings. The programme focused on the expression of affect, in particular the experience of shame. Kaufman (1985) eloquently defines shame as: "a wound felt from the inside, dividing us both from ourselves and from one another" (pp. ix–x). Much research and writing on the subject suggests that shame and an inability to tolerate difficult feelings binds a person to the addictive behaviour. The groups were open groups and consisted of members at various stages of their treatment, thus people were arriving and leaving the group throughout the process. Those close to graduating from the programme were often a source of inspiration for newcomers and modelled how to use the group.

Working together

We met in 1990 on a TA psychotherapy training programme and soon developed a working relationship. We were both inspired by Berne's

(1966) writing on group work. He seemed to be suggesting that it was necessary for practitioners to be willing to share themselves with the group, which he demonstrated by his emphasis on congruence and transparency; this felt radical. We see his statement: "The patients have as much right to hear what the staff have to say as the staff have to hear what the patients have to say" (1968, p. 158) as a forerunner to relational principles.

Key to Berne's thinking was the contracting process; patients would make an explicit behavioural contract that would define their work in the group. An example of this would be, "I will stay out of hospital" (1968, pp. 286–293). There was implicit expectation that people could learn to tolerate and manage psychic pain. This seems to fit with our current thinking to do with "cure" and the therapeutic process. We perceive cure as including an ability to tolerate existential angst and suffering without harming self or other.

We began facilitating residential psychotherapy marathons. These were weekend workshops drawing participants from our practices. We would have up to twenty-one group members and three facilitators. The main focus would be on individual work within the group using a variety of skills and theoretical concepts, including re-decision work (Goulding & Goulding, 1979), multiple chair work (Stuntz, 1973), psychodrama (Moreno, 1964), and a variety of Gestalt (Perls, 1969) techniques. However, we also considered the need for process sessions within these workshops, in order for members to account for their experience of taking part or observing the individual work. These early process sessions went *some* way towards addressing and naming the underlying feelings of envy and competition between group members. However, we started to feel uncomfortable with the queuing system in the individual slots. It felt pressurized, as the hungriest members would sit at the top of the queue, "fighting" for the psychotherapist's attention. There was a desperate feeling of "Will I get what I need from this group/mother/father and siblings?" This of course fed into our own vulnerabilities about being enough. As we processed our own experience of these workshops, we considered that at best we were midwives pushing for the birth or breakthrough of a new experience through the expression of affect. At its worst, we pondered on our potential for less benign, more punitive, exploitative, and voyeuristic motives. The shadow side of this way of working was beginning to emerge for us. We struggled with a growing sense of our own sadism, which manifested itself in a variety of ways including voyeurism, impatience, and in the power to both gratify and withhold; an internal conflict emerged between the usefulness of these groups (the individual work within the group) and the deeper disturbance that we felt needed to be acknowledged and expressed. We came to recognize through in-depth reflections and discussions, by sorting through what was countertransference and what was a here and now concern about the limits of the methodology, that some of the more primitive and primal experiences could not be worked through in this way.

This coincided with the end of our training and a shared sense of ambivalence towards classical transactional analysis, with its emphasis on concepts and diagrams. We, as did others at the time, recognized that TA's greatest strength, i.e. to simplify and make psychological information accessible, was also its greatest weakness. We experienced the primacy of *"knowing"* to be reductive, and began to consider the emergent psychoanalytical position of *"not knowing"*. Through our experience, we were realizing that we knew less than we thought we did, and some psychoanalytic ideas allowed us to tolerate this. Jung, for example, suggested: "Not knowing is not a lack of knowledge" (2008, personal communication by supervisor) but an ability to sit with what Casement (2007) calls *"non-certainty"*. We consequently made a move in our practice to "take the lid off" and put our focus onto the unconscious processes in our groups. We felt liberated in holding the stance as it allowed for something bigger than "me and my omnipotence"; we believe that we can never fully know what a group experience will hold or how it will unfold.

We experienced this change in our focus as powerful and transformational and saw how, through the re-creation of something familial, possibly even tribal, groups can help people to reach somewhere within themselves that would not be possible alone or in individual therapy. Through their normalizing capacity, effective groups can be used to move individuals from a position of shame, fear, and isolation towards connection and belonging, a place where feelings of alienation can be truly challenged: "I can be seen, tolerated, and accepted. There are others like me." Clarkson (1992) voices some of our thinking when she states: "Human beings are born into groups, live in groups, and have their being through groups. Since the human being's first exposure to the human group will be his family, this is the matrix for his long lasting and profound injuries and permissions. It is by virtue of these facts that the group is probably the most potent vehicle for individual and societal change" (p. 205).

As we more explicitly focused on the essential nature of the collective and unconscious aspects of groups, we began increasingly to notice the ways in which words, voice tones, and other unconscious communications could trigger archaic emotional responses in others including ourselves. This aspect of the work became central. We were also recognizing the transferential impact of our joint working, both as role models but also as objects: "How do you need to use us/me and who are we for you?" We were beginning to be aware of the containing aspect of boundaries and the ways that these could be negotiated, passively acquiesced to, or attacked. This also paralleled the collective thinking of others within our community and signalled a move towards the emergence of a relational approach.

As we developed our own version of a relational approach, it felt important for us to hold on to the humanistic traditions of emotional self-disclosure, congruence (Rogers, 1959), and transparency or Adult-Adult transactions (Berne,1961). At the same time, we wanted to welcome the analytic traditions of holding (Winnicott, 1963) and containing (Bion, 1963), working with emerging processes and maintaining the primacy of the frame in recognition of the ever-present shadow (Jung, 1946). We embraced the concept of the "depressive position" (Klein, 1932), recognizing that within human beings there are always a combination of creative and destructive forces. In line with Jung's (1959) thinking of the collective unconscious, there are both individual daemons (Kalshed, 1996) and collective demons: "The Trickster is a Collective shadow figure, a summation of all the inferior character traits in individuals" (Jung, 1934, p. 270).

We also became interested in the ways in which group participants would engage in what Bleger (1967) calls "attacks on the frame" as well as attacks on facilitators and participants. This, in turn, led us to explore the concept of the demon/Trickster (ibid.) and to link these ideas to relevant TA theories.

Kalshed (1996, p. 11) says: "The word 'daimonic' comes from *daimonai*, which means to divide." He goes on to say: "Our daimon appears to personify the psyche's defences in those cases where early trauma made psychic integration impossible."

Fairbairn (1941) calls this intrapsychic phenomenon "the internal saboteur", and within transactional analysis we know it as P_1 (Berne,

1961) or the Pig Parent (Steiner, 1966). Berne's (1972) writing on the Little Fascist could equally well apply to the sabotaging demon: "He, who pretends that theses forces do not exist, becomes their victim" (p. 270).

We came to believe that by recognizing and coming to terms with our own destructiveness the beast that guards the doorway to the script (Berne, 1972) can be laid to rest, giving us the opportunity for transformation, rebirth, and integration. With its "larger than the sum of its parts" phenomenon, what appears to be "cooked up" is a tribal experience which puts participants powerfully in touch with their destructiveness, existential guilt, and transformative potential and, through this engagement offers something reparative in response. This phenomenon applied equally to us as facilitators.

We began to experiment with these ideas with an enhanced investment in the unstructured life of the group. We had in-depth discussions to do with our change of philosophy and methodology. We made a conscious decision, supported by relevant literature and our own experience, to move away from a soothing, reparative/re-parenting approach to one that welcomed conflict and negative transference and allowed for frustration as a way of working into the deficit (Clarkson, 1992). This culminated in our piloting a workshop for a TA conference in Swansea (2002), during which we ran four unstructured groups throughout a day. Each session aimed to map the life of the group with the life cycle. We named this workshop and model "The Four Seasons of Group Life". This was a seminal workshop for our group practice, setting the direction for our future work together. We realized that all groups go through processes linked to their age, from birth to death, irrespective of their time span, thus also relating to nature's life cycle.

Spring

The opening season in group life is spring, which encapsulates the process of an emergent group self or group identity. This stage of the group is typified by statements and concerns that relate to a primal sense of alienation, the capacity for trusting in others, and the capacity for survival; as with spring there is also the potential for frost. There is an inherent desire and fear of meaningful connections and belonging. In these early stages, archaic relational patterns are evoked. This is a time of both hope and terror: decisions are to be made about how to be a group together with an emerging confidence that the group can manage existential tasks. Corresponding with Berne's (1963) and Tuckman's (1965) ideas of the early stages of group process, this is a time for testing and pushing. When these essential tasks of "forming" and "storming" (Tuckman, 1965) are achieved, then there is time for relief and an unconscious hope that this group, like life, will last forever. Facilitators actively prepare the ground for the work, with a focus on holding (Winnicott, 1963), containing (Bion, 1963), and creating a new "good enough" (Winnicott, 1963) environment. Facilitators must demonstrate their ability to survive, needing to be both flexible and firm (Clarkson, 1992, p. 217). As the group moves towards the end of spring, early individuation is evident, a move from a narcissistic stance (it is all about me) towards an "us and them" experience. This nascent split will often typify this stage. Negative and positive transferences towards the facilitators and other members can emerge. This represents potential rather than a problem, and while conflict is never comfortable, it is nevertheless essential. "An adaptable member will not begin to play his games until he thinks he knows how he stands with the leader" (Berne, 1963, pp. 224–225).

Summer

The transition from one season to another always involves some early pull to the previous one. No transition is orderly or sudden, as all transitions involve leaving something behind. There is a sacrifice to be made. This appears to be true in the movement between the stages of group work.

This stage of the process often contains the beginnings of meaningful contact. The group experience takes on a more vibrant and optimistic feel, like a flowering or fruition, as the participants develop the courage to say what is on their minds, involving a sense that they have decided to commit to the process. Corresponding to Tuckman's (1965) norming stage, members decide to trust more and allow their thoughts to be communicated freely. There is also room for ambivalence to be expressed.

We experience the next part of the process to have a smooth flow feel where participants demonstrate a willingness to embrace the uncertainty of the unfolding process. Tuckman (ibid.) names this stage "performing". This brings a feeling of having settled into the group tasks. Facilitators can begin to sit back, moving in and out while paying attention to individuals and the group process. Our task here is to tolerate and name the negative transference in order to embrace the entirety of the individual and the group as opposed to the "persona" (Jung, 1971, para. 800, p. 465) or the adapted self. We recognize that individuals as well as groups have a persona. The function of this adapted good self is to keep hidden such unpalatable truths as our capacity for envy, hate, competitiveness, rage, and terror. Now the task as facilitators is to tolerate the attacks without retaliation or defensiveness(Winnicott, 1958; Clarkson, 1992). These attacks feel different from those in the storming stage, but nevertheless are likely to reduce the group's capacity to work at deeper levels if not adequately contained. We believe that therapists must have experienced sufficient therapy themselves to manage this task. We also need the courage to challenge. We believe co-facilitation makes this task more possible. We offer a balance of the masculine and the feminine, thus allowing for the creative and destructive aspects of both these archetypes (Jung, 1959).

Autumn

At this stage of the group's life, there is an acknowledgement of what the individual (including the facilitators) are getting from the experience— the harvest if you like. Conflicts tend to be managed without a threat to group survival and there is often a deepening sense of gratitude. We have observed there to be an appreciation of self and others and an investment and commitment to the growth of fellow group members. This we experience as an expression of love and generosity.

The autumnal stage also contains a sense of urgency, with participants realizing they have a finite amount of time to get things done. There is a greater impetus to live before death rather than "waiting to live". Here, we observe a shift from unconscious passivity to responsibility. Towards the end of autumn, there will be some recognition of the oncoming winter. People will perhaps face their own attitude to death and dying and to what extent they deny the finality of death. At this stage, we think the facilitators need to challenge the view that there is only one way of "performing" or getting on with the task (Tuckman, 1965). We need to support and encourage the group's own norms, thus acknowledging the uniqueness of *this* group by reflecting on what the group does. No two groups, like individuals, are ever the same. Here, we often observe the consolidation of a move from adaptation to a true group identity. On the one hand, a group member can acknowledge the importance of being an individual and part of a community, yet they also recognize that this entails compromise.

Winter

At this final stage, the group stays "performing" (Tuckman, 1965), but this necessarily includes a period of "mourning" (Clarkson, 1992). There will be expressions of appreciation and gratitude as well as disappointments, regrets, and guilt: "I should have done more." This also holds true for the facilitators. This is a time to revisit other deaths or endings. Some will resist or deny the finality of the experience and suggest: "We'll all meet again." Perhaps some are also fantasizing about a new spring.

This remains a vibrant time and holds its own aliveness, as does a setting sun. People are more able to acknowledge the poignancy of the moment. This seems to fit with Ram Dass's (1971) writing about the importance of developing an ability to experience the sacred in everyday life. The group ends, and people go their own way. Now is the time to leave home recognizing that death is the final individuation.

Conclusion

Our intention has been to share something of our journey as group therapists in order to emphasize the development of our relational identities, from working with conscious material, to being with and working with the unconscious. This is a twenty-five year work in progress, a forever evolving and changing landscape. Unlike Berne, we have found that we can do more together as facilitators than we can do alone. We feel fortunate to have found each other. We would like to acknowledge this as synchronistic and fruitful yet also not without its difficulties. We have described the way our practice has reflected the collective TA movement towards a relational approach, from the illusion of certainty and working with conscious material, to working with the unconscious. This represents a move from the therapist's application of skills and knowledge, towards a willingness to suspend these and be responsive to the here and now, with the courage to face the unknowable and name the unthinkable.

CHAPTER TWENTY FOUR

Is relational transactional analysis psychotherapy terminable?

Birgitta Heiller

Introduction

At the end of his life, in his paper "Analysis Terminable and Intermi-nable" (1937), Freud discussed the criteria of a successful analysis and whether it was indeed something that can ever be achieved. He starts by saying that "experience has told us that psychoanalytic therapy [...] is a lengthy business" (p. 373). External factors might influence the perception of this length—for example, "the impatient contempt with which the medical profession of an earlier day regarded the neuroses", and he continues by saying, "... if you were obliged to deal with them, you simply aimed at getting rid of them with the utmost despatch" (Freud, 1937, p. 373).

He questions Otto Rank's motives for espousing expediency in "Das Trauma der Geburt" (Rank, 1924), challenging his suggestion that "The cardinal source of neurosis was the experience of birth and [...] once this trauma was cleared up [...] the whole neurosis would clear up, so that this one small piece of analytic work, for which a few months should suffice, would do away with the necessity for all the rest." He continues, "Rank's argument was certainly bold and ingenious, but it did not stand the test of critical examination" (Freud, 1937, p. 373).

Freud deemed it "a premature attempt, conceived under the stress of the contrast between the post-War misery of Europe and the 'prosperity' of America, and designed to accelerate the tempo of analytic therapy to suit the rush of American life [...]. The theory and practice of Rank's experiment are now things of the past—as is American 'prosperity'" (ibid., p. 373).

Freud's allusion to "prosperity" is still relevant to the demand for brief term work today. Limited funds are a major factor for people seeking help. Where sessions are paid for by third parties, the aim frequently is to return a "human resource" back to work, to perform again to required standards. Financial considerations have been openly introduced as the rationale for particular types of short-term therapy on a national level in the UK (Layard, 2006). In circumstances pertaining to litigation, the prospect of insurance pay-outs plays a role in how a client might respond to treatment, and, especially, the alleviation of symptoms.

Historical context

Otto Rank was not the first, nor the last, psychoanalyst to champion brief term therapy within a psychoanalytic framework. In fact, as Neborsky and Solomon (2001) point out, most of Freud's original cases were treated for months rather than years. The conductor Bruno Walter "described a successful six-session therapy with Freud [... and ...] Freud successfully treated Gustav Mahler's psychogenic impotence in a single four hour session" (Neborsky & Solomon, p. 5). It was only later, when his theoretical formulation and, accordingly, his technique had changed, that psychoanalysis became "a lengthy business". Hence a shorter format was always inherent in, or even formed the basis of, psychoanalysis. Mander (2000) summarizes the models developed by Alexander (Alexander & French, 1946), Malan (1963), Balint (1972), as well as Mann (1973), and Davanloo (1980), all of which challenged Freud's later views, and insists that by focusing on affect expression and inviting transference phenomena from the outset, therapy can be reduced to a series of sessions of a duration between weeks to a few months. Beck (1976) as well as Ellis (1962) produced bodies of theory that also emerged from psychoanalysis, but focused on conscious cognition and action. More recently, theorists, including psychoanalytic writers, have turned their attention to techniques like EMDR and "Energy

Psychology" methods that speed up, in particular, the treatment of trauma (e.g., Solomon & Siegel, 2003; Mollon, 2008).

Transactional analysis—a brief or long-term treatment approach?

Berne fits neatly into the above chronology. He published the first manual on TA only twenty-four years after Freud's 1937 paper (1961). Transactional analysis, with its close observation of patients' behaviours, lies somewhere between CBT and the dynamic approaches.

Berne (1966) saw TA as a precursor to psychoanalysis. His first systematic description of its theory and practice (1961) was called "Transactional Analysis in Psychotherapy". Berne did not live to see the development of TA in a direction that fully integrated the cognitive-behavioural aspects of his technique with his psychodynamic theory of personality. On the contrary, there has been a growing trend towards reclaiming psychodynamic roots as transactional analysts struggle to develop methodology for deconfusion and complete psychotherapies.

TA practitioners, then, may feel as if they are faced with a dilemma—in remits requiring working with clients between six and twelve sessions it might at first seem difficult to apply relational principles. Does short-term work mean confining oneself to the "CBT elements" of TA, leaving deconfusion to long-term, painstaking psychoanalysis (which might well never happen)? And what does this mean for "the Relational"?

The relational in brief term work

The relational approach has been defined as being chiefly a "point of view" (Ghent, 2001) rather that a set of techniques, so it seems reasonable to assume that it can also make a difference to time-limited work. As Hargaden (2002) states, all therapy is, in a way, brief therapy (p. 45)—maybe it is never completed and our work is time-limited under any circumstances. The only difference is that in so-called brief, sometimes called "time conscious" (Elton Wilson, 1996) therapy, we have a reasonable expectation of knowing how long, or for how many sessions, we shall see a client. So does this alter the approach of a relational therapist?

"The carpenter has a hammer, the surgeon has a scalpel, the clinician has the self. The clinician's professional experience, theoretical knowledge, clinical skills, and personal history will shape the therapeutic self, and, in turn, affect the process of therapy" (Hayes & Gelso, 2001, in Dworkin, 2005).

How, then, can our "self" be used effectively in six or twelve sessions, and for what purpose?

Relational principles and their relevance to short-term work

A relational viewpoint starts with the first meeting, and remains a lens through which the work is seen. Benjamin (2002), in describing a relational approach during a conference address, suggests that "being recognized by another mind" is crucial to the process of healing. This recognition is not the exclusive province or hallmark of long-term work. Below I explore some of the relational principles as outlined in the introduction to this book and look at their relevance and compatibility to short-term work, using as context my own experience of working with victims of accidents, and people utilizing their company's employee assistance programmes (EAPs).

The centrality of relationship

The simple fact of my presence makes a difference, independent of the technique used. Keeping this in mind is crucial, even if I use, for example, EMDR (Shapiro, 2001) for the treatment of post-traumatic stress. EMDR is an intensely intimate experience. The client takes me in both as a person and the way I relate to them. No amount of technique, even if fairly narrowly circumscribed, can replace the human encounter. It begins with the setting, which is very different from the clinical surrounds that, for example, accident victims come to expect. Clients know that the consultations are confidential and private which often comes as a welcome relief.

Even if I see someone for only six sessions, I have to be able to relate to them in an empathic way, explore enough of their background to get a sense of their personhood, and be able to attune to their subjective experience. The kind of client who comes through an EAP or via an insurance company is different from the client who actively seeks psychotherapy or psychological services. Often it will have been suggested to them, and they feel under a certain amount of pressure. Frequently these clients are not very psychologically minded and indeed wary of the process.

On the other hand they might have unrealistic expectations of the kind of help I offer. They might have been told about the type of therapy they can expect. Regularly, I am given the brief of using cognitive behavioural interventions, which are compatible with "classical TA". However, TA goes much further because it makes explicit use of the psychodynamic model of the personality (e.g., Blackstone, 1993). The client experiences the level of involvement I offer, including, for example, making myself available between sessions if abreactions occur.

Clients who are advised by their EAPs to seek help often have no concept of what it might mean to be in therapy, however briefly. It provides a private space that most people do not ever imagine they could have, in any set of circumstances. To quote Adam Phillips (2009), "People organise their lives to avoid the imagined catastrophe of certain conversations; and they come into analysis, however fluent they may be, because they are unable to speak. But some people have had unspeakable experiences, or experiences that have been made unspeakable by the absence of a listener" (p. 97). While Phillips has long-term psychoanalysis in mind, the same is true for short-term clients, with the added sadness of the good-bye that has to happen, often after only a few sessions. The impact of having been listened to, however, can be major. Coming to therapy is in many ways frightening to short-term clients. Therapy remains an alien concept to most people outside the profession. While this perception is slowly changing, the expectation of the effect of therapy is skewed by notions of practical help, implying that a set of techniques can change how they feel or think. Even in six or eight sessions, clients eventually learn that it is the personal encounter which makes a difference. What most do not notice is the impact they have on me.

One of the most moving examples of this was a client who came with work-related issues and who, after eight sessions, told me that he thought of me as "one of the five people he was going to meet in heaven". I was informed that in a book of this name (Albom, 2003), a person dies and learns that the afterlife is not a location, but a place in which your life is explained to you by five people who affected, or were affected by, your life. The turning point in this client's brief therapy with me came when he, a high-flying executive, broke down in tears and admitted that he felt unable to cope. I had until then felt rather distant from him and could not relate to his particular concerns. His expression of emotion moved me profoundly and the remaining three sessions were conducted in an atmosphere of closeness and emotional intimacy. No one else was to know that he had cried for the first time since childhood, least of all his wife. The secret was kept between us and was significant enough for him to allocate me a space in his own private universe. I learnt a lot during the only eight sessions I had with this man, including facing up to issues in my own personal life which had biased my perception of his anxieties.

The importance of experience, engagement, and the significance of nonconscious as well as unconscious patterns

Especially where trauma is concerned, cognitive insight is not sufficient to alleviate the symptoms of stress clients are experiencing. The conditioned fear response (Le Doux, 1996) overrides everything. As Stolorow (2011) states, two interweaving themes tend to appear—painful emotional experiences can become enduringly traumatic in the absence of a relational context and, secondly, trauma is "built into the basic constitution of human existence" (p. 11). After initial concern, oftentimes victims of trauma are met with impatience and exasperation if they have not "got over it" yet. If two members of a family are traumatized by the same event, isolation rather than sharing is sometimes the result. Contemporary treatments including EMDR (Shapiro, 2001) or EFT (e.g., Mollon, 2008) are effective ways to ease the effects of a traumatic incident. How, then, are such methods compatible with a relational stance? Dworkin (2005) not only endorses the relevance of the relationship but suggests a "relational imperative". He writes: "I believe that people want to be known. When they feel received, they open up to doing the healing work. Once the information gathering is done and we move into active trauma work, I am a co-participant in the trauma processing" (p. 25).

EMDR engenders powerful experiences and can end up as "free association—fast-forwarded" (Richman, 2011, personal communication). The embodied, physically experienced fear resulting from a car accident can lead to the uncovering of previous incidents of abuse and physical or emotional trauma. In fact, Verhaeghe and Vanheule (2005) argue that PTSD only develops in individuals who have an underlying "actual neurosis". Powerful methods like EMDR allow for a direct re-experiencing of traumatic material, and the fact that I am bearing witness to the client's experience is crucial for a person to feel sufficiently held and supported. I cannot undo the harm that was done. At the same time I am taken in as a benign object through empathically attuning myself (Erskine et al., 1999; Tudor, 2011) and "being with" the traumatized individual. Clients might hate me on one level because I ultimately cannot help them; at the same time they experience me as being there for, and with them. I am perceived as able-bodied and pain-free, which can lead to powerful feelings of envy which, more often than not, are not actually expressed but projected into me. I have found that transformational transference phenomena (Hargaden & Sills, 2002) can occur within even a few weeks. All the while I am dealing with my own subjective cognitive, physical, and emotional reactions, which usually I cannot share directly. However, through subtle responses, my availability to be impacted upon and, crucially, my willingness to metabolize the unbearable on behalf of the client, I trust that I am able to make a difference.

The importance of uncertainty

Heiller and Sills (2010) describe the impact of a relational stance in view of existential givens. In my work with accident victims this comes to the fore most poignantly. The abiding notion of people surviving an RTA is the fact that their mortality has come into sharp relief. The meaning of their lives often changes, the significance of certain aspects, e.g. work, family, financial success gets reassigned. Things are no longer what they were before. Uncertainty, or indeed the "unbearable lightness of being" (Kundera, 1984) can no longer be denied. New meaning has to be made in the face of the ever-present danger of the road, which was hitherto seen as a space to enjoy a new car, demonstrate the power of an engine, or represent the freedom to escape at will. When someone's perceived degrees of freedom are curtailed by crippling anxiety, the reality of existential angst becomes unavoidable. The client and I are in this together, thrown into the world at random (Heidegger, 1927), with the task to find some kind of map to the territory. I often have strong reactions to the stories I hear, and the injuries I am presented with. I have been affected by vivid descriptions of a course of events. I feel less safe on roads myself, having heard one too many accounts of an articulated lorry shoving a small car off the motorway. Stolorow's (2011) "second theme" is often the subject of sessions towards the end of treatment.

My visceral response forms part of the countertransference I need to pay attention to. I have to bear the revulsion I feel at certain kinds of damage, and the horror some narratives engender in me. They rake up my own fears about safety, conjuring up scenarios of irreparable damage; lives being changed forever. This brings the relational attitude into sharp relief—how am I to use my subjectivity, my countertransference, for the benefit of the client? What do I do with my terror at the idea of scenarios that I have not (yet) encountered? This situation constitutes a condensed version of what we are dealing with in therapy no matter how long it lasts, and no matter what issues are being dealt with.

Concluding thoughts

Transactional analysis was conceived as a short-term therapy. Was Berne in 1961 motivated by the same motives as Rank in 1924? His argument was different, yet mirrored it to a point by suggesting that there was the psychological equivalent of a splinter, which caused a whole sequence of problems, and the skill of the transactional analyst was to locate the splinter and pull it out. Prosperity had again arrived in the USA. We can only speculate about how larger societal and political dynamics influence psychological theories. The focus on the relational in all of our endeavours can point us in a direction which avoids the battle between long- and short- term psychotherapy of any persuasion, under any circumstances, for we never know what is around the corner, and when therapy might end.

PART III

THE IMPLICATIONS
FOR PROFESSIONAL PRACTICE

CHAPTER TWENTY FIVE

Relational transactional analysis and ethics—minding the gap

Sue Eusden

Despite considering myself well boundaried and knowing the distress and vulnerability of Rachel, I somehow kept missing her when she knocked on my door. I was there, waiting, but somehow I did not hear her knock. I was preoccupied for the few minutes that ticked by as she waited for me, teetering on the edge of herself and her window of tolerance. Despite knowing I had done this once and it had been terrible for her, I did it again, and again. Not every time, but many times. My intention was the very opposite. Yet, here I was, in the enactment, replaying between us the dynamics of a woman full of fear of abandonment and a neglectful other.

Relational psychotherapy is a risky business. I would like to consider myself an ethical practitioner. I have been part of writing ethics codes, sat on ethics committees, and dealt with many ethical dilemmas in my practice and with supervisees. However, as I delved more deeply into my clinical work, particularly with certain clients, I found that I would fall into a state of ethical disorganization. Being an ethical practitioner involved a deep practice of mindfulness and attention to the microcosm of relating that meant acknowledging and exploring my "unethical" practice and becoming more interested in how I might be, what I term, ethically disorganized, rather than defensively ethical.

269

I want to clarify here that I am not exploring gross ethical misconduct. I am interested in the small, transaction by transaction, edges of clinical practice that may end up in a formal ethical complaint (for further discussion see Eusden, 2011).

One seminal moment occurred when I "found myself" up a tree, working with a young man of thirteen. He had just been placed with new foster carers and had had many placements in a short time. He was a long-term non-attender at school and was spending twenty-three hours a day in bed, depressed. I had no idea how I would work with him. At our first meeting I "found myself" having a vigorous (plastic) sword fight with him, in which I caught him with my sword and cut him on his hand very slightly. I was horrified and he was delighted and proud. As a consequence of this encounter he agreed to see me and we worked together for many years, and he always referred proudly to this tiny scar as a mark of our connection. I was aware that I could be open to criticism for this work. However, I suspected that my willingness to immerse myself in a real fight, where blood was drawn, and yet stay thoughtful with him about it, was a useful, albeit dis-regulating start. Anyway, back to the tree. We worked together at the carers' home, so I would arrive and he would set the theme for our session. On this day it was to climb trees. I was half way up and he was out on a branch no thicker than my wrist. I became acutely aware of the risk of him falling and being hurt, of me falling from my job and profession, and of a longing for a nice safe office to sit in. As I talked with him about my fear he talked with me about not knowing fear. He had a long history of violence in his family of origin and then in his adolescence, using it to escape any confines of school, carers, groups, etc. From high up a tree we co-regulated each other and explored how fear might be a friend, something useful to help us in times of trouble. He came in off the branch and we both got our feet back on the ground with a powerful experience between us of fear being our friend.

I already knew that relationship is a significant medium for change. What this young man taught me was the importance of taking risks, and in our work together he helped me to think about how our ethical codes support my work as a therapist and at times left me vulnerable. What I learned was that there were ethical implications if I took risks and ethical implications if I did not. What was important to me was that the value of the therapeutic work was not closed down by normative ethics.

What I needed in order to do the work was a shared responsibility for co-constructing an ethic that is supportive of therapy, therapeutically informed, and actively engaging in risks and uncertainty for therapeutic transformations. I engaged in this with my manager, supervisor, the team working with this young man, and most importantly, with him.

Ethically challenged

In her seminal paper, McGrath (1994) describes a method of applying moral principles (non-maleficence, beneficence, fidelity, justice, fairness, autonomy, and universality) to ethical dilemmas. Crucially, she highlights two difficulties that may emerge as therapists apply ethical guidelines:

> "First, therapists may confuse intentionality with good ethical practice, that is, they may assume that because they do not intend to hurt or exploit their clients that their clinical work must be ethical. Second, the fear of legal or professional liability may lead therapists to be so cautious that the potency of the clinical work is impaired, and the client is not offered the best possible treatment" (1994, p. 8).

McGrath proposes the use of moral principles to navigate ethical complexity. However, I think, while these offer an excellent framework for thinking about our work, the assumptions inherent in this approach are that we can be conscious enough to articulate and manage the ethical dilemmas we face and that the frame is solely focused on the therapist as potentially objective rather than immersed in a mutual process of subjectivity. McGrath hints at the implicit in her writing, and I think this needs exploring further in order to expand our frame to account for the intersubjective and implicit relational knowing that is foundational to current understanding of what goes on between people and in the therapy room. We need more than good intention and "safe practices" to do this work.

My thesis is that particularly when working with states of distress, trauma, and dissociation, enactments and ethical disorganization are inevitable and at times important/necessary aspects of the work. As therapists, and as relational transactional analysts, there is a need to develop formative ethics in ways that stretch and deepen an appreciation of the relational dimensions of therapy. There is a gap within ethics that needs examining if we are to work with ethical disorganization.

If we are to understand ethical disorganization as central to the work, we need a wider engagement with ethics to ensure that the core normative ethics are attended to while the work can unfold at the unconscious level and the therapist and client still have a framework for thinking and meaning making. The very nature of working with the unconscious cannot be proscribed or ethically cleansed. It is an emergent process, as is the disorganization that occurs. Our ethical codes need to help us find our way through and help guide us at these times of dis-regulation. They need to account for enactments.

One of the great difficulties of therapists' engagement with ethical disorganization is that we often do not want to talk about it. We can be swamped by shame, fear, and professional vulnerability. (Consider, in your own practice, what you do not talk about with your peers, supervisors, and trainers.) Gradually, as we gather courage as a profession, therapists are talking more honestly about their transgressions, case failures, and moments of madness in the work. Again, I stress that I am not talking about a scale of gross misconduct, but at the level of realization that we are not in charge of the work. It is bigger than us and we get into difficulties that we can not anticipate, but which we can use in the service of the work if we can keep our minds. In a recent book called *Taboo or Not Taboo? Forbidden Thoughts, Forbidden Acts in Psychoanalysis and Psychotherapy* (Willock, Curtis & Bohm, 2009), the contributing writers name and bring their minds to ethical dilemmas that have impact on all our practices. They model opening a dialogue by speaking with courage about more taboo subjects. It is inspiring to see this project reaching out to challenge us all, both individually and collectively, to consider our blind spots, self-deceptions, and disjunctions between our clinical stance and our actual clinical work.

So, how can we account for all this when working relationally, endeavouring to stimulate working with implicit process, primitive process, deep distress, and dangerous waters? I suggest four points of orientation, which are not discrete entities, but overlap and co-influence.

Ethical disorganization—a deepening of the work

Tim Bond (2006) writes about how ethics have traditionally been about making the client and work safe. This is necessary, but what about beyond that? What do competent practitioners working with deep disturbance and primitive process use as a moral lens and compass?

I think we need a framework that accounts for working with the unconscious, with clients who stimulate a level of enactment and powerful co-transferential relating. How do we hold an ethical framework when our theory and methodology invites us to acknowledge that we spend significant moments of our working time in unconscious enactments?

The implications of this are that allowing and seeking an edge of risk in the work opens possibilities in relationship. This needs exquisite attention from the therapist in terms of our own therapy and supervision. I believe we also need to develop an ethical sensibility through consideration of potentially conflicting principles. Bond (2006) defines an ethic of trust as one that "supports the development of reciprocal relationships of sufficient strength to withstand the relational challenges of difference and inequality and the existential challenges of risk and uncertainty" (p. 82).

Building on Tim Bond's work on an ethic of trust, I propose that shared responsibility for managing necessary safety and necessary risk is explored with clients in the course of the therapeutic work. This shifts the ethical thinking and responsibility from a one-person ethical frame to a two-person ethical frame. This is a significant move from the traditional view of ethics as solely the domain of the therapist. Whilst I believe that normative ethics are the primary domain of the therapist I also think that we need to stretch beyond this to embrace a two-person ethic for a two-person frame, which encompasses two-person work (Stark, 1999).

In my opening above, I describe two examples of working with clients where I am ethically disorganized. For me these are the interesting moments, exciting, terrifying, or worse, but they now feel like progression in the work rather than disaster.

In the sword fight I had harmed my client. What had happened to "Do No Harm" (non-maleficence)? Would I be challenged or complained about for my unorthodox therapeutic engagement? I was both swarming with feelings of shame, fear, and excitement, and thoughts of the importance of someone being willing to meet this young man at a vigorous edge. I considered the risks (to me) if I engaged with him therapeutically and the risks (to him) if I did not. We were both considering the challenges of risk and uncertainty and it was important to share these, and as the client was a young person, for other appropriate adults to be engaged in this thinking too.

With Rachel, I am curious about the subtle ways the disorganization appears. I can be full of awareness of her fragility and traumatic history, yet at times I am not aware enough to avoid intruding or re-creating micro-environments that re-stimulate traumatic associations. The more attention I bring to this, the more I see. I am endlessly in an internal dialogue about the intent and impact of my interventions or lack of them. In some ways (within the obvious caveats) it does not matter what I do; what seems most important is how I think about what I do and what emerges between us, and an open dialogue with my client. Intent and impact must both be examined together. As McGrath says above, good intent is not enough. This is the excitement of ethics that can support deeper engagement for therapeutic purposes. However, courage needs a thinker, and Bion's (1967) writing about having a mind, holding in mind, and the capacity for thinking and linking has been important in my development of what I call "Minding the Gap".

Minding the gap is, for me, about attending to my interventions and the impact of them, staying exquisitely curious about what emerges and being available to explore the dynamic disturbance that may unfold. It is often at the edges of the relationship that the deeper, more unconscious forms of relating emerge. The working edge is often in the misattunements, absences, and ruptures rather than the attunements and empathic enquiries.

Exquisite attention to minding the gap

Daniel Stern and the Boston Change Process Study Group (2010) set out a well-researched outline to the therapeutic process, which they describe in four phases. The first phase is referred to as "moving along". This is when the work is just ticking over nicely; probably most transactions and co-transferences are complementary. Then comes the "now" moment. This is when the rapture is broken and perhaps a rupture occurs. Such a moment can lead to what Stern et al., following a Gestalt tradition (Hycner, 1991) describe as a "moment of ,meeting" and Hargaden and Sills (2002) associate with the transformational transference; or it can lead to defence, and realignment back to the comfort of "moving along". If the "moment of meeting" is achieved, then Stern suggests it is followed by an "open space", which allows a sense of integration for both parties.

The potential of the Now to reach the Moment of Meeting is what I refer to as the gap, an intersubjective, raw, tangy experience of the other. It is what occurred between Rachel and me in the vignette above, as I rush to the door, racked with puzzlement and frustration at myself. It is what Peter presented me with in that tree. A gap appears and we are confronted with ourselves, our client's history and the question, "What the hell do I do now?" Such enactments entail an externalization of the war within the patient's internal object world, and the therapist is:

> immersed, at least for a time, in a dissociative process of his own that is linked with the patient's and is objectifying his patient no less than his patient is objectifying him. It is because of the relative absence of intersubjectivity during enactment that an analyst will often concretise the event as something taking place within the patient. (Bromberg, 2011, p. 34).

At such moments what can happen, as Bromberg so clearly names, is that we might use theory to define and pathologize the client, to defend rather than reflect. Rather than plugging the gap with theory (as with filler to a crack in the wall), I believe our challenge is to bring our minds to reflect on the relational possibilities presented. Such Now moments hold both the potential for enactment and transformation: the cracks that open up in the relational field can allow light to emerge if both client and therapist can bear to look at it.

One foot in, one foot out—co-existence of unconscious and conscious relating

"One foot in, one foot out" refers to the capacity to reflect on the intrapsychic and interpersonal dance. It brings together the intersubjective space and the tension between enactment and transformation. It is the crucial capacity that the therapist seeks in order to help the dyad understand and learn from their own unique processes.

This means being available to all experiences in the dyad. The subtle ongoing dynamics that are inevitable and desirable involve transference and countertransference relating. With one particular client the transference can be a silent withdrawal, which may stimulate the therapist to work harder. The client may feel defined and boxed in and the therapist may pursue, seeking understanding, but also fearing the rupture. Both dance the enactment of the impasse between revenge and compassion, co-creating an old but familiar routine. The relating has an I-It (Buber, 1923) mutually objectifying quality and the therapist has "both feet in" the countertransference at this point. They have fallen into an inevitable mindlessness. Such moments capture the ethical tensions of our work. A crack appears and offers light.

The therapist takes "one foot out" by adopting an attitude of curiosity and mindfulness and asks, what is going on here? What am I enacting of my own and what is the client showing me and what am I, as therapist, not understanding? How have I stimulated this in them and vice versa? So the therapist takes their mind to the dyad in a different way. The aim, in so doing, is to also invite the client into wondering. The unconscious and the conscious are a dynamic duo, each needing the other in order to be meaningful.

Capers (1999) argues how two distinct capacities must come together within the analyst—the union of their receptivity to the client's projection with the analyst's capacity to distance himself from them: "The analyst tends to fall spontaneously into a countertransference illness as part of his receptivity to the patient's projections, and he must cure himself of it if the analysis is to progress" (Capers, 1999, p. 114). This corresponds with Siegel's (2007) explanation of reflectiveness: receptivity, self-observation, and reflexivity. These are three essential elements for Minding the Gap.

Capacity to use a third

As therapists our ethical responsibility is to pay attention to enactments. The notion of "the third" has been defined in many ways (see e.g., Ogden, 1994). Here I want to use the concept more broadly to explore the provision of another space. There are three thirds that I believe are useful ways of thinking in relation to Minding the Gap.

The three thirds are:

Reflectiveness—described by Siegel (2007) as encompassing receptivity, self-observation, and reflexivity. Our capacity to reflect (upon ourselves, others, and the in between) can become the third. It is also common for the client to introduce a third to the dyad by way of a story of "out there" to supervise the work "in here".

Supervision—the need for the therapist to seek a third mind, usually a supervisor. As a supervisor I request that supervisees attend to and bring the edges of their practice to supervision. During my work on the ethics committee, I often heard that qualified and experienced therapists considered they needed less supervision than when they were in training. There seemed a narcissistic difficulty with seeking a third, and a lack of understanding of the vital function a clinical supervisor holds in the protection of the work, the therapist, and the client. This is not something to pay lip service to; it is rooted in the deepest sense of respect for our clients, the profession, and ourselves.

Ethical consultation—when the rupture has gone too far for the client to bear, the third may be that of consultation, mediation, or an ethics committee to bring a mind or minds to bear witness and help make sense and meaning from the therapeutic rupture. In our present litigious culture this often becomes a painful and terrible event, rather than an ordinary reflective accounting. What I have learned is that there is great benefit in the possibility of having a third attend to the therapeutic relationship that is in deep trouble.

The therapist's need for clinical supervision and therapy is central. In doing this kind of relational work it is incumbent on us to reflect deeply and be in regular reflective supervision. Our post-qualification guidance on this is unhelpful in its underestimation of the need, supporting a growing community of practitioners who believe that supervision is for beginners as opposed for the clinically serious.

Conclusion

In this chapter I describe how working relationally and at the edges with clients who bring deep and/or early disturbances to our consulting rooms demands a practice of ethical mindfulness. I propose four principles to support this, which are: the normalization of enactments and therefore ethical disorganization in the therapist and the dyad; exquisite attention to minding the gaps; keeping "one foot in and one foot out", and finally the capacity to use a third.

These principles need to be included in the training of relational therapists, our supervision and supervision of supervision, and in our work in writing and considering ethical codes as practitioners, colleagues, and ethics committees.

CHAPTER TWENTY SIX

Reflections on a theme of relational supervision

Suzanne Boyd and Carole Shadbolt

Introduction

In this chapter we seek an atmosphere and space which is impression-istic, reflective, suggestive, rather than definitive, dogmatic. Conse-quently we will keep discussions on models of relational supervision to a minimum. Also, although influenced by teachers and others, whom we will be naming, we will report only briefly on their ideas. Our aim is to tempt the reader to associate to our wonderings and use them as one uses art—as a means of expanding their creative mind. This space is our idea of what relational supervision provides to our supervisees.

As a way of exploring all this, we wish to introduce a metaphor, which we hope will be useful. There is a series of well-known paint-ings by Monet, "The Houses of Parliament", all different but all unmis-takably about the same subject. In a description about the series we learn that the paintings are all the same size and all are from the same viewpoint, but painted at different times and under different weather conditions. Although Monet's paintings are all varied and impression-istic, to our mind there is an unmistakable discipline in them. Most importantly they all have a frame, which holds the painting, unique though each is. The frame both limits and contains the painting, an idea originally about contracting from our colleague Jean Maquet (2010). Because the frame is there, the painting can move around freely, yet it is held. The frames themselves seem heavy, but they are beautiful, traditional. They are paintings where paint was applied in a particular way, a brush held this way or that. The painter, a master of his profession, a teacher from whom we can learn, is also a pupil of his own creativity, who is his teacher. The paintings are not photographic reproductions of the subject; they are reflections on a theme and they have emerged from his involvement with his environment, in this case the Houses of Parliament in London.

This has many parallels with what we mean by relational supervision. Each session and series of sessions is broadly about the same subject, but each supervisory encounter will be different, as in Monet paintings. All have a frame which holds, limits in some ways, allows in others.

To begin, we want to engage with two questions. First: what do we mean by supervision? Then, what do we mean by relational supervision? In *The Supervisory Relationship* (2001), Frawley-O'Dea and Sarnat quote Fiscalini, who describes supervision as "a relationship about a relationship about other relationships". This simple phrase belies the intricate, complex process that supervision can sometimes be. At its simplest, supervision is the place we go to talk through our professional endeavours. It can also be a source of support, an experience of challenge, an opportunity for insight, a profoundly moving personal journey, a delight, a disappointment, and much more besides.

Supervision at its best is a vibrant and alive process where more becomes possible; our minds can stretch and our hearts can soar. At its worst, it can evoke feelings of shame and humiliation. As reflected in the quote above, at the heart of supervision is a relationship, or rather a series of relationships. Two people sit in the room together—more if it is a supervision group—and they engage. How they engage is informed by several factors, not least of which is the model/theories used in the work being discussed, along with the ethical principles and philosophy which underpin and inform their work in the first place. We might think of this as the frame. Within this frame, many relational elements come into play: power, authority, control, mutuality, and assessment to name a few, and these of course are tempered by the experience of both the supervisor and the supervisee.

Although there are two people (at least) in the room, supervision is not necessarily a two-person endeavour. Stark (1999) describes a one-person, a one-and-a-half-person, and a two-person approach and applies them to the task of psychotherapy. This idea seems easily transferable to the supervisory relationship. She does not value one mode over another; each is relevant in its own way. A traditional model of supervision as used by, for example, Mazzetti (2007) in his reworking of Clarkson's (1992) procedural checklist for evaluating supervision sessions, may well fit within the one- or one-and-a-half-person frame. Within this model, the supervisee seeks help from a more experienced supervisor. The supervisor listens, interprets, shares knowledge, and stays relatively separate. Used to this day as a checklist for examining TSTA candidates, Clarkson's list has proved to be a highly effective tool in many ways, but it is a frame. The danger, if used by rote as the work of supervision (rather than a frame), is that a supervisory encounter risks becoming a painting by numbers endeavour. The frame becomes the dictator of the work, rather than the enabler of something more creative. Growth, or indeed thriving, cannot really happen. We do not go to see Monet's frames, important though frames may be.

Relational supervision

When working relationally, including in supervision, the endeavour moves towards a two-person mode, although not exclusively, depending on the circumstances and the contract. Within a two-person mode, what goes on between all persons present is central to the supervisory endeavour. The "agent of change" moves away from cognitive insight, important though that is, and instead uses "affective, co-creative, nonconscious and unconscious relational interactions as a primary means of growth, change and transformation" (International Association of Relational Transactional Analysis (IARTA) website, 2009).

Gilbert and Evans (2000) describe relational supervision as "always interpersonal" (p. 7). It is a process of enquiry that takes into account the dynamics of the present relationship and is open to the ways in which this may reflect and parallel the talked-about relationship. It is a process of enquiry that uses what is present in the room, a process of co-creation that allows for the emergence of insight that is never a search for "the truth" (p. 7). This framework of mutual understanding is always partial and open to deconstruction and reconstruction in the light of new experiences. The task is to attempt to find out what is going on and to take the risk to ask.

Two major themes we consider central in this approach to supervision are *risk* and *self-reflection*. We now reflect on these and on the implications of supervising with these elements at the core of the work, which includes working at the controversial teach/treat boundary.

Risk

What do we mean by risk, and what are some of the ethical considerations to be taken into account when working in this way? When we are open to what is present in the room, and value and see this as a natural part of the supervisory work to be undertaken, the likelihood is that the people involved will be able to be insightful, open, and non-defensive about themselves and their internal, unconscious processes. Acknowledging this process and creating and transforming these struggles in an honest way inevitably, we believe, involve risk. What we risk in this process is that our internal, perhaps private experience becomes public and therefore potentially shaming. Life can be risky … life *is* risky and sometimes dangerous. No less in psychotherapy, but risk is different from recklessness. The difference between risk and recklessness is captured in a quotation by the medieval philosopher, Maimonides. He is quoted as saying that "courage is the mid-point between cowardice and recklessness" (2011, BBC Radio 4). Could it be that there is no courage without there first being fear, anxiety, uncertainty, or apprehension? If so, the reckless person, practitioner, or supervisor probably does not think about risk and has no anxiety, uncertainty, or apprehension; she is presumably therefore unaware of needing courage. To our way of thinking, the "thought about risks" at the heart of relational supervision are the risks we take to challenge, to reveal, and to question. These risks are based on trust and courage to stay in relationship and, for example, to work through ruptures even though the path may become rocky at times. Tim Bond's (2006) work on the missing ethic of trust within psychotherapy, between client and therapist, illustrates the balance required of us when considering risk or recklessness. To our mind when applied to supervision the issues are the same. What we understand this means is the development of a mutual trust in the integrity and significance of the here and now process, as we have stated above. The absence of this relationship of trust makes supervision an overly secure or indeed a frightening place, where true exploration or risk is sacrificed to safety beyond all uncertainty: "A fundamentally dishonest and existentially infantilizing approach" (Bond, 2006, p. 83). It amounts to a sanitization of risk, where creativity and more importantly robustness have little hope of flourishing. This is not to say that safety and ethics are not important; they are all the more so when working at the edge of experience, with nonconscious processes where wondering rather than knowing is the order of the day. Working without knowledge of an ethical frame is also what we mean by recklessness. We might say that Monet took risks in his paintings of the Houses of Parliament but he was not reckless. He was not a beginner when he painted his series. He knew, appreciated, and thought about the basics and underpinning principles of painting and art. In this sense as well as literally his work was solidly framed.

Self-reflection

Self-reflection deepens the now clichéd notion of parallel process (for a review see Mothersole, 1999), hitherto seen as insight into the psychodynamics, and sometimes diagnosed as the psychopathology of the client, made object by the supervisee. We suggest it is not the supervisor's job to catch the parallel process or to necessarily expose it, but to see it and to use it as part of the work. Seen through a relational lens, self-reflection on the parallel process regards the emotional experiences, disturbances, and sometimes odd thoughts of the supervisee and the supervisor themselves as vital to the transformational potential of relational TA supervision. Here, both become subjects, and the felt experience of the parallel process, rather than having a cognitive hunch about it, is central to gaining awareness and insight.

It is easy to see how a capacity for self-reflection on the part of all concerned is paramount, together with the willingness to be profoundly impacted by the other. If relational supervision is an exploration without necessarily "a right answer", then part of the risk, as we have discussed above, for the supervisor can be to expose themselves and perhaps aspects of their own internal world—maybe unwittingly—in order to gain insight into the process between the therapist and the client. This emergence is then the subject of self-reflection. Suzanne gives this example from her own supervisory practice.

"In a recent supervision session with a long-qualified and experienced therapist, the supervisee describes feeling numb, blank, and disinterested in response to a quite harrowing story from a young woman she had been working with for a while. She reports not even being sure whether she believes what her client is telling her, and this is disturbing to her. She tells me virtually nothing of the harrowing story and yet as I sit with her I begin to experience a profound somatic response of fear and anxiety. I have a sense of wanting to leave the room, to get away, and I even glance at the clock to see how long we have left of the session. Some moments go by as I sit with my discomfort and begin to think about what might be happening. This was not at all how I usually feel when working with this person. Am I wanting to get away from disturbance in me, disturbance in her, disturbance in the client, or some combination of all of that? I struggle with myself and wonder what will happen if I dare to reveal something of my internal process. If I own up to feeling frightened, will I alienate her? Will she think less of me? I feel on a precarious edge. I take the risk and begin to talk with her about what I am experiencing and share my curiosity about what is happening between us. As we begin to talk and explore, my sense of tension and unease lessens as she gradually allows herself to remember an incident in her own life from many, many years ago that she has deeply buried. She realizes that her disconnection from her client is in some way a defence against the impact of her own experience. In an attempt to think about and understand this process that is occurring between us, I go to the idea that my experience is a countertransference phenomena, perhaps a projective identification, and that I experience the feelings that she, in that moment, is unable to allow herself to feel. As we connect to each other and explore and think, my supervisee can reconnect to herself and to her client, and what has been frozen and hidden from view becomes available. This, in turn, is a parallel to what may be happening in her relationship with her client. The numbness and inability to allow the impact of the experience produces a deadness in the relationship. As our encounter becomes alive again, so possibilities emerge for the therapeutic work".

The intersubjective process described above takes us into the realm of the teach/treat boundary.

The teach/treat boundary

Before we turned our minds and practice to discovering what a relational TA supervision might involve for us, and embracing it, we struggled with what we regarded then as a curious phenomenon, which, sad to say, we pathologized. Supervisees would at times struggle to maintain their Adult (Berne, 1961), and in response, our supervision sometimes turned into mini therapy sessions. Similarly, we had personal experience of this as members of a long-standing supervision group where we learned our craft. Early on in this group, times without number, we observed each other and our struggle with emerging emotions as we brought our work to the group and were observed by our colleagues; we would then discuss and sometimes dissect the work in terms of Clarkson's checklist: a group supervision model very familiar to the TA community. It would not be too much of an exaggeration to call the emotions, that sometimes emerged when we were doing supervision, tumultuous and disturbing. The manner in which we dealt with these moments and emotional experiences in supervision could be shaming at worst and unsatisfactory at best.

It was as if these wonderful, albeit tortuous processes, major unconscious or pre-conscious communications, opportunities to understand something of the process, presented themselves and, unattended to, marched by us like a silent retreating army. Despite originally discounting these communications, by either pathologizing them or trying to fit them into a model, to do so was like "pushing against a river"; always, in our experience, authentic truths of the heart cannot be denied. Gradually we learned, along with many others who were becoming of a relational mind, to read these emotions differently. We now saw them not as our shameful inability to keep "in" Adult or to avoid Script (Berne, 1961), but as the potential embodiment and emotional revelation of the very stuff of the supervisees and clients struggle, the key issue, if you will, right there in the room between supervisor and supervisee. Acknowledging, making space and meaning of, and transforming these emerging relational dynamics is what we mean by working at the teach/treat boundary—that fluid edge between learning and personal work.

Sometimes of course the emergence of feelings and emotions is indeed our own and nothing to do with the work. There is a danger of viewing everything of an emotional nature that occurs during a supervision session as a co-created enactment. Sometimes a cigar is indeed just a cigar, as Freud is reputed to have said.

What may be uncovered in working at the teach/treat boundary is what might previously be understood as a cultural double contamination (Berne, 1961) concerning the nature of strong emotions. If we understand

and believe strong feelings and emotions solely as regressions into Child or Parent, and regard our clients as pseudo-children rather than as adults, who are able to manage strong emotions between us and understand them in the service of the work, then it follows, does it not, that when these moments happen, our delusion may consequently be that they belong in the therapy room and have no place in a thinking adult approach to supervision? To our minds this is a facing backward rather than a reaching forward for an understanding of those strong feelings.

Knowing the difference between these two views of strong emotion is the art of an adult-to-adult relational supervision. In one, they are relegated to the realm of Script or Child and the supervisor is always in an authoritative position, having the answers or superior expertise. In the other, there is a mutual, if asymmetrical, exploration of the dynamics between those in the room. The transformational potential of this process is exciting in that it is rather reminiscent of Jessica Benjamin's (2002) ideas of the therapist rather than the client being the one that does the changing. For example, it is not unusual for us to have worked on an issue in supervision about a dynamic that is occurring with a client only to find that, at the very next session, the client has either changed or emerged from a stuck place without a word having passed between us about it.

Reflecting together on the meaning and implications of emotions that are felt in response to the work is what distinguishes this type of supervision from therapy. In our view, it is this reflecting process and the emphasis on mutuality that may go some way to settling the controversy within psychotherapy circles, including TA, about whether it is an ethical or clinical mistake to do what is called therapy in supervision. It is not teach or treat, but it is both teach and treat. The therapy, if therapy it be, turns out to be the therapy of some aspects of a relationship about a relationship about other relationships rather than an individual.

Conclusion

In ending, we return to Monet's paintings as a metaphor for working in this way with supervisees. There is discipline and vigour. There is structure and a frame. But at the centre of things there is a space that allows for the emergence of what has been hitherto unknown. This creative space is for us the heart of relational work and we think it born out of the intersubjective processes we have been addressing.

CHAPTER TWENTY SEVEN

Exploring the relational meaning of formula G in supervision and self-supervision

Jill Hunt

In this article, I will show how I use formula G (Berne, 1972) to make sense of a re-enactment between therapist and client. I demonstrate this by describing how I have used it in my own practice as a psychotherapist and also as a supervisor, helping therapists to uncover the unknown elements of their countertransference.

Formula G was Berne's final description of a game. He described it as a sequence and stated: "Whatever fits this formula is a game, whatever does not fit it is not a game" (p. 24).

A criticism of formula G has been that it is a formulaic way of approaching and understanding games. I will show, however, how it can be used creatively, as a way of understanding the subjective experiencing of the therapist and the possible implications for the inter-subjective experiencing, between therapist and client.

In her article, "The Ongoing and Bilateral Nature of Games", Hine (1990, p. 28) suggests that "we are giving lip service to Berne's (1964) definition 'it takes two to play a game', as long as we continue to use this model to analyze only one of the participant's motivations". She describes an ongoing interweaving of two people's games, each step of the formula G representing a transferential engagement in the interaction. She states, "Each party to a game is playing his or her version,

287

which is complementary to the version played by other participants" (p. 29). In other words I attempt to get my longing or unmet need met, while you attempt to get yours.

I propose that Hine's development of the formula G theory offers a powerful tool in therapeutic work, a way of highlighting the here and now, relational dynamics of the therapist and client dyad, particularly in terms of the countertransference of the therapist and what this might mean with regard to the transferences impacting on the therapy.

I focus particularly on the con and gimmick, as I see these as describing key aspects of the relationship, particularly the longings/unmet needs of both members of the dyad. The con is the unconscious intent to engage the other in some way, in the participation of meeting desires; the gimmick is the subjective vulnerability of that other. Another way to describe this may be to see the con of the therapist as the therapist's pro-active countertransference (Clarkson, 1992), or, as Martha Stark (1999) says, "a story about the therapist's unresolved past" (p. 57), and the gimmick as the therapist's reactive countertransference (Clarkson, 1992). In my experience, careful exploration reveals that each person is usually looking for something remarkably similar, which is why the therapist responds strongly to the con (transference) of the client.

In supervision, I invite the therapist who feels in the grip of a game to draw two formula G equations—one under the other, as below (see Figure 15):

Client: Con + Gimmick = Response → Switch → Cross up → Pay off
Therapist: Con + Gimmick = Response → Switch → Cross up → Pay off

Figure 15. Formula G (Berne, 1972).

They then identify what they know of their countertransference, which I explore with them using questions to elicit information such as:

- How did you feel?
- What did you want to do?
- How do/did you want your client to see you?
- What do you know about this for yourself?

Example: A supervisee brought her work with a male client in his 40s whom she experienced as impenetrable, as if made of steel.

She felt unable to have an impact upon him. He had said that people saw him as a "smart aleck". He had no friends and although married, had problems in his relationship. I encouraged my supervisee to become deeply in touch with her response to her client. She realized that she felt competitive for the "smart" position and persecutory towards the client. This was her gimmick; she competed with "smart" people for the position of being the smartest. I encouraged her to consider what she knew about this for herself and she realized that being smart was the way she obtained attention from her father. She also realized that it left her feeling lonely, as her peers did not respond well, and that she was longing for friends. Her unknown con was her desire for the client to like her and see her as a friend.

I wonder whether a game occurs when the therapist is unable to contain their response to their client, for example, overwhelming sadness, fear, or strong erotic feelings.

If a game continues unchecked, the switch occurs. Indeed, as Berne (1972, p. 24) makes clear, this is the defining feature of a game. However, the nature of the switch and the reason for it are subtle. It may represent the breakdown of an unspoken promise between the two people, much that both may have wished it to be otherwise. In the therapist's desire to offer something different to the client they may unwittingly have given the client a message that they can do something *for* them. Therefore, interestingly, a switch may also happen when the therapist has the humility to acknowledge their part in the dynamic and withdraws engagement from the symbiosis (Schiff et al., 1975).

I believe that the therapist's countertransference is both something of their own experience and an embodiment of something that is happening between therapist and client. In other words, the therapist's response reveals something of their self, the client's self,and the relationship. The therapist brings their self to the encounter with the client, as the client brings their self to the encounter with the therapist. When there is a game dynamic—emerging either as enactment or as being stuck a careful analysis of the countertransference will reveal important information about the therapist's script and that of the client's script.

Example: Another supervisee was closing her practice to move house and begin a new phase of her life. She was concerned that her client was not talking with her about the forthcoming ending. My supervisee was waiting for the client to initiate the conversation. She had not brought it up as she considered her client to be too fragile, not ready to face what was happening. I invited my supervisee to consider what this situation meant for her. She realized that she could not bear what she was doing to her clients, that she was not behaving in her usual way of being the person who looks after and does what others want, she was making a "selfish" decision and choosing to pay attention to herself. We identified her con as a need for her not to appear "bad" and selfish, to be "good" and helpful, her gimmick her own vulnerability in doing something that someone else did not want her to do and the possible emotional responses of her client.

My supervisee said, "I have to face my own daemon and accept what I am doing to my client."

Berne (1972) states, "A con only works if there is a weakness it can hook into, a handle or gimmick in the respondent, such as fear, greed, sentimentality, or irritability" (p. 23). I see the sequence in Berne's formula G diagram as a way of separating out the various elements of the dynamic, in order for the contribution of each to be understood. Thus, the therapist is able to identify their gimmick if they are caught by the client's con. The starting point is: what is it in the person of therapist that is evoked? And, what is more, what is the therapist's con in relation to their client?

Gradually, the supervisee is able to become skilled at self-analysis, reflecting into their own experience the questions: what's my con, what's my gimmick, how does this "catch" me? This reflective attitude becomes a form of self-supervision.

Example: Self-supervision. My client arrived and rang my doorbell. I opened the door expectantly, and saw someone I was not expecting. I was surprised and must have shown it on my face. My client moved back away from the door. Her look changed, and she said to me "You were not expecting me," and turned as if to leave. Fortunately my diary was in my hand, and I saw that the client I usually saw at this time had cancelled and the client standing in front of me had rearranged.

I felt terrible. This was the client I would most wish not to have forgotten. As well as a terrible history full of abandonment, her previous therapist had forgotten to let her know that she had left her place of work. I asked her to come in. In my consulting room, I apologized, having realized that this moment had been quite devastating for my client. She stated that she was considering leaving and not returning. I told her that I wished that it had not happened and that I would be willing to look at the meaning in the situation; she agreed to stay, as she was relieved that I had accepted my contribution to her distress. The question I continued to grapple with was, why did I feel so awful, as the session continued? I began to realize I had been attempting to be the antithesis of the therapist who forgets her client, to prove that I was the good therapist, that I would not abandon her. I had now to bear being a therapist who had abandoned her client, for that was certainly her experience in that moment. My con had been my need to be seen as caring, and my gimmick (my subjective vulnerability) was my need to be seen as the good therapist, perhaps even to the extent of protecting my professional reputation. I had not thought well of the therapist who had left and not let her client know. (I am aware that there are many reasons why this might happen and possibly if I knew the circumstances I would feel different.)

We spoke in depth about what this meant for her and how she had been abandoned in numerous and awful ways in her life.

Conclusion

Far from being formulaic, I consider formula G to offer a visual and technical representation, which provides a method of separation of the aspects of the transferential dynamics between therapist and client. The therapist is able to develop their knowledge of themselves and their desires—their subjectivity—to increase their understanding of what happens between them and their client—the intersubjective. Through this, they may come to know something more of their client(s).

CHAPTER TWENTY EIGHT

Relational supervision

Keith Chinnock

Introduction

In this chapter, I will consider the supervisory process and relationship from a contemporary relational perspective where, alongside the usual tasks of supervision, what is central to the supervisor's attitude is a curiosity and engagement with the relational vicissitudes of the supervisory dyad.

Contracting

The use of contracting (Berne, 1966) has been a cornerstone of a transactional analysis approach since Berne developed his innovative theory and psychotherapeutic methods. There is also strong evidence (e.g., Bordin, 1994) that supports the use of contracts in creating effective working alliances and successful therapeutic outcomes. If we accept the same as true of the supervisory relationship, as discussed by Proctor (2006), then the use of contracts in supervision can serve to support, enhance, and facilitate effective supervision.

Sills (2006, and in this volume) offers a contracting matrix, which describes four types of therapeutic contract that can be negotiated and re-negotiated in a way that allows flexibility and fluidity as the work unfolds. I have adapted and developed this for the supervisory context (see Figure 16 below). This differs from Sills's original model in that the emphasis in the horizontal axis is on the approach or attitude the supervisor takes with the supervisee. It represents, in the form of a continuum, what Stark (1999) has described as a movement between a one-, a one-and-a-half-, and a two-person psychology. At one end of the continuum is facilitating the supervisee's thinking, understanding, emotional processing, or insight within the Clarifying and Exploratory contract: a one-person psychology. At the other end is a relational engagement with the supervisee in the Practice Based and Relational Field contracts, representing Stark's two-person psychology. Put simply, this axis represents the amount of himself or herself that the supervisor brings in to the work. This leaves the one-and-a-half-person approach in the centre of the horizontal continuum, and I suggest that this be viewed as the relationship alliance between supervisor and supervisee where the supervisee and client dyad is held and supported by the supervisor's containing (Bion, 1959) function.

Working within a two-person approach takes the supervisory dyad into what is referred to as the teach/treat boundary. This is an area of contention within different supervisory models, where it is often argued that focusing on the supervisee's/therapist's personal issues oversteps a line between supervision and therapy. By shading this area in the matrix, I acknowledge the importance of containment and respect for the supervisee's personal therapeutic privacy, whether working within the more traditional (one-person) or relational (two-person) approaches.

The four types of contract

I shall briefly outline the main focus of these four types of contract, for a fuller discussion and explanation (see Chinnock, in press).

Practice Based—Usually this is a clear outcome-based contract where the supervisee recognizes the need for information or guidance from the supervisor. Here, the supervisor discloses something of herself, often in the form of advice or suggestions. Personal experiences (disclosures) are sometimes shared to support understanding and serve to normalize or contain the supervisee's anxieties.

Clarifying—The supervisee is often seeking some guidance: for example, an understanding of the key issues (Clarkson, 1992), an

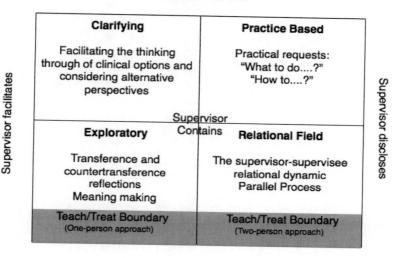

"Hard", observable,
outcome-focussed

Clarifying Facilitating the thinking through of clinical options and considering alternative perspectives	**Practice Based** Practical requests: "What to do....?" "How to....?"
Exploratory Transference and countertransference reflections Meaning making	**Relational Field** The supervisor-supervisee relational dynamic Parallel Process
Teach/Treat Boundary (One-person approach)	**Teach/Treat Boundary** (Two-person approach)

Supervisor
Contains

Supervisor facilitates

Supervisor discloses

"Soft", subjective
emergent, process orientated

Figure 16. Supervision contract matrix. (Adapted from Sills, 2006)

exploration of options for treatment direction, or a consideration of different types of empathic intervention (see the revisioning of Berne's therapeutic operations (1966) by Hargaden & Sills, 2002) to support deconfusion. The supervisor's task is to facilitate the supervisee's thinking and consideration of options.

Exploratory—This contract offers space to explore transference and countertransference experience including sensations, thoughts, dreams, and images. This is the area where the unconscious aspects of the client or client-supervisee relationship emerge and meanings are made. When addressing the teach/treat boundary from within an Exploratory contract the supervisee's issues are seen as located inside her and the supervisor acts as a facilitator who helps to identify the supervisee's personal difficulties, including pro-active countertransference (Clarkson, 1992) and transference issues.

Relational Field—This area represents working with the "overlapping dynamics of patient, supervisee and supervisor" (Driver, in Henderson, 2009, p. 176), and in particular with the supervisee's, and the supervisor's, own unconscious script (Berne, 1961) processes and how they may be facilitating or hindering the therapeutic work. Within the Relational Field, we are more concerned with bi-directional processes, where the supervisory pair maintain a curiosity about the relational processes between them that can act as supporting the supervisee in recognizing their "deaf, dumb and blind spots" (Ekstein, 1969). This I view as a relational approach to the teach-treat boundary where two persons' subjectivities are involved. I consider that this approach enhances the supervisee's ability to work at relational depth and can increase their capacity to hold or contain their client. In doing so, I would go so far as to suggest that this also has the potential to reduce the possibility of harm to the client (Clarkson, 1992).

Relational field diagram

To support me in this relational supervisory approach, I use the analytic model of the Triangle of Insight originally developed by Menninger (1958), and amalgamate this with Jacob's (1988) more simplified version (see Figure 17). It shows with elegant simplicity the link between past relationships and present ones—both in and out of the consulting room. It recognizes three distinct poles or aspects of a person's experience, the Analytic, the Reality and the Childhood situations, and in addition includes dream material.

Past Back Then (Childhood Situation)—The early history and ego-relational unit (Little, 2004) configuration of each person.

Present Out There (Reality Situation)—The current difficulties, experiences, and relationship dynamics in the person's life.

Present In Here (Analytic Situation)—Where the intrapsychic becomes interpersonal; a dynamic interplay of the here and now conscious, unconscious, and nonconscious (Cornell, 2008) experiences between both participants in the relational encounter: The Relational Field.

Dream Connections—The unconscious representation and expression of events, experiences, and the attendant affect drawn from our waking hours, and their potential connections with our historical or childhood experiences, which are then symbolized in the dream material.

The supervisor-supervisee relational field diagram

I have adapted the ideas in Figure 17 further by recognizing that there are two triangles at play in any relationship. I link the two triangles

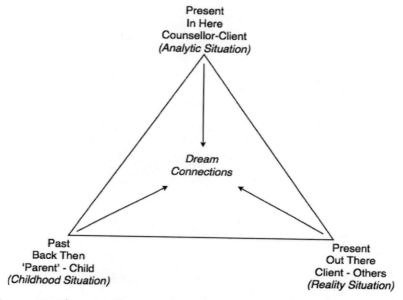

Figure 17. The triangle of insight. (Jacobs, 1988 with additions from Menninger's original (*in italics*) 1958)

together and rotate them to represent the relationship between supervisor and supervisee (see Figure 17). Of course, this model can also be applied to the relationship between therapist and client.

The relational field

The Relational Field represents the mutuality and bi-directional nature of the relationship between supervisor and supervisee or supervisee/ therapist and client. Within this, what becomes figural is the exploring of the relationship between supervisee and supervisor including the willingness to engage with the sharing and exploration of dream material. This also allows space for a modelling of the process of supervision (Clarkson, 1992), and an acknowledgement of the supervisory relationship as being central to influencing the development of the supervisee; it is "... second only to the therapist's own analytic relationship in potentiating the supervisee's development as an analytically informed clinician" (Frawley-O'Dea & Sarnat, 2001, p. 70).

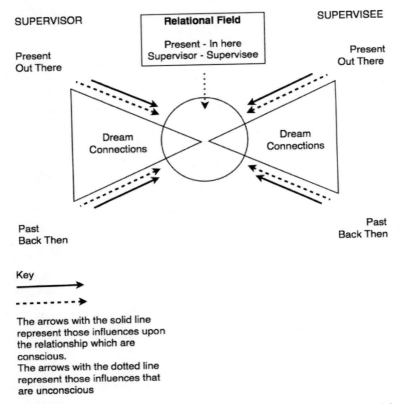

Figure 18. Supervisor-supervisee relational field diagram. (Adapted from the triangle of insight diagram from Jacobs, 1988, with original material from Menninger, 1958)

Dream connections

I propose three ways that dreams from either the supervisee or supervisor can be understood and expand on them in my second client example. The three ways are:

Client Communication—dreams may represent an unconscious communication from the client: a form of projective identification (Klein, 1975/1988).

Personal Issue—dreams may bring an unresolved issue from the supervisee's (or supervisor's) past or present into consciousness that needs resolution or working through.

Relationship Alliance—dreams that include the supervisor or supervisee, or an aspect of the relationship in symbolic form, may reflect something from the therapeutic or supervisee-supervisor relationship that is seeking expression or needing to be attended to and that is pressing at the boundary of consciousness.

Case example one

In the first session of a newly formed supervision group, Sally had become distressed about her work, trying to offer empathy to a challenging client. Ajani suddenly and brusquely said: "Why do we need to have empathy?" There was a palpable feeling in the room of discomfort and disquiet, and I noticed my internal response of wanting to criticize him. I gathered myself, saying: "I'm curious about your question and wonder what your thoughts were?" Ajani just sat back and said he had heard the question asked in another supervision group and thought he would ask it here. His body language communicated the sense that he was not willing to say anything further. I decided to continue to ask him about his question and after some coaxing Ajani responded by acknowledging that he was seeing how I would respond to him.

It seemed that Ajani had initiated the opening con (Berne, 1972) in a game (Berne, 1964), an early attempt at storming (Tuckman, 1965): testing out the authority of the leadership role. Having contained a threat to the major internal boundary (Berne, 1966), the rest of the session continued without incident. I wondered about the issues of difference as Ajani was the only African in a group of four white British people, three of whom were women. In particular, the directness of Ajani's comment may have been culturally syntonic or part of a personal style. His comment had seemed to set himself apart from the others in the group and myself. I needed to be mindful of this.

The supervision then settled down into a norming stage (Tuckman, 1965). However, there were further incidents that led to me having to reflect more deeply about how to work with Ajani and the group. In the first, Ajani and I agreed a Practice Based contract about how to work with Zack, a seven-year-old boy. Ajani described Zack as very angry and uncontained; he was "fed up with him" and was thinking about leaving the placement. The other group members began to intervene, expressing their concerns for Zack and telling Ajani that he couldn't leave the work in the middle.

I stepped in at this point and asked the group to reflect on their feelings. This marked a shift to an Exploratory contract focusing on the intersubjective Relational Field (Therapist-Client Relational Field Diagram) and using the members' subjectivities, drawing upon the multiplicity of meanings from their differing processes. I wanted to move the group from intervening to reflection on their own counter-transference. My thinking was that Ajani was experiencing a powerful countertransference or projective identification (Klein, 1975/1988; Ogden, 1982/1992) in relation to his young client.

This creation of space for Ajani to listen to the group members' internal process helped him to reflect on his feelings and to think about how he was experiencing a pressure to repeat Zack's history of abandonment. The theoretical explanation seemed to support Ajani's thinking and highlighted that his learning edge seemed to be about the need to develop the capacity to think about and reflect on his countertransference.

In a later session Ajani began by describing a client with a small physical deformity that troubled her. He reported having no feelings of empathy, not understanding why she had come to therapy and how he had said to her at the end of the session: "If you decide that you don't need counselling then you don't need to come back next week." I felt a deep sense of alarm and was also aware of the strong invitation to shame Ajani. As before, he sat back in his chair, arms folded, and my attempts to invite him to reflect were met with: "I don't know."

I wondered if this was another opening con or if Ajani really did lack a capacity for empathy. I asked Ajani if it would be useful for him to hear how the other group members imagined the client may have felt (an attempt to use an Exploratory contract to help develop a reflective capacity among the group and in Ajani). Ajani listened to their responses and replied again that he didn't see what the problem was. I responded in quite an immediate and instinctive way saying: "You don't think your client would have felt rejected?" Ajani reacted quite angrily to my parental response, and I realized we were in the middle of a game.

I was thankful for the tea break. When we returned I spoke with Ajani about how I had reflected on my own feelings. I owned that I had indeed contacted a critical part of myself (my own Past-Back-Then surfacing in the relationship), and that I was curious about this, as it was unusual for me. I wondered if we could explore further what had happened between us (Relational Field contract and two-person teach/ treat boundary) and what this might mean for him and me, and for him and his client—especially were she to return. This led to a fruitful discussion about the difficulties he had experienced with not feeling anything for her. Ajani was also able to let me know that he hadn't felt that I had contained him with his concerns and we processed his hurt and my sadness about this.

Following this session I reflected on my concerns for Ajani and his clients. I explored and processed some of my reticence about speaking directly to him due to my concerns about the cultural differences between us, issues of power and white-black oppression, and my fear of my feedback being seen purely as criticism within a cultural, perhaps racist dimension. The owning to myself of these fears freed me to be more direct with Ajani, to move to "functional helping" (Batts, cited in Henderson, 2009, p. 76); to own my authority (Henderson, 2009, p. 123).

In the next session I described what I saw as Ajani's process, how he would say something quite provocative and then sit back. I had a very potent and curious image, that I now understand as an unconscious communication from Ajani, that I chose to share with him. I commented on how at times in supervision it was as though he brought a bomb into the room and sat back to watch the resulting chaos. Ajani then told us that a previous job, in security settings, was to literally bring explosives into buildings to test the security systems. This disclosure of Ajani's I understood as a probable link to his internal object world, perhaps at the level of protocol (Berne, 1972). I recognized we were exploring issues relating to the one-person teach/treat boundary and his Present-Out-There and Past-Back-Then experiences.

This continued when, in relation to a client who was ending, Ajani described wanting to understand why the ending process of therapy was so important. I explored with him his experiences of endings and he described being sent by his parents from one West African state to another as a child to attend boarding school, that he "just had to get on with it", that there was not space for feelings. To Ajani this was the cultural norm as many people he knew had similar experiences. Loss was just part of life and had to be "got on with". When we explored Ajani's feelings towards his own son and how he would feel towards him if there were a similar situation, he was able to recognize his emotional connections and attachment. This marked a significant turning point as Ajani was able to recognize that his early experience was having an impact on his capacity to be with his clients. He continued to work with Zack and other clients with more empathy, sensitivity, and containment.

Case example two

A peer supervision group, of which I am a member, recently had to change its venue for meeting. Whilst on the social level (Berne, 1961) all members were in Adult agreement to this change, a number of unconscious feelings and processes began to emerge that had not been fully considered or accounted for and became the subject and process for the group's attention. These were revealed in a dream from the member I call Tamara, who lived furthest from the new venue.

Tamara is trying to get to the supervision group; she keeps losing her way; no-one is answering their door. Eventually she gets in. I and the other members of the supervision group are busy talking to each other and she cannot get to us. I have a hair-band around my head with fruit attached to it. Tamara described a feeling of exclusion in the dream.

As Tamara told the dream, she was able to connect to a recent experience of feeling excluded at a meeting, which also resonated somewhat with her Past-Back-Then experiences as a child, of sometimes not being included or taken seriously by others.

The group, although offering support for her experience in the interview, became caught up in the comic image of me with a hair-band on my head! This image seemed to become the main aspect that we were engaging with, and after a while I began to feel some discomfort about this. I suggested to Tamara and the group that while the image was funny, we seemed to have lost the more serious themes of exclusion, that perhaps were reflecting something about her experience at the meeting, but also about our change of venue. I wondered about other feelings relating to who was included/excluded and the meanings this may have for us (the Present-In-Here). The other members of the group resonated with this, and we began a reflective process to explore our less conscious feelings about the change.

Tamara was able to recognize how the "hair-band image" in the dream reflected her own tendency to make light of her own feelings and undermine her very real capabilities and competence. The focus on exploring what meaning the dream might have for us as a group brought up Oedipal issues of participant and observer relationships

(Britten, in Britten et al., 1989); who was in and who was out, who was special, and who was not. The themes of sibling rivalry (Mitchell, 2003), of envy, competitiveness, and ambivalence around involvement in professional activities, were explored. Each of us was able to identify with feeling both included in the group and excluded. One member spoke of the difference between intention and impact: in that it seemed that none of us had any conscious intention to exclude but the impact was of a feeling of being forgotten and excluded. We all became more aware of how painful that feeling can be. Our understanding, through experience, of exploring the multiplicity of meanings and in being willing to explore our own subjectivities with one another was both deeply intimate, moving, and theoretically rich. There was certainly a sense of us individually and collectively expanding our conscious, Adult selves, which helped us develop a greater understanding of how these themes are constantly present in our clinical work and in our own supervision groups.

Conclusion

What I hope to have conveyed in this chapter is a sense of how a relational approach to supervision involves the supervisor in a constant curiosity, confrontation, and engagement with their own internal process and subjectivity, and a capacity to use this to surface emergent themes, processes, and relational dynamics from the Supervisor-Supervisee and Supervisee/Therapist-Client dyads. It also involves facilitating the development of these same capacities in the supervisee.

CHAPTER TWENTY NINE

Research and relational psychotherapy

Biljana van Rijn

Introduction and basic principles

Research is not often associated with relational psychotherapy. The gap between psychotherapy research and practice separates the two disciplines and has consequences for both. Although psychotherapists use clinical supervision to reflect on their practice, research methodologies contain strategies which can also deepen insight and develop practice. Overt evaluation of practice is also increasingly important as a way of evidencing effectiveness. Relational methodologies in psychotherapy research and the relevance of quantitative findings have a potential to bridge the research/practice gap and develop both clinical practice and its mainstream credibility.

The aim of this chapter is to show that all research has the potential to be relational and useful for clinical practice. I will give a broad overview of research methodologies, their principles and design, and invite reflection on how they can be used in relational practice.

Every research project is based on philosophical concepts about the nature of reality (ontology), and the search to know it (epistemology). The methodology that we are drawn to in relation to this is influenced to a large extent by our philosophy, and whether we believe that reality is objective and constant or ever changing, being based on a co-creation between the individual, their context, and relationships.

There are two broad and often polarized approaches to research. One is based on positivist science related to quantitative methodologies and the other on post-modern philosophical principles and qualitative methodologies. A recent development of mixed methodologies uses both, in order to gain multiple views of a phenomenon. Mixed methodologies move beyond the polarities of quantitative versus qualitative debate and use both with post-modern sensibilities.

Different methodologies use different standards to determine what constitutes valid knowledge, based on their underlying philosophy. A question of validity refers to truthfulness. Are the findings really about what they appear to be about? Are they true?

Another standard relevant to different methodologies is generalizability of the findings. Each methodology has limitations in terms of both truth and generalizability, and these limitations need to be made overt.

Quantitative methodologies

Quantitative methodologies have had a major role in the development of Western science. The aim of quantitative methodology is to establish knowledge that can be generalized to wider populations. The research design aims to answer questions that can give insight into the broader trends and efficacy of treatments. The outcomes are statistically analysed and tend to be conducted on large samples. This means that research projects are meticulously designed so that they can be replicated by other researchers, and their conclusions can be independently confirmed. Quantitative methodologies can be broadly described as surveys of variations of the experimental design.

A survey design gives a numerical description of trends by examining a sample of the population. For example: how satisfied are the clients receiving TA in comparison to other treatments (Novey, 2006)?

An experimental design tests the impact of an intervention on the outcome by controlling for all other factors that might influence the outcome. Variations of experimental designs are Quasi Experimental and Correlational Studies.

These are some examples of research questions that might be tested by an experiment:

- Is psychotherapy effective?
- What is the best way to treat depression?
- How many sessions are optimal for treatment?

It has been possible to compare different research studies by using the statistical methods of meta-analysis (Lambert & Bergin, 1994; Luborsky, Singer & Luborsky, 1975; Wampold, 2001). Meta-analytic studies in psychotherapy have given us insight into the so called "common factors in psychotherapy", which stress the importance of the therapeutic encounter and the comparative efficacy of theoretical approaches.

In 1994, the review of studies into the effectiveness of psychotherapy by Lambert and Bergin summarized that:

- Psychotherapy helps clients to develop coping strategies and recover from their symptoms. The effects of psychotherapy are lasting and surpass placebo.
- There is little consistent evidence for the clinical superiority of one therapy over another.
- Interpersonal and affective factors within psychotherapy are relevant in achieving successful outcomes. Lambert and Barley (2002), in their review of research, suggested that a non-blaming attitude, an accepting therapeutic stance, and a strong therapeutic alliance were all associated with successful outcomes.
- The therapist's ability to relate is a significant factor in overall effectiveness, and there are wide variations in effectiveness between individuals. Lambert and Bergin (1994) suggest that training programmes should emphasize the development of therapists as individuals in order to increase their effectiveness. Further research emphasizes the importance of therapists' responsiveness to clients and their own attachment styles (Meyer & Pilkonis, 2002; Mohr, Gelso & Hill, 2005).

The outcomes of these studies, although conducted using "non-relational" methodologies (in other words, based on the philosophy of objective reality and a neutral researcher/observer), give a research base which emphasizes the quality of the therapeutic relationship. Both generalizability and validity of quantitative research such as this can help to inform practitioners about therapeutic strategies which are effective, and those that might not be. For example, a therapist using the term "game" might be perceived by a client as blaming. Could there be another way they could use this theory to engage, rather than alienate the client? Allen and Allen (1997) suggest a constructivist approach, where theory is used to create a dialogue and develop a new narrative through the therapeutic process.

Qualitative methodologies

In designing qualitative research projects, researchers accept the existence of multiple realities (Creswell, 2009). Their aim is to discover, understand the meaning, and give voice to different individual realities, an aim which is wholly in keeping with relational principles and the practice of psychotherapy. The concept of validity is defined in terms of the trustworthiness, credibility, and authenticity of the research and the researcher. Sometimes this is done by having an additional researcher to check the interpretations, or by developing rich layered narratives using transparent and credible strategies, which could in principle be checked and repeated by others. The relationship between the researcher and the participants is transparent and collaborative.

Creswell (2009) gives the following characteristics of qualitative research, which have been expanded to include clinical examples:

Natural setting. In order to understand the subject's reality, researchers aim to get as close to the participants as possible. The studies are normally conducted in the "field" (such as a therapy room), rather than the laboratory setting.

Researcher as a key instrument. This places a particular emphasis on the researcher to account for their subjectivity, and to develop trustworthiness. A researcher needs to demonstrate reflexivity and transparency and have procedures to check their understanding. In psychotherapy, this may mean using supervision, personal psychotherapy, or a confidential peer group, to understand, for example, the therapists' part in a game process (Hine, 1990).

Multiple sources of data. Qualitative researchers usually use multiple data sources. These could be interview transcripts, diaries, discussion groups. For example, Etherington (2000) used her own treatment diaries, notes, and a journal, as well as notes, diaries, and artwork provided by clients, to create a multilayered narrative of her work with men who were sexually abused.

Inductive data analysis. Qualitative researchers build their understanding in layers, starting from the content of the transcripts, rather than an abstract (theoretical) concept. This practice in TA psychotherapy could involve developing layers of interpretation, based on what happened in each transaction, before arriving at the theoretical categories such as ego states (Berne, 1966).

Participants' meanings. Need to be a part of the analysis, and this involves a consideration of ethical principles, such as beneficence and non-maleficence (Bond, 2004). Where a researcher has used transcripts, the participant (client) would normally give their view on them before the analysis is completed. In clinical practice this could involve a staged consent, checking agreement at each stage of research and publication.

Emergent design. The full design of the research project is not determined at the outset but develops through the process of research. For example, a therapist may have a question about developing her work with male clients. She may start by reading the literature, using it to introduce gradual changes to her practice and evaluate the impact of each change before proceeding further.

Theoretical lens. Qualitative researchers often use a theoretical lens or a rationale to view their study. Theoretical concepts need to be overtly defined in qualitative studies. For example, if a therapist is using a concept such as ego states (Berne, 1961), it is important to make this overt and clarify the definition used.

Interpretative. Interpretations made in qualitative studies cannot be separated or made separately from the researcher's background, subjectivity, and experiences. They need, therefore, to be identified, accounted for and made transparent.

Holistic. Qualitative researchers try to develop a complex picture of the problem, reporting on and from multiple perspectives, identifying a number of factors, and sketching the larger picture which emerges. For example, in the reflective inquiries described by Fowlie elsewhere in this book, practitioners use reflection in supervision, their own psychotherapy, and the cultural context of their practice, as well as detailed reflection of what happened within the session, in order to develop an in-depth understanding of their research question. In a supervision group, for example, each group member could listen to a session recording or a presentation and offer their own understanding of the process, to help the therapist develop their analysis.

There are several qualitative methodologies. Each has its own aims and methods, and each is suitable for different types of research questions. They include ethnography, grounded theory, qualitative case studies, phenomenological inquiries, etc. All of these methodologies adhere to the characteristics outlined above.

Mixed methods

A mixed method approach to research has gained popularity in recent years. Like qualitative research, it is based on post-positivist, social constructionist philosophy, and it aims to address the complexity of phenomena in the social sciences. Creswell (2009) suggests different types of mixed method approach.

Overall, by using mixed methods, the researcher seeks to expand on the findings discovered using one method of research, by employing another. For example, the findings from a quantitative analysis of a standardized questionnaire which identified clients' responses about the working alliance (Bordin, 1979) can be used to inquire into effective therapeutic processes.

Two of the examples of mixed methodologies are:

Action research (Reason & Bradbury, 2001) where a researcher engages in reflective cycles of observation, action, implementation, and reflection, and might use both quantitative and qualitative methods in different cycles of enquiry. For example, in the research project which evaluated a psychotherapy training design, researchers used focus groups with tutors and students for qualitative analysis of the training process and quantitative evaluation of students' clinical practice as one of the outcomes (Van Rijn et al., 2008). Each focus group was conducted after a training module by the researcher; feedback was given to tutors, who used it to evaluate and develop the next training module. This is an example of an action cycle in action.

In clinical practice action research could be used in different ways. The therapist might use it to reflect on a particular emerging theme, use supervision to analyse it and develop new strategies, apply them in the next session, and evaluate the outcomes. At the research clinic at Metanoia Institute, action research engages clients directly. They complete short standardized questionnaires (i.e., PHQ9, GAD 7, WAI) during the week between sessions. When they bring them back, questionnaires are used to reflect on the week and develop a contract for the next session. The therapist and the client also use the question-naires to jointly evaluate the impact of the work. In this way quantitative methods are used relationally to develop collaboration, empower clients, and bring the therapeutic relationship to the fore by opening it up for exploration.

The reflective enquiries described by Fowlie (in this book) show further how an action research methodology can be used to develop reflexivity within clinical practice.

Case study. McLeod (2010) presents different types of case study research, using mixed methods and multiple data sources, from standardized questionnaires to reflexive accounts. Case study research can be used to develop theories and evaluate practice.

Why is research important to relational practice?

Psychotherapists will already be familiar with many of the strategies described in this chapter and have the ability to use them systematically to incorporate different research methodologies and develop their work. The methods they use to do this will depend on several factors, including the settings in which they work, their aims in using research, the resources available to them, and their philosophical sensibilities.

Qualitative and mixed methodologies lend themselves more easily to relational practice, because of their shared philosophy and the fact that they are usually conducted on small samples. Qualitative research and relational practice are both interested in developing a shared, in-depth insight into the process of psychotherapy. Some of the methods, such as detailed reflection in supervision, the use of a two-person psychology, and the embracing of subjectivity are shared between the two practices. In addition, research methodologies contain a rigorous structure that calls psychotherapists to deepen their knowledge and increase their reflexivity and questioning. This particularly relates to the qualitative analysis of transcripts and the process of coding (i.e., identifying significant themes and their recurrence) in qualitative research.

Quantitative methods could also be used by a single practitioner, even when not conducting a larger scale research project. Standardized questionnaires are available (often free of charge) and can enable a therapist to engage in a different sort of dialogue with their client. Transparency and collaboration are principles that can inform how we use these instruments to add a layer of shared dialogue with a client. For example, using a CORE Outcome Measure (CORE Information Management Systems) even in long-term treatment could be another way for a client to communicate their experiences to the therapist as well as to evaluate practice.

CHAPTER THIRTY

Reflective inquiries

Heather Fowlie with Sarah Brown, Rachel Cook, Rob Hill, Judy Sleath, and Maja Zivkovic

Introduction

In the introduction of this book we elaborated principles of relational TA, each of the chapters exploring one aspect in depth of the theory and method in practice.

This chapter explores the implications of these principles for designing a training course. As head of department of TA training at the Metanoia Institute in London, I and the staff team faced the question: how can training support students not only to learn relational theory and method but to deepen their ability to work within it?

Following an in-depth research project looking at "developing effective psychotherapy training" (Van Rijn et al., 2008), we decided, in keeping with the findings, that one of the ways we could respond to this question was through the use of reflective inquires. We felt that these inquiries would provide practical and creative opportunities for students to develop their awareness and their reflective capacities and to realize their own solutions to the issues they were finding in their clinical work.

The ability to think critically, to reflect, to challenge one's stance, to stay with experiences, to be curious about processes as they unfold, to hold multiple meanings, to stay with uncertainty, to engage in collaborative exploration, and so on are all at the heart of what it means to work relationally. Taking part in a reflective inquiry not only has the advantage of developing the students' capacity to reflect on their practice but also can mirror, create, and familiarize the student with many of these relational processes. The following quote by Schon (1983) elaborates this:

> The practitioner allows himself to experience surprise, puzzlement, or confusion in a situation which he finds uncertain or unique. He reflects on the phenomenon before him, and on the prior understandings, which have been implicit in his behaviour. He carries out an experiment which serves to generate both a new understanding of the phenomenon and a change in the situation (p. 68).

Implicit in the relational principles, and in the processes that working in this way can produce, is a demand for the therapist to commit themselves to a depth of engagement that can at times be personally taxing. In particular, this translates into the therapist being able to recognize, contain, and effectively use their countertransference responses in service of the work. Here again we thought that, alongside their personal therapy, taking part in a reflective inquiry could help develop this capacity. The very act of reflecting so intimately on their work requires students to question and challenge their own stance and then cope with any personal changes that they encounter as part of this, as the following quote by Bager-Charleson (2010) suggests: "Managing change usually involves confronting a loss of self, or at least the loss of elements that made up parts of what we used to be in terms of attitudes, habits and/or deep-seated values about ourselves or others" (p. 14).

Acknowledging the many experiential as well as practical opportunities that taking part in a reflective inquiry provides, we believe that it is a powerful and pro-active way of encouraging and fostering relational abilities and sensibilities in students. Reflective inquiries have been a central part of the relational TA training programme since 2007 and are, as we see it, in keeping with Berne's words: "True knowledge is to know how to act rather than to know words" (1958, p. 28).

In this chapter, I will provide a brief explanation of the structure of a reflective inquiry, describe the stages involved in such a study, and explain how they are used in training. Following that are some examples of reflective inquiries undertaken by students from different stages in their training.

The reflective inquiry

The value and importance of self-reflection has long been emphasized by learning theorists as a central part of the learning process. Reflective observation, for example, is one of the stages of the Kolb (1984) learning cycle and Schon's (1983) seminal work, *The Reflective Practitioner*, has been hugely influential in developing the theory and practice of professional learning in the twentieth century.

Reflective inquiry comes under the broad umbrella of action research (Lewin, 1946)—a form of research that pursues both action and research at the same time. Following these principles, a reflective inquiry involves a planned and purposeful reflection on practice, with the purpose of discovering new or deeper understandings, which will effect change. As Bager-Charleson writes (2010, p. 143): "Reflective Learning involves moving from noticing a problem to transforming it into something that is of practical use".

Using a variation of the Kolb (1984) learning cycle, we teach the students a basic framework for their reflective inquiry, which involves four stages (see Figure 19):

Stage 1—OBSERVE—This involves students looking at their clinical practice and seeing what issues are challenging them, stimulating them, exciting them at the current time, and helping them to make these into a question that they can reflect upon.

We call the second year of training "Becoming an effective practitioner", and students at this stage are new both to this form of inquiry and to seeing clients. We recommend that they frame their inquiry within the theme of the year and generate a question around personal blocks that could limit their effectiveness. As a result, a typical question during this year might involve exploring how their tendency to rescue might affect their effectiveness. This helpfully narrows the field a little for the student, but also emphasizes the need for the psychotherapist's own therapy and encourages students to begin thinking about how they might use themselves in the work, a central concept in a two-person (Stark, 2000), relational therapy.

Third and fourth year students decide on their own questions. Interestingly, many continue with the same theme that originated in

1. OBSERVE

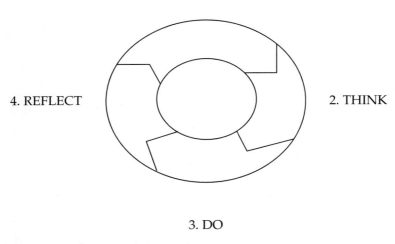

4. REFLECT   2. THINK

3. DO

Figure 19.   Reflective inquiry cycle.

their second year only at a deeper and more advanced level of cycling. For instance, the tendency to rescue inquiry leads the student to understand that they rescue when they anticipate conflict, which leads them to focus on the importance of rupture and repair in therapy, etc.

Stage 2—THINK—This involves the student in planning out their reflective inquiry, including incorporating the concept of validity. In recognition of the fact that action research does not necessarily lend itself to the forms of validity often used in quantitative research, Van Rijn (2010) states: "Validity in this context depends on the ability of the participant to be reflexive and transparent about their knowledge. We do not aim to find absolute truths but to engage in ongoing cycles of inquiry and change" (p. 106).

While we have not set these inquiries up as validated pieces of qualitative research, due mainly to the additional time demands this would place on the student, we do expect them to think about designing their inquiry in such a way that it involves some form of triangulation—that in the terms of relational psychotherapy they include a third in their investigations. Students usually do this through involving their supervisors and supervision group, and sometimes their therapist, in both planning out their inquiry and reflecting on their findings. For instance, in the example above, the student decides to explore her rescuing tendencies by taking tape recordings of her work to supervision and asking her supervision group to help her identify and look for patterns of when she moves into a rescue, etc.

Stage 3—DO—This involves the student in immersing themselves fully and actively in their reflective inquiry. Often, as a part of this process, they begin to make tentative connections and realizations about themselves and their chosen topic of inquiry, which lead them to modify or expand their original question in some way. The student may identify things that they want to do differently. For example, the student who is finding it hard to finish sessions on time resolves to end the session regardless of how they feel or what the client is doing, and see what happens.

Stage 4—REFLECT—This involves the student in reflecting on their experiences, and out of this experiential learning drawing conclusions or constructing a meaningful explanation or solution to what they have discovered. Additionally, this stage and also stage 2 may involve the student in critiquing the findings and opinions of previous theorists. To continue our example, in her later exploration, the therapist's discovery about her avoidance of conflict led her to investigate the literature (see for example, Guisolise, 1996) on the inevitability of therapist error in the important work of therapeutic repair.

"This is the stage of learning where the initial problem has become an asset, something to be incorporated as a valuable experience; almost like 'recycling' something that was previously useless. It can be compared to wisdom and deep insight" (Bager-Charleson, 2010, p. 149).

Students may recycle back and forth through the stages outlined above several times, deepening and learning anew as they discover and embrace new meanings.

Student examples

Space restriction does not allow us to reproduce the examples in full. They have had to be considerably shortened. However, they serve as a snapshot of how the process of articulating the inquiry deepens and enriches the student's learning.

Rob—2nd year student

Stage 1—Rob decided to consider whether his own emotional experiences arose out of an "intuitive connection with the other and their emotional process or whether they were merely his own response to the other".

"I was attracted to the choice of project because I was sceptical about my capacity (in fact anyone's capacity) to make this sort of connections reliably. I have a lot of 'scientific', 'positivist' thinking which is sceptical, of intuition in general and 'transpersonal' connections in particular—a sense overall that 'thinking is safer and more trustworthy than intuition'. At a deeper level, in my Child, however (it feels like P_1 and C_1), there are doubts about my ability to connect emotionally with others; a self-image of myself as someone who 'cannot make connections'. Perhaps also an uncertainty about whether my own feelings are reliable; a sense of 'Do I know what I feel?'"

Stage 2—Rob decided he would examine his question by reading relevant literature and "mentally logging" instances "in which I was able to assess my own internal emotional responses to others" and to check out with the other whether there was a connection.

Stage 3—He noted a few of the many experiences that he had and how he had checked them out with people when appropriate:

1. Feeling scared while a training group member talked about her frustration;
2. Feeling a sense of defiance when a training group member struggled to locate what he felt;
3. Feeling an absence of emotion while a training group member wept;
4. Feeling overwhelming sadness while a client recounted a story with a complete absence of emotion;
5. Feeling stuck as a client "rambled" disjointedly through a session; and
6. Feeling anger and irritation at a client's unreliability and self-absorption.

Stage 4—As I reflected, I became interested in why it was that my internal emotional response seemed to "match" the emotion of the other person in some situations and in others seemed to "counter-balance" it.

In other words, why was it that in example 2 above my feeling of defiance was "matching" the other person (who also felt defiance), whereas in example 6 my feeling of (Parental) irritation was counter-balancing the client's feeling of neediness.

Rob found Novellino's concepts of "conforming identification" and "complementary identification" (1984) useful as "they seemed to align with the matching and counter-balancing experiences that I refer to above. They matched Racker's (1957) concepts of concordant identification and complementary identification, and also Hargaden and Sills's (2002) discussion of different kinds of transference".

In hypothesizing about why one type of transference arises rather than the other, he felt that this could be influenced by the "client's level of congruence. Where the client was not congruently and fully 'inhabiting' their feelings—then I would almost be attempting to fill that space for them by 'supplying' the emotion that they were not fully congruent with or embracing. Conversely, if they were congruently in touch with their feelings (for example my client being in touch with his 'unboundaried neediness' in example 6 above) then that would leave me the space to experience my own reaction to that 'unboundaried neediness' (and feel irritation, etc.)."

As a result of this inquiry cycle, Rob deepened his question to explore "what it feels like to bring my own feelings directly into the therapy. Early on I recognized I had a lot of caution, reluctance, and fear in this respect, part of which I am sure was inexperience. As time passed I became less cautious, but what remained was an underlying discomfort with 'imposing myself' on the client—a felt sense of narcissistically inserting myself into the session, of taking the client's space. Yet, on the other hand, I felt a strong desire to make a connection and share something with the client, be impactful, be potent, to take some place in my client's space." His questioning continues.

Rachel—3rd year student

Stage 1—"When considering my research question I was questioning the very purpose of therapy. My defences were being stripped away in my deeply searching psychotherapy and training, making me question my lifelong faith and highlighting my perceived emptiness. I wondered whether it would have been better keeping my old defences rather than face the harsh existential truths of life that therapy surfaced, and questioned whether therapy could offer a reparative, positive, life-changing experience—the Script cure that Berne aimed for (1961).

Relational therapy started to seem cruel and disturbing, even unethical, if it could not. I therefore decided to research 'Can relational TA therapy result in positive personal change?'"

Stage 2—Rachel decided to address her question in the following ways—through reading, discussion in supervision and therapy, and reviewing the written responses of her clients, via an agency questionnaire that they completed at the end of their therapy.

Stage 3—In terms of the questionnaire, she states,—"The results showed positive evidence for change. Interestingly, for some change consisted of tolerating their situations better, whilst all mentioned the importance of the therapeutic relationship. One client stated the greatest catalyst for change had been her anger at me for not understanding her situation. It seemed that she had been able to use our differences and my failings to experience repressed emotions and confront contaminations (Berne, 1961), that 'To feel (anger, sadness) means you are going crazy.' I was intrigued that even though I'd failed her, just as her parents had done, something different about the experience had been 'life-transforming'. Perhaps in surviving her angry attack without becoming hostile I had modelled a way of containing what was most threatening and engulfing for her (Hargaden & Sills, 2002, p. 68), and I began to question whether it was the apparent 'cruelty' of therapeutic ruptures that was necessary for change in therapy."

As a result, of her findings, Rachel modified her research question to "Are ruptures necessary for effective therapy?' and decided as before to read around the subject, to discuss with peers and in supervision, and also to be open to her experience of exploring the consequences of ruptures and repairs with her own therapist and clients.

In terms of her reading, she noted that there was "general consensus amongst theorists from many different models that ruptures are inevitable in therapy and can be therapeutic. Still needing evidence, however, I became quite agitated (one of Schiff et al.'s passive behaviours, 1975) and critical of my therapist when she did not soothe me but allowed me to sit with my uncertainty. Feeling dismissed by her I decided to leave, only staying because of her encouragement to work though the rupture we'd co-created."

Stage 4—Rachel discovered that she felt a deep change inside her, when her "therapist non-defensively explored" with her a difficult re-enactment that had happened between them. "I became aware that although such ruptures seemed to be repetitions of historical ruptures, the crucial difference was that they were acknowledged and addressed differently. My historical lack of repair was not repeated when my therapist, rather than withdraw, validated my feelings and committed to making sense of these difficult experiences."

Rachel's conclusion was that "relational TA therapy can indeed lead to positive change: perhaps not Berne's Script cure but increased insight, integration, and the ability to tolerate more of the pain and joy of life and relationships. Sometimes, if not always, this can only happen through the 'cruelty' of disturbance and rupture in the therapeutic relationship. If therapy is too kind, too soothing and empathic, it would seem that Cornell and Bonds-White (2001) are right—we might be 'anaesthetizing' the work, giving our clients an opiate in an attempt to soothe ourselves (p. 77)."

Sarah—3rd year student

Sarah's inquiry focused on examining the somatic responses she had been experiencing in relation to her clients and had settled on a "soft" question of "What does all this mean and what can the body says to us—nonverbally?"

Stage 2—"In terms of how I approached my enquiry, I have used my supervision time to find useful publications and discuss bodily responses that have occurred with my clients. I have also used my personal therapy time to explore where these nonverbal reactions I have may come from and what this may mean for me and in my work."

Stage 3—Sarah noted a number of bodily responses that she was experiencing when sitting with clients: a "hypnotic effect"; "a woolly minded sensation"; "I feel worn out and distant"; "there is an almost soporific feel to the room".

"This client has begun to sigh frequently in sessions. She says that it brings her relief, as she often feels stressed. I had noticed when I listened to my tapes that I too sigh occasionally."

"I had a sensation in a part of my body that I had an operation on some years ago. I sat with the pain and thought it was my own. This continued for a number of weeks. My client then brought to the session that she was fearful of having exactly the same operation that I had and told me that she was in constant pain. We talked about her fear, and she resolved to have the operation. Since her operation, neither of us has experienced this pain."

"On another occasion I found myself pressing my fingers against my temples. The client, at the same time, also did this and screwed up her eyes as if trying to reach some thought and verbalize something that was proving unreachable, and therefore difficult. In that moment, I had felt confused and anxious. I too had screwed up my eyes. The client said that she was feeling anxious and had a slight headache. By pressing her temples, she felt she was getting some relief."

Stage 4—Sarah recognized that often her somatic experiences seemed to match with something that was happening for the client, which set her off on a series of further questions: "Does this hypnotic induction feel like her mother's behaviour or could it be how she reacted to it? My client was often sent to her room as a child: did she sleep there? I discovered that she did—this could explain the heavy, sleepy atmosphere created in the session. I feel I understand better how she deadened her feelings in order to cope. This, more than her words, has helped me understand on a different level what it must have been like for her at this time. There is much meaning in silence."

Sarah also noted that she experiences strong somatic experiences when she shuts out her own emotions and so wondered what was hers and what was the clients—"Who is influencing whom?"

"So, I will continue to learn to sit with these varied feelings and link them to the client's life story, whilst at the same time exploring in my personal therapy whether part of what is going on links into my script, which is why I sense some of these things so keenly."

Maja—4th year student

Maja decided to inquire into the question, "How do I account for my apparent difference to the majority of my clients and its impact on the therapeutic relationship?"

"Having a foreign name and an accent is self-disclosing on its own and naturally triggers curiosity in clients. Very often during the initial session, clients would inquire about my accent and country of origin. At some point, I became aware that answering the question, 'Where are you from?' often evoked a sense of uneasiness in me, and I felt reluctant to inquire about how they felt working with a therapist who is culturally different to them."

"Thinking about my reluctance to be open with clients puts me in touch with my sense of shame. Given the recent civil war in my country where people of my nationality committed atrocities, I somehow wanted to avoid being seen in the light of these horrible events. It became clear to me how my mother's family's experience after WWII, of being punished for just being German, and the necessity for their 'fitting in', for they were a minority in my country of origin, was in the core of my issues of belonging and acceptance."

"I became conscious that my way of coping with the negative political image of my country was by 'fitting in', discounting (Schiff et al., 1975) my cultural identity in the same way my mother's family did in order to cope with their not-so-popular nationality. This awareness prompted me to think about how my tendency to hide parts of myself might affect my work with clients."

Stage 2—Maja decided to explore her question initially by reading around the subject and by reflecting on her discomfort in therapy and supervision.

Stage 3—"I reflected on numerous articles by various authors (Hargaden & Sills, 2002; Shivanath & Hiremath, 2003; Shadbolt, 2004, and Widdowson, 2010) who emphasize the importance of accounting for and acknowledging differences. I realized as a result that by discounting my cultural identity, I was probably losing potency as a therapist and missing the opportunity to learn more about my clients through reflecting on my countertransference responses in relation to our cultural meeting."

"I noticed with some clients, usually those with perfect English accents, that I felt inferior to them, doubting my ability to express myself properly in English. I felt a pull to 'do things right' and was finding it difficult to be challenging. As a result, I started to wonder if this meant that I was denying clients the opportunity for negative projections and integration of bad experiences. I decided that when clients raised this issue with me, instead of doing my usual 'Hmm' and 'Thank you', I would explore with the client the meaning of it and share my feelings about it, which I did."

Stage 4—"Reflecting on my experience after this, it became clear to me that in gaining an understanding of my family cultural background and how it influenced the way I was, I was able to own my countertransferential responses and explore them with the client. In accounting for my countertransferential response of 'doing it right', I understood how my feelings were often matching with the client's experience. In this way I realized that my countertransferential feelings were a part of objective countertransference (Winnicott, 1975), and not only the result of my unresolved cultural issues. In some way, by owning my vulnerability I was able to understand the client's vulnerability."

Judy—4th year student

Stage 1—Judy's research question was "What does it mean when I do not like a client?"

"I became interested in this question because I noticed it coming up in my work with clients, both in a persistent way with particular clients, and in a more random manner with others. Playing in my mind was Carl Rogers's tenet of unconditional positive regard (1961), and I had difficulty reconciling the thoughts and feelings I sometimes had towards my clients with Rogers's stance. I wondered about the impact of my 'not liking' a client for the psychotherapeutic work, and I was also concerned about the ethical dimensions of the dislike. I felt an ethical obligation to look at this issue and thought it could potentially undermine the psychotherapeutic work if left unexamined. I was interested in how and if it is possible to work ethically and effectively with a client that I did not like and still view them with'unconditional positive regard."

Stage 2—"I decided to note my thoughts, feelings, and behaviour specifically around not liking a client, before and after each session and review the findings to see what emerged. I also used tapes to see if I could hear what was triggering feelings of 'not liking' in me and to monitor my responses. From this I hoped to gain insights, which I could then actively use both in the work and relationship with the client and also in supervision. I also imagined that I would find issues and themes, which I could explore in my own therapy."

"I was aware of my own sense of this being a 'not talked about' topic in my psychotherapeutic circle and decided concurrently to research what has been written about it, to support my thinking and exploration. In terms of the validity of my approach, I had concerns that it risked being subjective, being based principally on my own internal process and yet, at the same time, this is partly what the question was about. I decided to use peer discussion and supervision to give some perspective to my approach, together with my literature search."

Stage 3—The student began to note down her feelings as she suggested, and found that as well as noticing the times when she had feelings of dislike for a client, she also felt more in touch with the times when she liked a client. As a result, she modified her research question to become "What do I notice in myself when I like or dislike a client?"

Stage 4—Providing two detailed client examples, the student began to reflect on her feelings: "I noticed that there were particular feelings, which surfaced for me which I associated with not liking certain clients at certain moments. The most frequent feelings were either of anger or fear. From my own therapy, I knew that anger and fear can easily become mixed for me."

"I began to think not only about what thoughts and feelings I had towards my clients, but also what was triggering them. My thinking was that there was both the possibility that I was transferring archaic feelings onto my clients, not seeing them for who they were, and also that my feelings were countertransferential (Racker, 1988) and something the client needed to trigger in me so that I could either understand something about them or confirm something for them."

"Having begun to make some meaning of my like or dislike of clients and, in addition, being able to use it to think about the work, I became interested in what I did (or could do) when I experienced dislike. This formed the basis of my next research loop."

Judy, used the same method of data collection as before and found that her "most frequent response to feelings of dislike was to withdraw into myself. Through supervision, I realized that I was experiencing difficult feelings (anger, boredom) and was tucking these feelings out of sight—I stayed physically present, aware of my thoughts and feelings, but was at a loss as to how to use them, which seemed to reduce my potency as a therapist. When I compared this to what I did with more positive feelings (warmth, tenderness, joy) that I experienced when I liked a client (sometimes the very same client who I at other times disliked), then I was more active, more open to using these feelings."

"I realized that my emotional withdrawal with clients was an attempt at providing a 'corrective experience' (Cornell & Bonds-White, 2001 on Stark), as I was refusing to show or participate in the anger or fear that were familiar to my clients. At the same time, I was not being authentic and this, over time, risked having an impact on the work. Moursund (1985) expresses this as 'two individuals who risk themselves in a coming-together with an unpredictable outcome'. I realize that I need to risk myself (in the areas of dislike and difficult feelings) in order for my clients to risk themselves."

"This research project has enabled me to scrutinize my own internal process with regard to like and dislike of clients. It has shown me that it is not the fact of liking or disliking which is revealing, but rather what meaning the client and I can make of that. I realize that it requires courage to look at what sometimes seem to be inadmissible feelings for my clients. With courage and by stepping into that space between us, I can develop my potency as a therapist."

Conclusion

Working in accordance with the relational principles, whilst it can be rewarding, is most often a demanding process. Providing students with opportunities to develop the required capacities requires a response that is equal to the task. Thinking about, planning, taking part in, and reflecting on their findings, and then changing themselves in relation to what they discover, is a way that, we believe, affords them this possibility.

CHAPTER THIRTY ONE

The censorship process: from distillation to essence—a relational methodology*

Elana Leigh

Introduction

Relational psychoanalytic writings (of which relational transactional analysis is one) have flooded the field in recent years. Throughout this time, I have become increasingly aware of the absence of a sound methodology to support this theoretical, philosophical, and practice-based shift, all of which has inevitable implications for training.

In response to the relational turn, training in skills and methodology appear to have become background, even experienced by some as anomalous within the relational world. What has been privileged instead is the process of uncertainty and the emergence of unconscious dynamics. Over time, however, I have come to see that these notions are not necessarily paradoxical. The uncertainty we refer to within the relational approach need not invite "non-thinking", which can underpin a process of emergence, but rather invite us to develop the capacity both to tolerate a "not knowing space" and to think about this in clinical and theoretical terms. In fact, I would suggest it is vital that we do both.

---

* This chapter is dedicated to Dr Petruska Clarkson, whose mind and work were inspirational.

Working relationally brings the personal and the professional aspects of the psychotherapist's identity to the foreground, opening up a vulnerability to overstepping boundaries (see Eusden in this volume). Rather, therefore, than viewing skills and methodology as incompatible with working in this way, I suggest that this demands that we take greater responsibility for astute clinical thinking and method.

In this chapter, I will explore this dual process by focusing on what I view to be one of the most important tools that the relational therapist has, that of their countertransference. In particular, I will be exploring the psychotherapist's censored material. Ultimately, I believe that it is through the process of exploring this material and then lifting the censorship that the client's intrapsychic struggle becomes known.

Transparency and self-disclosure: challenges for contemporary practice

Countertransference refers to the use of the psychotherapist's pro-active and reactive (Clarkson, 1992) material in the service of the analysis. Transparency and self-disclosure of countertransferential material are often experienced as synonymous with a two-person (Stark, 2009) or relational approach. I suggest that these processes are not only part of the psychotherapist's relating to the client but also invite the psychotherapist to be transparent and disclosed to herself. The psychotherapist is required to find a balance between, at one extreme, intentional withholding or hiding behind their role, and at the other extreme, promiscuous transparency. The challenge within the relational position is to hold both these positions in a mindful, discriminative manner. Being available, being willing to be impacted, and using such impact in the service of the analysis is one of the core principles that guide relational and two-person clinical practice.

Censoring

> "All truths are easy to understand once they are discovered; the point is to discover them".
>
> Galileo (1564–1642)

Freud, the father of psychotherapy, perhaps left a legacy that transparency and disclosure are taboo. The effect of this has been that we have been trained to bracket and censor thoughts and feelings from the therapeutic space. *The Macquarie Dictionary* (2003) [of Australia] defines "censor" as "the official who removes parts for the purpose of suppressing those deemed objectionable on moral, political, military or other grounds" (p. 160).

Using the term censoring in the context of an intrapsychic dynamic refers to the moments when psychotherapists remove "potentially objectionable" parts of their countertransference repertoire, before making an intervention to the patient. Such censoring is carried deeply in our collective unconscious (Jung, 1959), and as such could provoke reactive intentional withholding or the opposite, reactive self-disclosure. Neither compliance with nor the reaction to the taboo is useful. Rather, it is sound methodology, which assists the necessary process of lifting the censorship, so that more can be known to the psychotherapist in the service of the analysis. The gap in methodology, however, is glaring.

Edge moments in psychotherapy

Censoring starts in moments when the therapist's professional and personal selves collide, the impact of which is often to feel stuck in a place of not knowing. Inspired by Ehrenberg (1974), I call these moments "edge moments". Ehrenberg refers to the "intimate edge" as "the point of maximum and acknowledged contact at any given moment in a relationship, without fusion, without violation of the separateness and integrity of each participant" (p. 424).

In these edge moments, anxiety is high. It is these moments that we back away from, as opposed to stepping into. It is these moments where the two unconscious processes are in alignment and need to be used in the service of the therapy. It is in these moments that aspects of the two selves are censored either through a conscious or unconscious process. Consequently, these aspects of self are disavowed, with the resultant disruption potentially leading to an enactment. If, however, the psychotherapist can become aware of their censoring and use these edge moments, they become golden opportunities.

It is in these moments, when we experience the censorship within us, that the process of "distillation" needs to begin. Distillation is the process that enables these moments to be understood and worked with, enables that which is not known to be known, and enables the selves of both psychotherapist and client to step back into the relationship and be present. It is only when both selves are fully present in the space that the therapeutic work can continue.

The distillation process

A filter is a device through which liquid passes in order to remove impurities. What is extracted is the pure essence.

Internal and external censoring are likely to occur in moments of unconscious interplay between therapist and client. They manifest in coded forms of communication that require decoding in order to find the hidden aspects of self. In such edge moments, the psychotherapist's censored feelings, thoughts, and observations that have been provoked need to be put through a metaphorical filter, a process that I call distillation. It is this process of filtering and analysing impurities (censored material) that talks to the heart of the work. What is distilled is the essence, which can then be transformed into a digestible intervention. In this chapter, I propose a method for carrying out this distillation process as well as a format for learning and practising it in training.

When to use the distillation process

The psychotherapist needs to be able to identify edge moments and when to use the methodology. Inevitably, it is at these moments that psychotherapists experience confusion of the boundary between their personal and professional selves and are likely to start the process of censoring.

Step 1: How do I assess when I am in an edge moment?

- The therapist feels provoked and experiences this at a physical and thinking level.
- This reaction feels unacceptable to the professional self of the therapist.
- The therapist feels provoked to either enact their own script or that of the client.
- The therapist feels provoked to cross a boundary that they would not otherwise cross.
- The therapist feels in an altered state of consciousness.

- The therapist feels slightly out of control (in an unfamiliar ego state) (Berne, 1961).
- The therapist feels internally disrupted.
- The therapist feels stuck or stunted.
- Communication between the client and therapist breaks down.
- The therapist feels upside down, turned inside out.

Once the psychotherapist has established that they are in an edge moment and accepts that the unconscious is at play, the transition to step 2 can be made.

Step 2: What to do/how to reflect?

At this point, the psychotherapist turns the window inwards. This is the moment when we walk the talk of being willing to be transparent to ourselves, beginning with a stringent process of examining our own *censoring* process as it is occurring in the moment.

The psychotherapist asks themselves:

- What am I feeling and thinking right now?
- What am I censoring?
- If I said what I really wanted to say without censoring what would it be? (It is important to dwell upon this last question—repeating it internally to allow the full impact.)

These steps will culminate in a clearer understanding of the essence of the censored material, and with further enquiry the meaning of the essence and to whom it belongs.

The psychotherapist now engages in further clinical thinking about how to bring this material into the therapeutic space. Turning point interventions, such as these, can take moments, weeks, or even months. Taking the time to turn inwards in order to have a clearer picture is a vital component in work such as this, and decisions about how to proceed need to encompass clinical considerations like timing, stage of treatment, diagnosis, context, etc.

Below I describe a training exercise that I have developed to help trainee psychotherapists deepen and develop their ability to engage in the distillation process.

Training in the distillation process

> "Knowledge is of no value unless you put it into practice".
>
> Anton Chekhov (1816–1904)

Context and contract

There is no replacement for having opportunities to practise psycho-therapy methods and techniques. Experimenting in a safe environment opens the internal space for real learning.

The context for this training exercise is a training group of interme-diate and advanced level trainee psychotherapists who are in ongoing supervision and their own psychotherapy. The group has some history of training together, which provides a level of safety with each other. However, the start of the exercise still demands reiterating the contract around confidentiality and confirming boundaries for safety.

Technical elements

Two trainees work in front of the group for a set time of forty-five min-utes; one is the psychotherapist and the other the client.

The trainee psychotherapist and the trainer agree that they both have a "pause button", which can be used at any time. The trainee psychotherapist usually presses the pause button when stuck. The trainer presses the pause button when edge moments are sensed. The combination of the two pause buttons keeps the process trans-parent and lively and allows the therapist to avoid trying hard to be perfect.

A word about the pause button. It is both a teaching tool and a meta-phor. The metaphor highlights the value of pausing to allow space to travel inwards, in search of the censored material that creates the rela-tional disruption.

The trainer states the learning task, which is to learn about and practise the distillation process. The main task of the trainee psychotherapist is to become aware of an emerging edge moment and to press the pause button in order to engage actively in the distillation process. The trainer encourages an attitude of curiosity, as opposed to judgement. Since the work is steeped in subjectivity, there is no right and wrong.

Both the client and psychotherapist engage in an authentic piece of therapy, as opposed to a role play, as the learning requires real thoughts and feelings. When the trainee psychotherapist experiences an edge moment, they press the pause button. The observers are invited to be active in their learning by noticing their own reactions and hypothesizing what they might do.

The working of the distillation filter

When either party pushes the pause button, the trainer takes the psychotherapist through a series of questions with the intention of lifting the internal censorship (within the psychotherapist). Once the censored material is articulated, further enquiry takes place as to the meaning the psychotherapist gives to this information.

The questions asked are the following:

- How are you feeling right now?
- What are you thinking about the process?
- Are you censoring your thoughts and feelings?
- How might the content and manner of your censoring relate to you and your client's script issues?
- If you did not censor yourself, what would you bring into the space?
- How would you imagine your uncensored information challenging you and your client's script?

These now uncensored thoughts and feelings go through the filter of the trainee psychotherapist's reflectivity, as they immerse themselves in reflecting on what the impact might be if these thoughts were uttered. They then become free to engage with thinking about whose story this is (the client's, their own, or both of theirs). With this knowledge, the psychotherapist can take a meta-perspective, attempting to focus on the essence of this information and wondering about what is being kept out of the therapeutic space; what cannot be thought, felt, or stated; what, possibly, is being enacted. The push to enact is of course what we experience in the heart of the edge moment.

Through this process, the trainer and the trainee therapist distil the essence of what is being said and not said. Coded and hidden language needs to be decoded and brought into the space. The distillation process aids this decoding and the information that is gleaned from this process helps to formulate the resultant intervention.

Once the trainee therapist has consulted the trainer, they return to the client (who has been listening) and the work continues till the time has been used.

Closing and evaluation of the exercise

On completion of the work, the trainer takes time to debrief with the trainee client who talks about their process without reopening the piece of work. The client is asked to state what was useful and less useful. This is important as success or usefulness is often best measured by the recipient. Then the trainee psychotherapist is invited to debrief and talk about their experience and what they found helpful about the process.

Finally, the space is then opened to the rest of the trainees to talk about what they learnt through the experience and to ask training questions. However, this is not an opportunity to reopen the therapeutic work or to play what Berne (1963) called a "game of psychiatry" (p. 135), thus avoiding competition and the danger of shaming.

Case example

The psychotherapist and the client are working; the central issue for the client is that she describes feeling despair with her daughter, who is in her final year of school and is disinterested in applying herself in her studies. The client is in an emotional quandary about what she should do and speaks disparagingly about her thoughts and feelings.

About ten minutes into the session, the psychotherapist pushes the pause button and engages in the questioning process with the trainer who facilitates her to talk in an uncensored way. In doing so, she expresses strong feelings of anger and feels disconnected from the client. She confesses that she does not want to engage with the client as she is scared of behaving in a persecutory way. The trainer explores the psychotherapist's rage as well as what she would want to say to the client, if she were uncensored. She courageously states, "Just leave her alone! Support and love your daughter and trust that she will find her way." She imagines saying this in a stern way.

The trainer explores what is stopping the psychotherapist from saying this. She says that she imagines the relationship will break down as a result of shaming her client. She cannot imagine that it is possible to be in a supportive relationship and also have strong feelings. She believes they should be censored. The trainer supports her to explore this idea more fully and together they agree that this is what needs to be taken back into the therapeutic work. The essence that has been distilled is that the mother (the client) was censoring her real feelings because she could not imagine that the relationship with her daughter could be sustained if she had her own thoughts and feelings. A hypothesis was made that the daughter of the client was probably experiencing similar feelings, namely struggling to be her own separate person and feeling angry about not being free to be herself. The mother, unable to be true to her own thoughts and feelings, was maintaining the symbiotic relationship.

The psychotherapist now feels equipped to re-enter the therapy space. This is what followed:

Psychotherapist: It seems that you might feel you cannot share your feelings with your daughter? What do you think about this?

Client: [Tears in her eyes.] I can't do that as that will be a burden on her and she will get angry and that is my worst nightmare. I am so scared to lose her.

Psychotherapist: You are grieving for your little girl and you are losing her and she you. You are losing who you once were for each other. Instead of being sad together you are angry.

Client: [Crying.] I know this is true and I feel so sad, I need to be myself so she can be herself.

The psychotherapist and client sit quietly together and the work ends. Both the client and the psychotherapist are deeply moved.

The intervention was formulated in the following way

The trainee therapist identified her disconnection, which was provoked by her censored anger towards the client. Through further exploration, she came to know that she believed that the relationships between her and her client could not withstand the expression of truthful strong thoughts and feelings. As a result of an exploration of this contaminated belief (Berne, 1961), she was able to acknowledge where this belief belonged in her history and to hypothesize about it in her client's.

Three enactments occurred through this belief:

Client: Her disconnection from her daughter, which manifested in her withholding her real thoughts and feelings.

Daughter: Her disinterest and withdrawal as a way to claim her separateness.

Therapist: Disconnection from the client and, therefore, feeling stuck.

Through this distillation enquiry, it was agreed that the resultant intervention needed to talk to the essence of this material. It needed to target the affect of the client and not be overly wordy or cognitive as this would perhaps maintain the defence. The intervention needed to speak to the essence of what was missing which was the disavowed thoughts and feelings of the client.

The intervention that the trainee therapist chose is an interesting intervention as it can appear to be an interpretation from a one-person approach; however, the process of reaching the intervention speaks to the heart of a two-person approach. The psychotherapist was transparent and self-disclosing to herself, and through this, came to know the censored material and therefore to grasp the essence. Other interventions, including those in which the psychotherapist disclosed more personal information relating to the process, may have been equally facilitative. The important rule is to have gone through the distillation process so that the intervention is clinically well supported.

Conclusion

Developing relational methodologies is the growing challenge in this field of psychotherapy. The distillation of the psychotherapist's censorship process as described in this chapter is a contribution to this development.

CHAPTER THIRTY TWO

Fostering the freedom for play, imagination, and uncertainty in professional learning environments

William F. Cornell

"This gives us our indication for therapeutic procedure—to afford the opportunity for formless experience, and for creative impulses, motor and sensory, which are the stuff of playing. And on the basis of playing is built the whole of man's experiential existence"

—(Winnicott, 1971, p. 64)

Transactional analysis, as developed by Eric Berne, was predominantly a theory and system for identifying and changing patterns of psychological and interpersonal defence, which he called games (1964) and script (1972). Berne's emphasis was on the therapist as an outside observer of the patient's internal and interpersonal dynamics. Believing that the thinking capacities of the Adult ego state (1972, p. 57) were the primary mechanisms of the treatment, Berne's use of group treatment, game theory, and the diagramming of transactions (1972, pp. 14–21) and scripts provided a set of predominantly cognitive tools for clients to develop insight and self-observation skills to foster change.

In his theory of games, Berne (1964, p. 64) distinguished between three levels (or degrees) of interpersonal defences which enact childhood script injunctions in a progression that he understood as increasingly destructive and difficult to change: 1) 1st degree, social; 2) 2nd degree, psychological; and 3) 3rd degree, tissue, i.e., held in the body and the most pathological and resistant to change. In differentiating these levels of defence, he invited transactional analysts to notice how defences are organized and expressed. But he never differentiated what styles and levels of intervention might be needed to work effectively with these different levels of defence. While Berne articulated these distinctions within a theory of defences, we can apply these levels of psychic organization through all domains of human experience. We have come to see through clinical exploration, as well as parent/infant observation and affective neuroscience research, that the levels of psychic organization Berne referred to as 2nd and 3rd degree are fundamental and vital aspects of being alive. Models based on implicit relational knowing (Lyons-Ruth, 1999; Fosshage, 2010), sub-symbolic experience (Bucci, 2001, 2010), script protocol (Berne, 1963; Cornell & Landaiche, 2006; Cornell, 2010), affective neuroscience (Panksepp, 2009), and body psychotherapy (Bloom, 2006; Anderson, 2008; Hartley, 2008) are among the emerging paradigms that underscore the necessity of recognizing and working *within* and *through* these pre-cognitive, affective, and somatic levels of organization.

The traditional reliance on strengthening the Adult ego state and its cognitive (and allegedly predictive) capacities is mirrored in much of our TA training and preparation for certification, which is heavy on theory, diagnosis, and treatment planning. As I teach in various TA communities and sit on oral examination boards around the world, I see the impact of this emphasis, which fosters a strong bias towards forms of attention and understanding that can be cognitively accessed and named by the professional and the client alike. Yet the 2nd and 3rd degrees of defences that Berne describes are not organized and maintained at the social/cognitive level, but rather at levels of nonconscious experience (Cornell & Landaiche, 2008; Pierini, 2008; Tosi, 2008), implicit memory, protocol (Guglielmotti, 2008), and bodily experience. Many aspects of evolving TA theory and technique, often now referred to as relational, are an effort to develop a systematic understanding of how to work at these levels. This broadening of our therapeutic repertoire necessitates a broadening of our training models as well.

In classical TA script analysis, the client and professional step *out of* the transference and analyse it through diagnostic labels (e.g., identifying a Don't grow up injunction) (Goulding & Goulding, 1979, pp. 34–38) and diagrams (the script matrix) (Berne, 1972, pp. 279–283). In conventional script analysis, as in genetic interpretations typical within a psychoanalytic frame, therapeutic attention is directed to the forces from the past and the psychological impact of historical figures. This is often sufficient for changing script beliefs and behaviours held at the 1st degree level, but is often not adequate to address script issues maintained at the 2nd and 3rd degrees. In more contemporary approaches to transactional analysis, the client and practitioner are more likely to *stay within* the transference/countertransference dynamics, seeking a more emotional and experiential understanding of what is going on, in the belief that it is only through these nonconscious processes that meaning can be discovered and enacted. The meaning and impact of one's script is now more likely to be explored as it is experienced (and repeated) moment to moment, between client and practitioner and/or among group members. Holding experience in the here and now is much more necessary for working at the 2nd and 3rd degree levels of defence. I want to emphasize that I do not believe that work of human relations professionals is only that of resolving script injunctions and other patterns of defence, but also to facilitate the capacity of individuals, groups, and organizations to live with more vitality, aggression, and depth of visceral and creative experience.

I believe that each of us needs to begin our professional work grounded in a theory or two and a set of basic techniques, as much for the security of the practitioner as the efficacy of the work and the learning of our clients. How do we move beyond this initial ground, so that we do not become overly identified with and dependent upon our favoured theories and the illusions of predictive knowing that they offer? How do we find the psychological space within ourselves and in relation to our clients to wonder, imagine, and not-know? How do we, as trainers and supervisors, create experiences that facilitate learning through lived experience, in which our theories are secondary containers to a more fundamental process of discovery?

My work as a teacher and consultant has been profoundly influenced by my readings of Thomas Ogden (2005, 2009) and my personal supervision and study with Christopher Bollas (1999, 2009). Both are elegant, thrilling writers and major contributors to the contemporary psychoanalytic attitudes. Neither affiliates himself with the relational zeitgeist, but neither shies away from fully immersing himself in the affective and unconscious domains of his patients or supervisees. Both steadfastly refuse to limit their groups to psychoanalysts or to associate with any formal, analytic training programmes. Each is committed through his writing and supervision to fostering the capacities for reverie, imaginative thought, and receptivity to unconscious communication, which I see as essential to working at the 2nd and 3rd degree levels of somato-psychic organization.

Ogden (2009), for example, sees his primary goals in supervision and teaching as creating atmospheres to maximize the freedom to think and imagine:

> The supervisor is responsible for creating a frame that ensures the supervisee's freedom to think and dream and be alive to what is occurring both in the analytic process and in the supervisory process. The supervisory process is a felt presence that affords the supervisee a sense of security that his efforts at being honest in the presence of the supervisor will be treated humanely, respectfully, and confidentially (p. 36).
>
> Everything about the seminars is voluntary. The groups are not associated with any training program; no certificate of participation is awarded; no one is required to present a case or even to enter into the discussions (p. 51).

Ogden's "to think and dream and be alive" captures, in a different language, Berne's own ideal outcome of "autonomy", which he defined as the capacities for "awareness, spontaneity and intimacy" (1964, p. 178). Berne describes awareness as "the capacity to see a coffee pot and hear the birds sing in one's own way, and not the way one was taught" (p. 178). For Berne, spontaneity represented "liberation, liberation from the compulsion to play games and have only the feelings one was taught to have" (p. 180), and "intimacy means the spontaneous, game-free candidness of an aware person, the liberation of the eidetically perceptive, uncorrupted Child in all its naïveté living in the here and now" (p. 180).

So much of transactional analysis training and supervision is now so profoundly tied to endless preparation for the examinations and certification that I seldom see this freedom of thought and experience within the TA communities where I work as an independent trainer. Even working with seasoned TA practitioners, years after they have been certified, I see sadly diminished capacities for free thought, imaginative exploration, and discovery, which I see as essential to working at 2nd and 3rd degree levels. I have come to further understand training and supervision in human relations work within these non-cognitive realms to be the creation and sustenance of the exploratory, intermediary space that Winnicott called "play" (1971, 1989).

Play, in Winnicott's conception, is not the exclusive terrain of childhood nor is it a matter of simply having fun, but rather an essential, exciting, and sometimes anxiety-inducing necessity for self development:

> ... *it is play that is universal*, and that it belongs to health: playing facilitates growth and therefore health; playing leads into group relationships; playing can be a form of communication in psychotherapy; and, lastly, psychoanalysis has been developed as a highly specialized form of playing in the service of communication with oneself and others (1971, p. 41, emphasis in the original).

While Winnicott often cast his discussions of play within the context of his own work with children and parent/child relations, it was an ongoing metaphor for creative adult relations and therapeutic activity. Play in this sense is not necessarily pleasant but represents the freedom and capacity for one to come *up against* other people and the external world in its various manifestations:

> Through play the child deals with external reality creatively. In the end this produces creative living, and leads to the capacity to feel real and to feel life can be used and enriched. Without play the child is unable to see the world creatively, and in consequence is thrown back on compliance and a sense of futility, or on the exploitation of direct instinctual satisfactions.
> ... in play an object can be
> destroyed and restored
> hurt and mended
> dirtied and cleaned
> killed and brought to life
> with the added achievement of ambivalence in place of splitting the object (and self) into good and bad (1989, pp. 60–61).

Here, in his emphasis on literal action into and against the external environment, Winnicott offers an important complement to the states of reverie and internal exploration emphasized by Bollas and Ogden.

I have come to conceive of my teaching and consultative groups as creating a sustained "play" space, providing opportunities to explore and challenge one's self image, professional ideals, theoretical assumptions and biases, fantasies, imaginative capacities, technical range, and interpersonal relations. In this way, I hope to foster the attitudes and skills needed to work effectively at the 2nd and 3rd degrees of psychic organization. I attempt to attend to experiences at intellectual, affective, and bodily levels as work unfolds. As a teacher, I need also be in a position to have *my* operating assumptions and supervisory understandings explored, discussed frankly, and challenged by a group or supervisee.

What does this look like in actual practice? To use a recent example, I was leading a two-day workshop on transference and countertransference in transactional analysis in a country I had only visited once before. It was a group of thirty, a mixture of psychotherapists, counsellors, teachers, child care workers, and organizational consultants. I had prepared a rather thorough set of notes on the topic as presented in the seminar description. As we began, I did a quick tour of the group to ask why people were there and quickly discovered that their interests had little to do with the workshop description. What emerged in the group was a concern and fear of their own emotional and bodily experiences, as well as those of their clients. Theory was not what they were seeking. So much for my notes! What followed was a kind of improvisational process between the group and me—an extended play experience.

I noticed my own bodily reactions as I listened to the initial tour of the group, my fantasies and associations as well. Rather unexpectedly, I started off with a case example of a young man, who came to my mind as I listened to the group talking about their anxieties about their own emotional and bodily reactions to their clients. I felt a strong erotic and affection bond towards this guy. He had terminated recently to move to another city. We decided to fully terminate rather than continue working by phone. I referred him on. I missed him a lot, hoped he was doing well, and hoped he was missing me. My body and feelings were certainly present in the room as I worked with this fellow and as we terminated. I did not have to tell him this in words, as he could sense it in my way of being with him. Unconsciously, and then consciously, I was showing the group, "This is OK, and this is what we're here to talk about. Such feelings don't mean there's something wrong with you, or that they'll all go away when you become more experienced."

I then broke the group into dyads who would be working pairs throughout the workshop. I led them on a guided fantasy of their bodily experiences (which could be framed as countertransference) of a session with their most favourite client (or group) and then of their most dreaded client (or group). The rich discussion in the group that emerged from the dyads then oriented my subsequent teaching. The didactic portions of the two days were guided by the thoughts, feelings, interests, and experiences that emerged from the experiential dyads and group discussions. The experiential dyads provided participants with the opportunities for working together, experiencing their anxieties, discoveries, and competencies in the here and now. My intention was to open multiple channels of receptivity and learning within the group. The experiential dyads underscored the competencies of the participants while grounding the theory and discussions in a lived encounter with self and other. Case examples from my own work emerged spontaneously in association to the group's interests, and the two clinical consultations with members of the group further elaborated the learning that emerged within the group.

What does it mean to think? Healthy thinking and learning goes well beyond our capacities for conscious cognitions. To be fully engaged with our clients in a depth of shared experience, I believe we need to be engaged at the levels of affective, bodily, and frequently unconscious receptivity.

Berne's emphasis on the Adult ego state, his use of diagrams, and many of the techniques he devised to distinguish transactional analysis from psychoanalysis, created a highly efficient mode of group and individual treatment to foster cognitive insight. What I have wished to outline here is a perspective that facilitates learning and change through training and supervision within the realms of nonconscious, imaginative, and somatic functioning, which I see as necessary for growth at the 2nd and 3rd degree levels of psychological organization.

REFERENCES

ABBA (1976). *Knowing Me, Knowing You.* "Arrivals" album. Universal International.

Abram, J. (1996). *The Language of Winnicott—a Dictionary of Winnicott's Use of Words.* London: Karnac.

Ainsworth, M. D. S., Blehar, M. C., Waters, E. & Wall, S. (1978). *Patterns of Attachments: A Psychological Study of the Strange Situation.* Hillsdale, NJ: Lawrence Erlbaum Associates.

Albom, M. (2003). *The Five People you Meet in Heaven.* London: Little, Brown.

Allen, J. R. (1989). Stroking: biological underpinnings and direct observations. *Transactional Analysis Journal, 19*: 26–31.

Allen, J. R. (1999). Biology and transactional analysis: integration of a neglected area. *Transactional Analysis Journal, 29*: 250–259.

Allen, J. R. (2000). Biology and transactional analysis II: A status report on neurodevelopment. *Transactional Analysis Journal, 30*: 260–269.

Allen, J. R. (2003). Concepts, competencies, and interpretive communities. *Transactional Analysis Journal, 33*: 126–147.

Allen, J. R. (2009). Constructivist and neuroconstructivist transactional analysis. *Transactional Analysis Journal, 39*: 181–192.

Allen, J. R. (2010). The neurosciences, psychotherapy and transactional analysis: A second look. International Association of Relational Transactional Analysis, www.relationalta.com

Allen, J. R. (2010). From a child psychiatry practice. In: R. G. Erskine (Ed.), *Life Scripts: A Transactional Analysis of Unconscious Relational Patterns* (pp. 151–178). London: Karnac.

Allen, J. R. (2011, in press). The experienced self. *Transactional Analysis Journal.*

Allen, J. R. & Allen, B. A. (1989). Ego states, self, and script. *Transactional Analysis Journal, 19*: 4–13.

Allen, J. R. & Allen, B. A. (1991). Concepts of transference: a critique, a typology, an alternative hypothesis, and some proposals. *Transactional Analysis Journal, 21*: 77–91.

Anderson, F. S. (Ed.) (2008). *Bodies in Treatment: The Unspoken Dimension.* Hillsdale, NJ: Analytic Press.

Aron, L. (1996). *A Meeting of Minds: Mutuality in Psychoanalysis.* Hillsdale, NJ: Analytic Press.

Aron, L. (2006). Analytic impasse and the third: Clinical implications of intersubjectivity theory. *Colloquium Series, 9*: October 30—November 19.

Bager-Charleson, S. (2010) *Reflective Practice in Counselling and Psychother-apy.* Exeter, UK: Learning Matters.

Balint, M. (1968). *The Basic Fault.* London: Tavistock.

Barnes, G. (2004). Homosexuality in the first three decades of transactional analysis: A study of theory in the practice of transactional analysis psy-chotherapy. *Transactional Analysis Journal, 34*: 126–155.

Bartholomew, K. & Horowitz, L. (1991). Attachment styles among young adults: A test of a four-category model. *Journal of Personality and Social Psychology, 7*: 147–178.

Batts, V. (1982). Modern racism: A TA perspective. *Transactional Analysis Journal, 12*: 207–209.

Batts, V. (2009). Developing trans-culturally sensitive theory and practice. In: P. Henderson (Ed.), *Supervisor Training: Issues and Approaches* (pp. 69–79). London: Karnac.

Beebe, B. (2004). Faces in relation: A case study. *Psychoanalytic Dialogues, 14*: 1–51.

Benjamin, J. (1999). Recognition and destruction: An outline of intersubjectivity. In: S. Mitchell & L. Aron (Eds.), *Relational Psychoanal-ysis: The Emergence of a Tradition* (pp. 181–210). Hillsdale, NJ: Analytic Press.

Benjamin, J. (2002). Principles of relational psychoanalysis. First biannual meeting of the International Association for Relational Psychoanalysis and Psychotherapy, New York.

Benjamin, J. (2006). The analyst's fear of doing harm. Paper presented at the London Voluntary Sector Resource Centre, sponsored by Confer, England.

Bentall, R. P. (2010). *Doctoring the Mind.* London: Penguin.

Berne, E. (1947). *The Mind in Action.* New York: Simon & Schuster.

Berne, E. (1958). Transactional analysis: A new and effective method of group therapy. *American Journal of Psychotherapy, 12*: 735–743.

Berne, E. (1961). *Transactional Analysis in Psychotherapy.* New York: Grove Press. Reprinted London: Souvenir Press, 1975.

Berne, E. (1962). Classification of positions. *Transactional Analysis Bulletin, 1*(3): 23.

Berne, E. (1963). *The Structure and Dynamics of Organizations and Groups.* New York: J. B. Lippincott.

Berne, E. (1964/2010). *Games People Play.* New York: Grove Press/London: Penguin.

Berne, E. (1966). *Principles of Group Treatment.* New York: Oxford University Press.

Berne, E. (1968). *A Layman's Guide to Psychiatry and Psychoanalysis.* New York: Simon & Schuster.

Berne, E. (1968). Staff conference papers. *American Journal of Psychiatry, 125*(3): 286–293.

Berne, E. (1970). *Sex in Human Loving.* New York: Simon & Schuster.

Berne, E. (1972). *What Do You Say after You Say Hello: The Psychology of Human Destiny.* New York: Grove Press.

Berne, E. (1973). *Sex in Human Loving.* London: Penguin.

Berne, E. (1977). *Intuition and Ego States: The Origins of Transactional Analysis: A Series of Papers* (pp. 1–31). San Francisco: TA Press.

Bion, W. R. (1959). Attacks on linking. *International Journal of Psychoanalysis, 40*: 3–10.

Bion, W. R. (1962). *Experiences in Groups.* London: Tavistock.

Bion, W. R. (1963). *Elements of Psycho-analysis.* London: Heinemann.

Bion, W. R. (1967). A theory of thinking. In: *Second Thoughts: Selected Papers on Psychoanalysis.* London: Heinemann.

Bion, W. R. (1967). *Second Thoughts: Selected Papers on Psychoanalysis.* London: Heinemann.

Bion, W. R. (1990). *Brazilian Lectures*: 1973 São Paulo; 1974 Rio de Janeiro/São Paulo. London: Karnac.

Blackstone, P. (1993). The dynamic child: Integration of second-order structure, object relations, and self psychology. *Transactional Analysis Journal, 23*: 216–234.

Bleger, J. (1967). Psychoanalysis of the psychoanalytical frame. *International Journal of Psychoanalysis, 48*: 511–519.

Bloom, K. (2006). *The Embodied Self: Movement and Psychoanalysis.* London: Karnac.

Boholst, F. A., Boholst, G. B. & Mende, M. M. B. (2005). Life positions and attachment styles: A canonical correlation analysis. *Transactional Analysis Journal, 35*: 62–67.

Bohr, N. (1963). *Essays 1958–1962 on Atomic Physics and Human Knowledge*. New York: Interscience Publishers.

Bollas, C. (1987). *The Shadow of the Object*. New York: Columbia University Press.

Bollas, C. (1989). *Forces of Destiny: Psychoanalysis and the Human Idiom*. Northvale, NJ: Jason Aronson.

Bollas, C. (1999). *The Mystery of Things*. London: Routledge.

Bollas, C. (2000). *Hysteria*. London: Routledge.

Bollas, C. (2009). *The Infinite Question*. London: Routledge.

Bond, T. (2004). *Ethical Gudelines for Researching Counselling and Psychotherapy*. Lutterworth, UK: British Association for Counselling and Psychotherapy.

Bond, T. (2006). Intimacy, risk and reciprocity in psychotherapy: Intricate ethical challenges. *Transactional Analysis Journal, 36*: 77–89.

Bordin, E. S. (1979). The generalizability of the psychoanalytic concept of the working alliance. *Psychotherapy: Theory, Research, Practice, 16*: 252–260.

Bordin, E. S. (1994). Theory and research on the therapeutic working alliance. In: O. Horvath & J. Greenberg (Eds.), *The Working Alliance: Theory Research and Practice* (pp. 13–37). New York: Wiley.

Boroditsky, L. (2011). How language shapes thought. *Scientific American*, February: 43–45.

Boston Change Process Study Group (2008). Forms of relational meaning: Issues in the relations between the implicit and reflective-verbal domains. *Psychoanalytic Dialogues, 18*: 125–148.

Boston Change Process Study Group (2010). *Change in Psychotherapy*. New York: W. W. Norton.

Bowlby, J. (1958). The nature of the child's tie to his mother. *International Journal of Psychoanalysis, 39*: 350–373.

Bowlby, J. (1969). *Attachment and Loss: Attachment*. New York: Basic.

Brandshaft, B. J. (2004). To free the spirit from its cell. In: R. Stolorow, G. Atwood & B. J. Brandshaft (Eds.), *The Intersubjective Perspective*. Oxford: Jason Aronson.

Bretherton, I. & Waters, E. (Eds.) (1985). Growing points of attachment theory and research. *Society for Research in Child Development, Monograph No. 209, 50*(1–2): 66–104.

Britton, R. S. (1989). The missing link: parental sexuality in the Oedipus complex. In: R. S. Britton, J. Steiner, H. Segal, M. Feldman & E. O'Shaughnessy (Eds.), *The Oedipus Complex Today: Clinical Implications* (pp. 83–101). London: Karnac.

Britton, R. S. (1998). *Belief and Imagination: Explorations in Psychoanalysis*. London: Routledge.

Britton, R. S., Steiner, J., Segal, H., Feldman, M. & O'Shaughnessy, E. (Eds.) (1989). *The Oedipus Complex Today: Clinical Implications*. London: Karnac.

Bromberg, P. (2011). *Awakening the Dreamer: Clinical Journeys*. London: Routledge.

Buber, M. (1923/1958). *I and thou* (2nd ed.) (R. G. Smith, Trans.). New York: Scribner.

Bucci, W. (1997). *Psychoanalysis and Cognitive Science: A Multiple Code Theory*. New York: Guilford Press.

Bucci, W. (2001). Pathways of emotional communication. *Psychoanalytic Inquiry*, 21: 40–70.

Bullara, M. (Ed.) (1979). *Before Speech: the Beginning of Human Communication*. London: Cambridge University Press.

Burck, C. (2005). *Multilingual Living. Explorations of Language and Subjectivity*. Basingstoke, NY: Palgrave, Macmillan.

Burke, W. & Tansy, M. (1991). Countertransference disclosure and models of therapeutic action. *Contemporary Psychoanalysis*, 27: 351–384.

Calich, J. & Hinz, H. (Eds.) (2007). *The Unconscious: Further Reflections*. London: International Psychoanalytic Association.

Capers, R. A. (1999). *A Mind of One's Own: A Kleinian View of Self and Object*. London: Routledge.

Carey, B. (2008). H. M. dies at age 82—neuroscience's most unforgettable amnesiac. http://neurosciencenews.com/hm-dies-amnesia.htm (last accessed: 14.03.11).

Carpy, D. (1989). Tolerating the countertransference: A mutative process. *International Journal of Psychoanalysis*, 70: 287–294.

Casement, P. J. (1982). Samuel Beckett's relationship to his mother tongue. *International Review of Psycho-Analysis*, 9: 35–44.

Casement, P. J. (2001). *On Learning from the Patient*. Hove, UK: Brunner-Routledge.

Casement, P. J. (2006). *Learning from Life. Becoming a psychoanalyst*. Hove, UK: Routledge.

Chekhov, A. www.brainyquote.com (retrieved March 8, 2011).

Cheney, W. (1971). Eric Berne: Biographical sketch. *Transactional Analysis Journal*, 1: 14–22.

Clark, B. (1991). Empathic transactions in the deconfusion of the Child ego states. *Transactional Analysis Journal*, 21: 92–98.

Clarkin, J., Yeomans, F. & Kernberg, O. (2006). *Psychotherapy for Borderline Personality: Focusing on Object Relations*. Washington, DC: American Psychiatric Press.

Clarkson, P. (1992). *Transactional Analysis Psychotherapy: an Integrated Approach*. Hove, UK: Routledge.

CORE Information Management Systems, L. Outcome Measure 34, accessible at http://www.coreims.co.uk

Cornell, W. F. (1988). Life script theory: A critical review from a developmental perspective. *Transactional Analysis Journal*, *18*: 270–282.

Cornell, W. F. (2001). There ain't no cure without sex: the provision of a "vital" base. In: W. F. Cornell & H. Hargaden (Eds.), *From Transactions to Relations: The Emergence of a Relational Tradition in Transactional Analysis* (pp. 213–224). Chadlington, UK. Haddon Press, 2005.

Cornell, W. F. (2003). Babies, brains and bodies: somatic foundation of the child. In: C. Sills & H. Hargaden (Eds.), *Ego States: Key Concepts in Transactional Analysis: Contempory Views* (pp. 28–54). London: Worth.

Cornell, W. F. (2008). *Explorations in Transactional Analysis—The Meech Lake Papers*. San Francisco: TA Press.

Cornell, W. F. (2010). Whose body is it? Somatic relations in script and script protocol. In: R. G. Erskine (Ed.), *Life Scripts: A Transactional Analysis of Unconscious Relational Patterns* (pp. 101–126). London: Karnac.

Cornell, W. F. & Bonds-White, F. (2001). Therapeutic relatedness in transactional analysis: The truth of love or the love of truth. *Transactional Analysis Journal*, *31*: 71–93.

Cornell, W. F. & Hargaden, H. (Eds.) (2005). *From Transactions to Relations: the Emergence of a Relational Tradition in Transactional Analysis*. Chadlington, UK: Haddon Press.

Cornell, W. F. & Landaiche, N. M. (2006). Impasse and intimacy: Applying Berne's concept of script protocol. *Transactional Analysis Journal*, *36*: 196–213.

Cornell, W. F. & Landaiche, N. M. (2008). Non-conscious processes and self-development: Key concepts from Eric Berne and Christopher Bollas. *Transactional Analysis Journal*, *38*: 200–217.

Cornell, W. F. & Rubin, L. R. (2006). Wilhelm Reich and the corruption of ideals: Idealization and ideology. Pittsburgh Psychoanalytic Society and Institute, October 13.

Cranmer, R. M. (1971). Eric Berne: Annotated bibliography. *Transactional Analysis Journal*, *1*: 23–29.

Crastnopol, M. (2002). The dwelling place of self-experience. *Psychoanalytic Dialogues*, *12*: 259–284.

Creswell, J. W. (2009). *Research Design. Qualitative, Quantitative, and Mixed Method Approaches*. London: Sage.

Damasio, A. (2010). *Self Comes to Mind*. London: Heinemann.

Davies, J. M. (2002). Whose bad objects are we anyway? Repetition and our elusive love affair with evil. A plenary paper presented to the first biannual meeting of the International Association for Relational Psychoanalysis and Psychotherapy, New York.

De Saint-Exupéry, A. (1943). *The Little Prince*. Florida: Harcourt.

DeYoung, P. (2003). *Relational Psychotherapy—a Primer*. New York: Brunner-Routledge.

Diamond, N. & Marrone, M. (2003). *Attachment and Intersubjectivity*. London: Whurr.

Dimen, M. (2003). Sexuality and suffering, or the "eeew!" factor. *Studies in Gender and Sexuality*, 6: 1–18.

Driver, C. (2009). Supervision: a psychodynamic and psychoanalytic perspective on supervisor practice and supervisor training. In: P. Henderson (Ed.), *Supervisor Training: Issues and Approaches* (pp. 175–184). London: Karnac.

Dufresne, J. (1999). *Love Warps the Mind a Little*. London: Vintage.

Duncan, B. & Miller, S. (Eds.) (2010). *Heart and Soul of Change in Psychotherapy* (2nd ed.). New York: Oxford University Press.

Ehrenberg, D. B. (1974). The intimate edge in therapeutic relatedness. In: *Contemporary Psychoanalysis*, 10: 423–437.

Ehrenberg, D. B. (1992). *The Intimate Edge: Extending the Reach of Psychoanalytic Interaction*. New York: W. W. Norton.

Ekstein, R. (1969). Concerning the teaching and learning of psychoanalysis. *Journal of the American Psychoanalytic Association*, 17: 312–332.

English, F. (1971). The substitution factor, rackets and real feelings. *Transactional Analysis Journal*, 1: 27–32.

English, F. (1988). Whither scripts? *Transactional Analysis Journal*, 18: 294–303.

Erskine, R. G. (1988). Ego structure, intrapsychic function, and defense mechanisms; A commentary on Eric Berne's original theoretical concepts. *Transactional Analysis Journal*, 18: 15–19.

Erskine, R. G. (1997). *Theories and Methods of an Integrative Transactional Analysis*. San Francisco: TA Press.

Erskine, R. G. (2001). Psychological function, relational needs, and transferential resolution: Psychotherapy of an obsession. *Transactional Analysis Journal*, 31: 220–226.

Erskine, R. G. (2010). *Life Scripts: a Transactional Analysis of Unconscious Relational Patterns*. London: Karnac.

Erskine, R. G. & Moursund, J. P. (2010). *Integrative Psychotherapy in Action*. London: Karnac.

Erskine, R. G., Moursund, J. P. & Trautmann, R. L. (1999). *Beyond Empathy: A Therapy of Contact-in-Relationship*. Philadelphia, PA: Brunner/Mazel.

Erskine, R. G. & Zalcman, M. (1979). The Racket system: A model for Racket analysis. *Transactional Analysis Journal*, 9: 51–59.

Etherington, K. (2000). *Narrative Approaches to Working with Adult Male Survivors of Child Sexual Abuse. The Clients', the Counsellor's and the Researcher's Story*. London: Jessica Kingsley.

Eusden, S. (2011, in press). Minding the gap. *Transactional Analysis Journal*.

Eusden, S. & Summers, G. (2008). Pre-conference institute: vital rhythms. Australasian Transactional Analysis Conference, Rotorua, New Zealand.

Fagan, J. & Shepherd, I. L. (Eds.) (1970). *Gestalt Therapy Now*. New York: Harper & Row.

Fairbairn, R. (1940). Schizoid factors in the personality. In: W. R. D. Fairbairn, *Psychoanalytic Studies of the Personality*. London: Routledge & Kegan Paul, 1952.

Fairbairn, W. R. D. (1952). *Psychoanalytic Studies of the Personality*. London and New York: Tavistock/Routledge, 1990.

Fletcher, J. (1998). Castrating the female advantage. Feminist standpoint research and management science. *Journal of Management Inquiry*, 3: 74–82.

Fletcher, J. (1998). Relational practice: a feminist reconstruction of work. *Journal of Management Inquiry*, 7: 163–186.

Fonagy, P. (1999). The process of change and the change of processes: What can change in a good analysis. Keynote address to the spring meeting of Division 39 of the American Psychological Association, New York, April 16.

Fonagy, P. & Target, M. (1997). Attachment and reflective function: Their role in self organization. *Development and Psychopathology*, 9: 679–900. Cambridge: Cambridge University Press.

Fonagy, P. & Target, M. (1998). Mentalization and the changing aims of child psychoanalysis. *Psychoanalytic Dialogues, 8*: 87–114. Fonagy, P., Gergely, G., Jurist, E. L. & Target, M. (2002). *Affect Regulation, Mentalization, and the Development of the Self*. New York: Other Press.

Fosha, D., Siegel, D. J. & Solomon, M. F. (Eds.) (2009). *The Healing Power of Emotion: Affective Neuroscience, Development, and Clinical Practice*. New York: W. W. Norton.

Fosshage, J. L. (2010). Implicit and explicit pathways to psychoanalytic change. In: J. Petrucelli (Ed.), *Knowing, Not-Knowing & Sort-of-Knowing: Psychoanalysis and the Experience of Uncertainty* (pp. 215–224). London: Karnac.

Fowlie, H. (2005). Confusion and introjection. A model for understanding the defensive structure of the Parent and Child ego states. *Transactional Analysis Journal*, 35: 192–204.

Frawley-O'Dea, M. G. & Sarnat, J. E. (2001). *The Supervisory Relationship: A Contemporary Psychodynamic Approach*. New York: Guilford Press.

Fredrickson, B. (2009). *Positivity: Groundbreaking Research Reveals how to Embrace the Hidden Strength of Positive Emotions, Overcome Negativity, and Thrive*. New York: Crown.

French, R. & Simpson, P. (1999). Our best work happens when we don't know what we are doing. http://www.ispso.org/Symposia/Toronto/1999french-simpson.htm (accessed February 2011).

Freud, S. (1895). Project for a scientific psychology. *S. E.*, *1*. London: Hogarth, 1950.

Freud, S. (1913). *The Interpretation of Dreams*. New York: Macmillan.

Freud. S. (1923). *The Ego and the Id. S. E., 19*. London: Hogarth, 1961.

Freud, S. (1940). *An outline of psychoanalysis. S. E., 23*. London: Hogarth, 1964.

Freud, S. (1974). The Clark Conference. In: S. Freud, C. G. Jung & W. McGuire, *The Freud/Jung Letters* (pp. 239–231), New Jersey: Princeton University Press, as referenced by Tansey, M. J. (1994), Sexual attraction and phobic dread in the countertransference. *Psychoanalytic Dialogues*, 4: 130–152.

Friedlander, M. G. (Ed.) (1991). Special Issues on Transactions and Transference. *Transactional Analysis Journal*, 21: 62–120; 122–192.

Friere, P. (2000). *The Pedagogy of the Oppressed*. New York: Continuum.

Gabbard, G. O. (1997). Nonsexual and sexual boundary violations between analyst and patient: a clinical perspective. Paper presented at Scientific Meeting of the British Psycho-Analytic Society, November 5 (pp. 1–8).

Gabbard, G. O. & Wilkinson, S. (1994). *Management of Countertransference with Borderline Patients*. Washington DC: American Psychiatric Press.

Galileo, G. (2011). www.thinkexist.com (retrieved March 8).

Gerrard, J. (1999). *Love In the Time of Psychotherapy, Erotic Transference and Countertransference: Clinical Practice in Psychotherapy*. London: Routledge.

Ghent, E. (2002). Relations. Unpublished manuscript of the introductory speech to the First Conference of the International Association for Relational Psychoanalysis and Psychotherapy, New York, January 18.

Gilbert, M. C. & Evans, K. (2000). *Psychotherapy Supervision: an Integrative Relational Approach to Psychotherapy Supervision*. Buckingham, UK: Open University Press.

Gilderbrand, K. (2003). An introduction to the brain and the early development of the Child ego state. In: C. Sills & H. Hargaden (Eds.), *Ego States: Key Concepts in Transactional Analysis: Contempory Views* (pp. 1–27). London: Worth.

Gill, M. M. (1994b). *Psychoanalysis in Transition*. Hillsdale, NJ: Analytic Press.

Goldberg, S., Muir, R. & Kerr, J. (Eds.) (1995). *Attachment Theory: Social, Developmental, and Clinical Perspectives*. Hillsdale, NJ: Analytic Press.

Gomez, L. (1997). *An Introduction to Object Relations*. London: Free Association.

Gorkin, M. (1987). *The Uses of Countertransference*. Northvale, NJ: Jason Aronson.

Goulding, M. & Goulding, R. (1979). *Changing Lives Through Redecision Therapy*. New York: Brunner/Mazel.

Goulding, R. & Goulding, M. (1976). Injunctions, decisions and redecisions. *Transactional Analysis Journal*, 6: 41–48.

Gramsci, A. (1971). *Selections from Prison Notebooks*. London: Lawrence & Wishart.

Green, A. (2001). *Life Narcissism Death Narcissism: André Green* (A. Weller, Trans.). London: Free Association.

Greenberg, J. (1986). Theoretical models and the analyst's neutrality. *Contemporary Psychoanalysis*, 22: 87–106.

Greenson, R. (1967). *The Technique and Practice of Psycho-Analysis*. London: Hogarth and the Institute of Psycho-Analysis.

Greenspan, S. I. (1989). *The Development of the Ego: Implications for Personality Theory, Psychopathology, and the Psychotherapeutic Process*. Madison, CT: International Universities Press.

Guggenbuhl-Craig, A. (1971). *Power in the Helping Professions*. New York: Spring Publications.

Guistolise, P. (1996). Failures in the therapeutic relationship: Inevitable and necessary? *Transactional Analysis Journal*, 26: 284–288.

Guntrip, H. (1962). The schizoid compromise and psychotherapeutic stalemate. *British Journal of Medical Psychology*, 35: 273.

Hanly, C. (2007). The unconscious and relational psychoanalysis. In: J. Calich & H. Hinz (Eds.), *The Unconscious: Further Reflections* (pp. 31–46). London: International Psychoanalytic Association.

Hargaden, H. (2001). There ain't no cure for love: The psychotherapy of an erotic transference. *Transactional Analysis Journal*, 31: 213–220.

Hargaden, H. (2002). Brief psychotherapy using psychoanalytic TA. In: K. Tudor (Ed.), *Transactional Analysis Approaches to Brief Therapy* (pp. 45–63). London: Sage.

Hargaden, H. (Ed.) (2005). Transactional analysis and psychoanalysis. *Transactional Analysis Journal*, 35: 106–213.

Hargaden, H. (2007). The evolution of a relational TA supervision group. IARTA website, www.relationalta.com (accessed April 2011).

Hargaden, H. (2010). The emergence of the relational tradition in transactional analysis. *The Psychotherapist: The Journal of the UKCP*, 46: 20–22.

Hargaden, H. & Fenton, B. (2005). An analysis of nonverbal transactions, drawing on theories of intersubjectivity. *Transactional Analysis Journal*, 35: 173–186.

Hargaden, H. & Sills, C. (2001). Deconfusion of the Child ego state. *Transactional Analysis Journal*, 31: 55–70.

Hargaden, H. & Sills, C. (2002). *Transactional Analysis: a Relational Perspective.* London: Brunner-Routledge.

Hartley, L. (Ed.) (2008). *Contemporary Body Psychotherapy: the Chiron Approach.* London: Routledge.

Haynes, J. (2009). *Who Is It that Can Tell Me Who I Am?* London: Constable & Robinson.

Hazan, C. & Shaver, P. (1987). Romantic love conceptualized as an attachment process. *Journal of Personality and Social Psychology, 52*: 511–524.

Hebb, D. O. (1949). *The Organization of Behavior: A Neuropsychological Theory.* New York: Wiley.

Heidegger, M. (1962). *Being and Time.* J. McQuarrie & E. Robinson (Trans.). New York: Harper & Row.

Heiller, B. & Sills, C. (2010). Life scripts: an existential perspective. In: R. G. Erskine (Ed.), *Life Scripts: a Transactional Analysis of Unconscious Relational Patterns.* London: Karnac.

Heisenberg, W. (1958). *Physics and Philosophy: The Revolution in Modern Science.* New York: Harper & Row.

Helman, G. C. (1981). Disease versus illness in general practice. *Journal of the Royal College of General Practitioners, 31*: 548–552.

Henderson, P. (Ed.) (2009). *Supervisor Training: Issues and Approaches.* London: Karnac.

Hine, J. (1990). The bilateral and ongoing nature of games. *Transactional Analysis Journal, 20*: 28–39.

Hine, J. (1997). Mind structure and ego states. *Transactional Analysis Journal, 27*: 278–289.

Hinshelwood, R. D. (1994). *Clinical Klein.* London: Free Association.

Hirsch, I. (1987). Varying modes of analytic participation. *Journal of the American Acadamy of Psychoanalysis, 15*: 205–222.

Hoffman, I. Z. (1998). *Ritual and Spontaneity in Psychoanalytic Process.* Hillsdale, NJ: Analytic Press, 2001.

Holtby, M. (1979). Interlocking racket systems. *Transactional Analysis Journal, 9*: 131–135.

Horvath, O. & Greenberg, J. (Eds.) (1994). *The Working Alliance: Theory Research and Practice.* New York: Wiley.

Hudson-Allez, G. (2008). *Infant Losses; Adult Searches: a Neural and Developmental Perspective on Psychopathology and Sexual Offending.* London: Karnac.

Hycner, R. A. (1991). *Between Person and Person.* Highland, NY: Gestalt Journal Press.

Hycner, R. A. & Jacobs, L. (1995). *The Healing Relationship in Gestalt Therapy.* Highland, NY: Gestalt Journal Press.

Jackson, P. Z. & McKergow, M. (2007). *The Solutions Focus.* London: Nicholas Brealey.

Jacobs, L. (1989). Dialogue in Gestalt theory and therapy. *The Gestalt Journal*, *12*(1): 25–68.

Jacobs, M. (1988). *Psychodynamic Counselling in Action*. London: Sage.

James, M. (1973). The game plan. *Transactional Analysis Journal*, 3: 14–17.

James, M. (1977). *Techniques in Transactional Analysis for Psychotherapists and Counselors*. Boston, MA: Addison-Wesley.

Johnson, S. (2010). Couple therapy in the 21st century. Keynote speech, Milton Erickson Brief Therapy Conference (Brief Therapy Lasting Solutions), Orlando, FL, December 9.

Jorgensen, E. W. & Jorgensen, H. I. (1984). *Eric Berne: Master Gamesman: A Transactional Biography*. New York: Grove Press.

Jung, C. G. (1946/1954). *On the Nature of the Psyche. Collected Works Volume 8*, paras. 343–442. London: Routledge & Kegan Paul.

Jung, C. G. (1959). *The Archetypes and the Collective Unconscious. Collected Works Volume 9*. London: Routledge & Kegan Paul.

Jung, C. G. (1971). *Psychological Types. Collected Works Volume 10*, chapter X. London: Routledge & Kegan Paul.

Kahler, T. & Capers, H. (1974). The miniscript. *Transactional Analysis Journal*, 4: 26–42.

Kalshed, D. (1996). *The Inner World of Trauma: Archetypal Defences of the Personal Spirit*. London: Routledge.

Keats, J. (2002). Letter to George and Thomas Keats, 21 December 1817. In: J. Mee (Ed.), *John Keats: Selected Letters* (pp. 40–43). Oxford: Oxford University Press.

Kellett, P. (2006). The enigma of desire, part 1: Lacanian psychoanalysis. *Transactions*, 5: 18–32.

Kellett, P. (2007a). The enigma of desire, part 2: The development of self-hood. *Transactions*, 6: 15–33.

Kellett, P. (2007b). Playing with theory: a relational search for self. In: K. Tudor (Ed.), *The Adult is Parent to the Child: Transactional Analysis with Children and Young People* (pp. 238–249). Lyme Regis, UK: Russell House.

Kellett van Leer, P. (2009). In your absence: Desire and the impossibility of intimacy. *Transactional Analysis Journal*, 39: 117–129.

Kelly, G. A. (1955). *The Psychology of Personal Constructs, Volumes 1 and 2*. New York: W. W. Norton.

Kenny, V. (1997). Constructivism: Everybody has won and all must have prizes. *Transactional Analysis Journal*, 27: 110–117.

Kernberg, O. (1965). Notes on countertransference. *Journal of the American Psychoanalytic Association*, 13: 38–56.

King, K. (2004). *Relational Practice in Consulting*. PhD dissertation. Bath University, UK.

King, K. (2011, in press). The challenge of mutuality. In: *Coaching Relationships*. London: Libri Press.

King, K. (2011, in press). *The Relationship and Executive Coaching*. London: Libri Press.

Klein, M. (1959). Our adult world and its roots in infancy. In: M. Klein, *Collected Works, Vol. III, Envy and Gratitude and Other Works*. London: Karnac, 1993.

Klein, M. (1959). *Collected Works, Vol. III, Envy and Gratitude and Other Works*. London: Karnac, 1993.

Klein, M. (1975/1988). *Envy and Gratitude and Other Works, 1946–1963*. London: Virago.

Koch, S. (Ed.) (1959). *Psychology: A Study of a Science*, vol. 3. New York: McGraw Hill.

Kohut, H. (1971). *The Analysis of the Self*. New York: International Universities Press.

Kohut, H. (1984). *How Does Analysis Cure?* London: University of Chicago Press.

Kolb, D. (1984). *Experiential Learning*. Englewood Cliffs, NJ: Prentice Hall.

Kraemer, S. (1999). *Infant observation*. London: BBC, Tavistock Institute videos.

Krueger, R., Densmore, J., Morrison, J. & Manzarek, R. (1968). No one here gets out alive. From the song *Five to One*. Los Angeles: Doors Music Company.

Kubler-Ross, E. (1973). *On Death and Dying*. London: Routledge.

Lacan, J. (1949). The mirror stage as formative of the I function as revealed in psychoanalytic experience. In: B. Fink (Trans.), *Ecrits* (pp. 75–81). New York: W. W. Norton, 2006.

Lacan, J. (1973). *The Seminar XX: Encore: On Feminine Sexuality, the Limits of Love and Knowledge*. J.-A. Miller (Ed.), B. Fink (Trans.). New York: W. W. Norton, 1998.

Lambert, M. J. & Bergin, A. E. (1994). The effectiveness of psychotherapy. In: A. E. Bergin & S. L. Garfield (Eds.), *Handbook of Psychotherapy and Behaviour Change* (4th ed.) (pp. 143–190). New York: John Wiley.

Lambert, M. J. & Barley, E. D. (2002). Research summary on the therapeutic relationship and psychotherapy outcome. In: J. Norcross (Ed.), *Psychotherapy Relationships that Work. Therapist Contributions and Responsiveness to Patients* (pp.17–32). New York: Oxford University Press.

Laplanche, J. (2007). Three meanings of the word "unconscious" in the framework of the general theory of seduction. In: J. Calich & H. Hinz (Eds.), *The Unconscious: Further Reflections* (pp. 31–46). London: International Psychoanalytic Association.

Lapworth, P. & Sills, C. (2011). *An Introduction to Transactional Analysis*. London: Sage.

Leary, T. (1970). *Politics of Ecstasy*. London: Paladin Press.

Le Doux, J. (2002). *The Synaptic Self*. New York: Viking.

Levin, F. (2009). *Emotion and the Psychodynamics of the Cerebellum: a Neuro-Psychoanalytical Analysis and Synthesis*. London: Karnac.

Lewin, K. (1946). Action research and minority problems. *Journal of Social Issues*, 2(4): 34–46.

Little, R. (2004). Ego state relational units and resistance to change: An integration of transactional analysis & object relations. *Transactions. The Journal of the Institute of Transactional Analysis*, 1: 3–10.

Little, R. (2005). Integrating psychoanalytic understandings in the deconfusion of primitive Child ego states. *Transactional Analysis Journal*, 35: 132–146.

Little, R. (2005). Relational transactional analysis: The therapist's stance. *ITA NEWS*, 18: 6–7.

Little, R. (2006). Ego state relational units and resistence to change. *Transactional Analysis Journal*, 36: 7–19.

Little, R. (2006). Treatment considerations when working with pathological narcissism. *Transactional Analysis Journal*, 36: 303–317.

Little, R. (2008). Working with the past in the present. Metanoia Relational Transactional Analysis Conference, London, July.

Little, R. (2010). The therapist's self-disclosure: A developing tradition, International Association of Relational Transactional Analysis, www.relationalta.com. Last accessed May 15, 2011.

Little, R. (2011). Impasse clarification within the transference-countertransference matrix. *Transactional Analysis Journal*, 41: 22–38.

Luborsky, L., Singer, B. & Luborsky, L. (1975). Comparative studies of psychotherapies: Is it true that everyone has won and all must have prizes? *Archives of General Psychiatry*, 42: 602–611.

Lynch, W. (1712). The Willie Lynch letter: The making of a slave. http://www.finalcall.com/artman/publish/Perspectives1/WillieLynchletterTheMakingofaSlave.shtml (last accessed March 25, 2011).

Lyons-Ruth, K. (1999). The two-person unconscious: Intersubjective dialogue, enactive representation, and the emergence of new forms of relational organization. *Psychoanalytic Inquiry*, 19: 567–617.

Lyotard, J. (1979). *La condition postmoderne: rapport sur le savoir*. Paris: Minuit.

Macquarie (2003). *Australia's National Dictionary*. Sydney: Macquarie University.

Mahler, M., Pine, F. & Bergman, A. (1975). *The Psychological Birth of the Human Infant: Symbiosis and Individuation*. London: Maresfield.

Maimonides (1135–1204). *In Our Time*. Presented by Melvyn Bragg, BBC Radio Four, February 2011.

Main, M. (1995). Recent studies in attachment: Overview, with selected implications for clinical work. In: S. Goldberg, R. Muir & J. Kerr (Eds.), *Attachment Theory: Social, Developmental, and Clinical Perspectives* (pp. 407–474). Hillsdale, NJ: Analytic Press.

Main, M., Kaplan, N. & Cassidy, J. (1985). Security in infancy, childhood and adulthood: A move to the level of representation. In: I. Bretherton & E. Waters (Eds.), Growing points of attachment theory and research. *Society for Research in Child Development, Monograph No. 209*, *50*(1–2): 66–104.

Mann, D. (1997). *Psychotherapy: an Erotic Relationship*. London: Routledge.

Mann, D. (Ed.) (1999). Oedipus and the unconscious erotic countertransference. In: *Erotic Transference and Countertransference: Clinical Practice in Psychotherapy*. London: Routledge.

Mann, D. (Ed.) (1999). *Erotic Transference and Countertransference: Clinical Practice in Psychotherapy*. London: Routledge.

Marber, P. (2006). *Notes on a Scandal* (film of the book by Zoe Heller, director, Richard Eyre).

Maroda, K. J. (2004). *The Power of Countertransference*. Hillsdale, NJ: Analytic Press.

Maroda, K. J. (2010). *Psychodynamic Techniques*. New York: Guilford Press.

Maslow, A. (1943). Psychology. In: J. A. Simons, D. B. Irwin & B. A. Drinnien (Eds.), *The Search for Understanding*. New York: West Publishing, 1987.

Masson, J. (1988/1990). *Against Therapy*. London: Fontana Paperbacks.

May, R. (1983). *The Discovery of Being: Writings in Existential Psychology*. New York: W. W. Norton.

Mazzetti, M. (2003). *Il dialogo transculturale. Manuale per operatori sanitari e altre professioni d'aiuto (The Transcultural Dialogue. Handbook for Health Workers and Other Helping Professions)*. Rome: Carocci Editore.

Mazzetti, M. (2007). Supervision in transactional analysis: An operational model. *Transactional Analysis Journal, 37*: 93–103.

Mazzetti, M. (2007). Cultural identities in movement in a world in movement: New frontiers for transactional analysis. *EATA Newsletter, 90*: 6–13.

Mazzetti, M. (2008). Trauma and migration. A transactional analytic approach towards refugees and torture victims. *Transactional Analysis Journal, 38*: 285–302.

Mazzetti, M. (2010a). Cross-cultural transactional analysis. *The Psychotherapist, 46*: 23–25.

Mazzetti, M. (2010b). Analyzing the impact of prior psychotherapy on a patient's script. *Transactional Analysis Journal, 40*: 23–31.

McGrath, G. (1994). Ethics, boundaries, and contracts: Applying moral principles. *Transactional Analysis Journal*, 24: 6–14.

McLeod, J. (2010). *Case Study Research in Counselling and Psychotherapy*. London: Sage.

Mee, J. (Ed.) (2002). *John Keats: Selected Letters*. Oxford: Oxford University Press. Mellor, K. (1980). Impasses. A developmental and structural understanding. *Transactional Analysis Journal*, 5: 295–302.

Menninger, K. (1958). *Theory of Psychoanalytic Technique*. New York: Basic.

Meyer, B. & Pilkonis, P. A. (2002). Attachment style. In: J. C. Norcross (Ed.), *Psychotherapy Relationships that Work: Therapist Contributions and Responsiveness to Patients* (pp. 367–382). Oxford: Oxford University Press.

Miller, E. (1998). Are basic assumptions instinctive? In: T. B. Talamo, F. Borgogno & S. Merciai (Eds.), *Bion's Legacy to Groups* (pp. 39–52). London: Karnac.

Mitchell, J. (2003). *Siblings*. Cambridge, UK: Polity Press.

Mitchell, S. A. (1988). *Relational Concepts in Psychoanalysis: An Integration*. Cambridge, MA: Harvard University Press.

Mitchell, S. A. (1993). *Hope and Dread in Psychoanalysis*. New York: Basic.

Mitchell, S. A. (1997/2005). *Influence and Autonomy in Psychoanalysis*. London: Analytic Press.

Mitchell, S. A. (2000). *Relationality from Attachment to Intersubjectivity*. Hillsdale, NJ: Analytic Press.

Mitchell, S. A. & Aron, L. (1999). *Relational Psychoanalysis. The Emergence of a Tradition*. Hillsdale, NJ: Analytic Press.

Mohr, J. J., Gelso, C. J. & Hill, C. E. (2005). Client and counselor trainee attachment as predictors of session evaluation and countertransference behavior in first counseling sessions. *Journal of Counseling Psychology*, 5: 298–309.

Moiso, C. (1985). Ego states and transference. *Transactional Analysis Journal*, 15: 194–201.

Moreno, J. L. (1945). *Group Therapy*. New York: Beacon House.

Moreno, J. L. (1964). *Psychodrama*. Volume 1. New York: Beacon House.

Morgan-Jones, R. (2009). The body speaks: Bion's protomental system at work. *British Journal of Psychotherapy*, 25: 456–476.

Mothersole, G. (1999). Parallel process: A review. *Clinical Supervisor*, 18: 107–121.

Moursund, J. (1985). Contact, intimacy, and need. *Transactional Analysis Journal*, 15: 116–119.

Nadel, J. & Camioni, L. (Eds.) (1992). *New Perspectives in Early Communicative Development*. London: Routledge.

Napper, R. (2009). Positive psychology and transactional analysis. *Transactional Analysis Journal*, 39: 61–74.

Noé, A. & Maquet, J. (2010). Les Entrelacs du Lien Thérapeutic: Trouble et Clarté. In conference papers entitled Les Rates et les Ruptures de la Relation: Entre Répétition et Dynamique. IFAT Paris, November 14 (pp. 32–41).

Norcross, J. C. (Ed.) (2002). *Psychotherapy Relationships that Work: Therapist Contributions and Responsiveness to Patients.* Oxford: Oxford University Press.

Norcross, J. C. (2010). The therapeutic relationship. In: B. Duncan & S. Miller (Eds.), *Heart and Soul of Change in Psychotherapy* (2nd ed.). New York: Oxford University Press.

Norcross, J. C. & Goldfried, M. (1992). *The Handbook of Psychotherapy Integration.* New York: Basic.

Novellino, M. (1984). Self analysis of countertransference in integrative transactional analysis. *Transactional Analysis Journal*, 4: 63–67.

Novellino, M. (2003). On closer analysis: a psychodynamic revision of the rules of communication within the framework of transactional analysis. In: C. Sills & H. Hargaden (Eds.), *Ego States: Key Concepts in Transactional Analysis: Contemporary Views* (pp. 149–168). London: Worth.

Novey, T. B. (2006). Myth and measurement. *Transactional Analysis Journal*, 36: 180–185.

Oates, S. (2003). A journey to the heart of ego states. In: C. Sills & H. Hargaden (Eds.), *Ego States: Key Concepts in Transactional Analysis: Contemporary Views* (pp. 247–259). London: Worth.

Ogden, T. H. (1982/1992). *Projective Identification and Psychotherapeutic Technique.* London: Karnac.

Ogden, T. H. (1991). *The Primitive Edge of Experience.* Northvale, NJ: Jason Aronson.

Ogden, T. H. (1994). The analytic third: Working with intersubjective clinical facts. In: S. A. Mitchell & L. Aron (Eds.), *Relational Psychoanalysis: The Emergence of a Tradition* (pp. 487–492). Hillsdale, NJ: Analytic Press, 1999.

Ogden, T. H. (2005). *This Art of Psychoanalysis: Dreaming Undreamt Dreams and Interrupted Cries.* London: Routledge.

Ogden, T. H. (2009). *Rediscovering Psychoanalysis: Thinking and Dreaming, Learning and Forgetting.* London: Routledge.

Oxford English Dictionary (2010). Oxford: Oxford University Press.

Panksepp, J. (1998). *Affective Neuroscience: The Foundations of Human and Animal Emotions.* Oxford: Oxford University Press.

Panksepp, J. (2009). Brain emotional systems and qualities of mental life: From animal models of affect to implications for psychotherapeutics. In: D. Fosha, D. J. Siegel & M. F. Solomon (Eds.), *The Healing Power of Emotion: Affective Neuroscience, Development, and Clinical Practice* (pp. 1–26). New York: W. W. Norton.

Papadopoulos R. K. (2006). *The Jungian Handbook. Theory Practice and Application*. Hove, UK: Routledge.

Perez Foster, R. M. (1998). *The Power of Language in the Clinical Process. Assessing and Treating the Bilingual Person*. Northvale, NJ: Jason Aronson.

Perls, F. (1979). Planned psychotherapy. *Gestalt Journal*, 2(2): 5–23.

Perls, F., Hefferline, R. & Goodman, P. (1951/1989). *Gestalt Therapy: Excitement and Growth in the Human Personality*. London: Pelican.

Petrucelli, J. (Ed.) (2010). *Knowing, Not-Knowing, & Sort-of-Knowing: Psychoanalysis and the Experience of Uncertainty*. London: Karnac.

Phillips, A. (2009), cited in Haynes, J. (2009). *Who Is It that Can Tell Me Who I Am?* London: Constable & Robinson.

Piaget, J. (1960). *The Child's Conception of Physical Causality*. Paterson, NJ: Littlefield, Adams. (First published in English by Routledge & Kegan Paul, 1950.)

Pierini, A. (2008). Has the unconscious moved house? *Transactional Analysis Journal*, 38: 110–118.

Plato (1920). *The Dialogues of Plato. Vol. 1* (B. Jowett, Trans.). New York: Random House.

Porges, S. W. (1995). Orienting in a defensive world: Mammalian modifications of our evolutionary heritage: A polyvagal theory. *Psychophysiology*, 32: 301–318.

Proctor, B. (2006). Contracting in supervision. In: C. Sills (Ed.), *Contracts in Counselling and Psychotherapy* (2nd edition) (pp. 161–174). London: Sage.

Racker, H. (1957). The meaning and uses of countertransference. *Psychoanalytic Quarterly*, 26: 303–357.

Ram Dass (1971). *Be Here Now*. Questa, NM: Lama Foundation.

Reason, P. & Bradbury, H. (Eds.) (2001). *Handbook of Action Research Participative Inquiry and Practice*. London: Sage.

Rizzolatti, G. & Craighero, L. (2004). The mirror-neuron system. *Annual Review of Neuroscience*, 27: 169–192.

Rizzolatti, G. & Fadega, L. (1998). Grasping objects and grasping action meanings: the dual role of monkey rostroventral premotor cortex (area 5). *Novartis Foundation Symposium*, 218: 85–95.

Rogers, C. (1951). *Client-Centred Therapy*. London: Constable.

Rogers, C. (1959). A theory of therapy, personality and interpersonal relationships as developed in the client centred framework. In: S. Koch (Ed.), *Psychology: A Study of a Science*, vol. 3 (pp. 184–256). New York: McGraw Hill.

Rogers, C. (1961). *On Becoming a Person*. Boston: Houghton Mifflin.

Rozensweig, S. (1936). Some implicit common factors in diverse methods in psychotherapy. *American Journal of Orthopsychiatry*, 6: 412–415.

Samuels, A. (1999). From sexual misconduct to social justice. In: D. Mann (Ed.), *Erotic Transference and Countertransference: Clinical Practice in Psychotherapy*. London: Routledge.

Sandler, J. (1993). On communication from patient to analyst: Not everything is projective identification. *International Journal of Psychoanalysis*, 74: 1097–1107.

Schaffer, H. R. (1996). *Social Development*. Oxford: Blackwell.

Schiff, A. W. & Schiff, J. L. (1971). Passivity. *Transactional Analysis Journal*, 11: 71–78.

Schiff, J. L., with Schiff, A. W., Mellor, K., Schiff, E., Schiff, S., Richman, D., Fishman, J., Wolz, L. & Momb, D. (1975). *Cathexis Reader: Transactional Analysis Treatment of Psychosis*. New York: Harper & Row.

Schon, D. (1983). *The Reflective Practitioner: How Professionals Think in Action*. New York: Basic.

Schore, A. N. (2003). *Affect Regulation and the Repair of the Self*. London: W. W. Norton.

Schore, A. N. (2009). Right brain affect regulation. In: D. Fosha, D. J. Siegel & M. F. Soloman (Eds.), *The Healing Power of Emotion: Affective Neuroscience, Development, and Clinical Practice*. New York: W. W. Norton.

Seligman, M. E. P. (2003). *Authentic Happiness*. London: Nicholas Brearley.

Shadbolt, C. (2004). Homophobia and gay affirmative transactional analysis. *Transactional Analysis Journal*, 34: 113–125.

Shivanath, S. & Hiremath, M. (2003). The psychodynamic of race and culture. In: C. Sills & H. Hargaden (Eds.), *Ego States: Key Concepts in Transactional Analysis: Contempory Views* (pp. 169–184). London: Worth.

Shmukler, D. (1991). Transference and transactions: Perspectives from developmental theory, object relations, and transformational processes. *Transactional Analysis Journal*, 21: 127–135.

Shmukler, D. (2003). Ego states: A personal reflection. In: C. Sills & H. Hargaden (Eds.), *Ego States: Key Concepts in Transactional Analysis: Contemporary Views* (pp. 135–148). London: Worth.

Shmukler, D. (2010). "It is all about you and nothing to do with you." Keynote address, International Association of Relational Transactional Analysis conference, London.

Short, D. (2010). *Transformational Relationships: Deciphering the Social Matrix in Psychotherapy*. Phoenix, AZ: Zieg, Tucker & Theisen.

Siegel, D. J. (1999). *The Developing Mind: Toward a Neurobiology of Interpersonal Experience*. New York: Guilford Press.

Siegel, D. J. (2007). *The Mindful Brain*. London: W. W. Norton.

Siegel, D. J. (2010). *The Mindful Therapist: a Clinician's Guide to Mindsight and Neural Integration*. London: W. W. Norton.

Sills, C. (2001). The man with no name: A response to Hargaden and Erskine. *Transactional Analysis Journal, 31*: 227–232.

Sills, C. (2006). Contracts and contract making. In: C. Sills (Ed.), *Contracts in Counselling and Psychotherapy* (2nd edition) (pp. 9–26). London: Sage.

Sills, C. (Ed.) (2006). *Contracts in Counselling and Psychotherapy* (2nd edition). London: Sage.

Sills, C. & Hargaden, H. (2003). Introduction. In: C. Sills & H. Hargaden (Eds.), *Ego States: Key Concepts in Transactional Analysis: Contempory Views* (pp. ix–xxiii). London: Worth.

Sills, C. & Hargaden, H. (Eds.) (2003). *Ego States: Key Concepts in Transactional Analysis: Contempory Views*. London: Worth.

Silverman, D. K. (1996). Arithmetic of a one- and two-person psychology: Merton M. Gill, an essay. *Psychoanalytic Psychology, 13*: 267–274.

Simons, J. A., Irwin, D. B. & Drinnien, B. A. (Eds.) (1943). *The Search for Understanding*. New York: West Publishing, 1987.

Simpson, J. A. (1990). Influence of attachment styles on romantic relationships. *Journal of Personality and Social Psychology, 59*: 971–980.

Soloman, C. (2010). Eric Berne the therapist: One patient's perspective. *Transactional Analysis Journal, 40*: 183–186.

Soloman, M. (2009). Emotion, mindfulness, and movement: Expanding the regulatory boundaries of the window of affect tolerance. In: D. Fosha, D. J. Siegel & M. Solomon (Eds.), *The Healing Power of Emotion: Affective Neuroscience, Development, and Clinical Practice* (pp. 232–256). New York: W. W. Norton.

Spinelli, E. (1989). *The Interpreted World. An Introduction to Phenomenological Psychology*. London: Sage.

Stacey, R. D. (1993). *Strategic Management and Organisational Dynamics*. London: Pitman.

Stark, M. (1998). When the body meets the mind: What body psychotherapy can learn from psychoanalysis. Panel presentation at the First National Conference of the United States Association for Body Psychotherapy.

Stark, M. (1999). *Modes of Therapeutic Action: Enhancement of Knowledge, Provision of Experience, and Engagement in Relationship*. Northvale, NJ: Jason Aronson.

Steiner, C. (1974). *Scripts People Live: Transactional Analysis of Life Scripts*. New York: Grove Press.

Steiner, C., Wyckoff, H., Goldstine, D., Lariviere, P., Schwebel, R. & Marcus, J. (1975). *Readings in Radical Psychiatry*. New York: Grove Press.

Stern, D. B. (1997). *Unformulated Experience: From Dissociation to Imagination in Psychoanalysis*. Hillsdale, NJ: Analytic Press.

Stern, D. B. (1999). Unformulated experience: From familiar chaos to creative disorder. In: S. Mitchell & L. Aron (Eds.), *Relational Psychoanalysis:*

The Emergence of a Tradition (pp. 77–108). Hillsdale, NJ: Analytic Press (originally published in 1983, *Contemporary Psychoanalysis*, *19*: 71–99).

Stern, D. N. (1985). *The Interpersonal World of the Infant: A View from Psychoanalysis and Developmental Psychology*. New York: Basic.

Stern, D. N. (2004). *The Present Moment in Psychotherapy and Everyday Life*. New York: W. W. Norton.

Stewart, I. (1992). *Key figures in Counselling and Psychotherapy: Eric Berne*. London: Sage.

Stolorow, R., Atwood, G. & Brandshaft, B. J. (Eds.) (2004). *The Intersubjective Perspective*. Oxford: Jason Aronson.

Stolorow, R., Brandshaft, B. J. & Atwood, G. (1987). *Psychoanalytic Treatment: An Intersubjective Approach*. Hillsdale. NJ: Analytic Press.

Stringer, E. T. (2007). *Action Research. A Handbook for Practitioners*. London: Sage.

Summers, G. (2008). The unfolding future—a co-creative TA vision. Keynote speech at Australasian Transactional Analysis Conference, Rotorua, New Zealand.

Summers, G. & Tudor, K. (2000). Co-creative transactional analysis. *Transactional Analysis Journal*, *30*: 23–40.

Symington, J. & Symington, N. (1996). *The Clinical Thinking of Wilfred Bion*. London: Routledge.

Szekacs-Weisz, J. & Ward, I. (Eds.) (2004). *Lost Childhood and the Language of Exile*. London, IMAGO Multi-Lingual Psychotherapy Centre and the Freud Museum.

Talamo, T. B., Borgogno, F. & Merciai, S. (Eds.) (1998). *Bion's Legacy to Groups*. London: Karnac.

Tansey, M. J. (1994). Sexual attraction and phobic dread in the countertransference. *Psychoanalytic Dialogues*, *4*(2): 130–152.

Temple, S. (1999). Functional fluency for educational transactional analysts. *Transactional Analysis Journal*, *29*: 164–174.

Temple, D. (2004). Update on the functional fluency model in education. *Transactional Analysis Journal*, *34*: 197–204.

Thierry, G. & Wu, Y. J. (2007). Brain potentials reveal unconscious translation during foreign-language comprehension. *Proceedings of the National Academy of Sciences*, July 24, *104*(30): 12530–12535.

Tilney, T. (1998). *Dictionary of Transactional Analysis*. London: Whurr.

Tokuhama-Espinosa, T. (Ed.) (2003). *The Multilingual Mind. Issues Discussed by, for and about People with Many Languages*. Santa Barbera, CA: Praeger.

Tosi, M. T. (2008). The many faces of the unconscious: A new unconscious for a phenomenological transactional analysis. *Transactional Analysis Journal*, *38*: 119–127.

Trevarthen, C. (1979). Communication and co-operation in early infancy. A description of primary intersubjectivity. In: M. Bullara (Ed.), *Before Speech: the Beginning of Human Communication*. London: Cambridge University Press.

Trevarthen, C. (1992). The functions of emotions in early infant communication and development. In: J. Nadel & L. Camioni (Eds.), *New Perspectives in Early Communicative Development*. London: Routledge.

Tuckman, B. W. (1965). Developmental sequence in small groups. *Psychological Bulletin, 63*: 384–399.

Tudor, K. (Ed.) (2002). *Transactional Analysis Approaches to Brief Therapy*. London: Sage.

Tudor, K. (2003). The neopsyche: the integrating Adult ego state. In: C. Sills & H. Hargaden (Eds.), *Ego States: Key Concepts in Transactional Analysis: Contempory Views* (pp. 201–231). London: Worth.

Tudor, K. (Ed.) (2007). *The Adult is Parent to the Child: Transactional Analysis with Children and Young People*. Lyme Regis, UK: Russell House.

Van Rijn, B. (2005). An enquiry into psychotherapy training. Challenges to developing a generic foundation year and links to clinical practice training. Unpublished D.Psych. dissertation, Metanoia Institute and Middlesex University.

Van Rijn, B. (2010). Evaluating our practice. In: S. Bager-Charleson (Ed.), *Reflective Practice in Counselling and Psychotherapy*. Exeter, UK: Learning Matters.

Van Rijn, B., Sills, C., Hunt, J., Shivanath, S., Gildebrand, K. & Fowlie, H. (2008). Developing clinical effectiveness in psychotherapy training: Action research. *Counselling and Psychotherapy Research, 8*: 261–268.

Verhaeghe, P. & Vanheule, S. (2005). Actual neurosis and PTSD. *Psychoanalytic Psychology, 22*: 493–507.

Vygotsky, L. S. (1962). *Thought and Language* (E. Haufmann & G. Vakar, Eds. and Trans.). Cambridge, MA: MIT Press.

Vygotsky, L. S. (1978). *Mind in Society: The Development of Higher Psychological Processes*. Cambridge, MA: Harvard University Press.

Wachtel, P. L. (2008). *Relational Theory and the Practice of Psychotherapy*. New York: Guilford Press.

Wallen, R. (1970). *Gestalt Therapy and Gestalt Psychology*. In: J. Fagan & I. L. Shepherd (Eds.), *Gestalt Therapy Now* (pp. 8–13). New York: Harper & Row.

Wallin, D. J. (2007). *Attachment in Psychotherapy*. New York: Guilford Press.

Wampold, B. (2001). *The Great Psychotherapy Debate*. Hove, UK: Lawrence Erlbaum.

Ware, P. (1983). Personality adaptations: Doors to therapy. *Transactional Analysis Journal, 13*: 11–19.

Watzlawick, P., Weakland, J. & Fisch, R. (1974). *Change: Principles of Problem Formulation & Problem Resolution*. New York: W. W. Norton.

Willock, B., Curtis, R. C. & Bohm, L. C. (Eds.) (2009). *Taboo or Not Taboo? Forbidden Thoughts, Forbidden Acts in Psychoanalysis and Psychotherapy*. London: Karnac.

Winnicott, C., Shepard, R. & Davis, M. (Eds.) (1989). *Psychoanalytic Explorations*. Cambridge, MA: Harvard University Press.

Winnicott, D. W. (1952). Anxiety associated with insecurity. In: *Collected Papers: Through Paediatrics to Psycho-Analysis* (pp. 97–100). London: Karnac, 1975..

Winnicott, D. W. (1952). Psychosis in child care. In: *Collected Papers: Through Paediatrics to Psycho-Analysis*. London: Hogarth, 1975.

Winnicott, D. W. (1953). Transitional objects and transitional phenomena. *International Journal of Psychoanalysis, 34*: 89–97.

Winnicott, D. W. (1965). Ego distortion in terms of true and false self. In: *The Maturational Processes and the Facilitating Environment: Studies in the Theory of Emotional Development* (pp. 140–152). New York: International Universities Press, 1965.

Winnicott, D. W. (1965). The theory of parent-infant relationship. In: *The Maturational Processes and the Facilitating Environment: Studies in the Theory of Emotional Development* (pp. 37–55). New York: International Universities Press.

Winnicott, D. W. (1965). *The Maturational Processes and the Facilitating Environment: Studies in the Theory of Emotional Development*. London: Hogarth.

Winnicott, D. W. (1971). *Playing and Reality*. London: Tavistock.

Winnicott, D. W. (1975). *Through Paediatrics to Psycho-Analysis*. London: Hogarth. Winnicott, D. W. (1989). Notes on play. In: C. Winnicott, R. Shepard & M. Davis (Eds.), *Psychoanalytic Explorations* (pp. 59–63). Cambridge, MA: Harvard University Press.

Wittgenstein, L. (1953). *Philosophical Investigations*. Malden, MA: Blackwell.

Yalom, I. (1991). *Love's Executioner*. London: Penguin.

Yontef, G. (1993). *Awareness, Dialogue and Process*. Highland, NY: Gestalt Journal Press.

Zvelc, G. (2010). Relational schemas theory and transactional analysis. *Transactional Analysis Journal, 40*: 8–22.

INDEX